Sage

Beginner's Guide

Unlock the full potential of Sage for simplifying and automating mathematical computing

Craig Finch

BIRMINGHAM - MUMBAI

Sage
Beginner's Guide

First published: May 2011

Production Reference: 1250411

Published by Packt Publishing Ltd.
32 Lincoln Road
Olton
Birmingham, B27 6PA, UK.

ISBN 978-1-849514-46-0

www.packtpub.com

Cover Image by Ed Maclean (edmaclean@gmail.com)

Credits

Author
Craig Finch

Reviewers
Dr. David Kirkby
Minh Nguyen

Acquisition Editor
Usha Iyer

Development Editor
Hyacintha D'Souza

Technical Editor
Ajay Shanker

Indexers
Tejal Daruwale
Rekha Nair

Project Coordinator
Joel Goveya

Proofreaders
Aaron Nash
Mario Cecere

Graphics
Nilesh Mohite

Production Coordinator
Adline Swetha Jesuthas

Cover Work
Adline Swetha Jesuthas

About the Author

Craig Finch is a Ph. D. Candidate in the Modeling and Simulation program at the University of Central Florida (UCF). He earned a Bachelor of Science degree from the University of Illinois at Urbana-Champaign and a Master of Science degree from UCF, both in electrical engineering. Craig worked as a design engineer for TriQuint Semiconductor, and currently works as a research assistant in the Hybrid Systems Lab at the UCF NanoScience Technology Center. Craig's professional goal is to develop tools for computational science and engineering and use them to solve difficult problems. In particular, he is interested in developing tools to help biologists study living systems. Craig is committed to using, developing, and promoting open-source software. He provides documentation and "how-to" examples on his blog at `http://www.shocksolution.com`.

I would like to thank my advisers, Dr. J. Hickman and Dr. Tom Clarke, for giving me the opportunity to pursue my doctorate. I would also like to thank my parents for buying the Apple IIGS computer that started it all.

About the Reviewers

Dr. David Kirkby is a chartered engineer living in Essex, England. David has a B.Sc. in Electrical and Electronic Engineering, an M.Sc. in Microwaves and OptoElectronics, and a Ph.D. in Medical Physics. Despite David's Ph.D. being in Medical Physics, it was primarily an engineering project, measuring the optical properties of human tissue, with a mixture of Monte Carlo modeling, radio frequency design, and laser optics. David was awarded his Ph.D. in 1999 from University College London.

Although not a mathematician, Dr. Kirkby has made extensive use of mathematical software. Most of his experience has been with MathematicaTM from Wolfram Research, although he has used both MATLAB™ and Simulink™ too.

David is the author of a number of open-source projects, including software for modeling transmission lines using finite difference (`http://atlc.sourceforge.net/`), design of Yagi-Uda antennas (`http://www.g8wrb.org/yagi/`) which can use a genetic algorithm for optimization, as well as software for data collection and analysis from electronic test equipment. David once wrote a web-based interface to MathematicaTM (`http://witm.sourceforge.net/`) which allows MathematicaTM to be used from a personal computer, PDA or smartphone.

Soon after the Sage project was started by Professor William Stein, Dr. Kirkby joined the development of Sage. He primarily worked on the successful port of Sage to the Solaris and OpenSolaris operating systems and encourages other developers to write portable code, conforming to POSIX standard, avoiding GNUisms.

Professionally, David's skill sets include computer modeling, radio frequency design, analogue circuit design, electromagnetic compatibility and optics—both free space and integrated. David has also been a Solaris system administrator for the University of Washington where the Sage project is based.

When not working on writing software, David enjoys playing chess, gardening, and spending time with his wife Lin and dog Smudge.

Readers wishing to contact Dr. Kirkby can do so via his website `http://www.drkirkby.co.uk/` where details of his consulting services may be found.

Minh Nguyen has been a contributor to the Sage project since December 2007. Over the years, he has worked on various aspects of Sage ranging from the standard documentation and modules such as cryptography, number theory, and graph theory to the Sage build system. He regularly maintains the Sage website and works on book projects that aim to provide in-depth documentation on using Sage to study cryptography and mathematics. More of his rantings can be found at `http://mvngu.wordpress.com`.

www.PacktPub.com

Support files, eBooks, discount offers and more

You might want to visit www.PacktPub.com for support files and downloads related to your book.

Did you know that Packt offers eBook versions of every book published, with PDF and ePub files available? You can upgrade to the eBook version at www.PacktPub.com and as a print book customer, you are entitled to a discount on the eBook copy. Get in touch with us at service@packtpub.com for more details.

At www.PacktPub.com, you can also read a collection of free technical articles, sign up for a range of free newsletters and receive exclusive discounts and offers on Packt books and eBooks.

http://PacktLib.PacktPub.com

Do you need instant solutions to your IT questions? PacktLib is Packt's online digital book library. Here, you can access, read and search across Packt's entire library of books.

Why Subscribe?

- Fully searchable across every book published by Packt
- Copy & paste, print and bookmark content
- On demand and accessible via web browser

Free Access for Packt account holders

If you have an account with Packt at www.PacktPub.com, you can use this to access PacktLib today and view nine entirely free books. Simply use your login credentials for immediate access.

Table of Contents

Preface

Results matter, whether you are a mathematician, scientist, or engineer. The time that you spend doing tedious mathematical calculations could be spent in more productive ways. Sage is an open-source mathematical software system that helps you perform many mathematical tasks. There is no reason to compute integrals or perform algebraic manipulations by hand when software can perform these tasks more quickly and accurately (unless you are a student who is learning these procedures for the first time). Students can also benefit from mathematical software. The ability to plot functions and manipulate symbolic expressions easily can improve your understanding of mathematical concepts. Likewise, it is largely unnecessary to write your own routines for numerical mathematics in low-level languages such as FORTRAN or C++. Mathematical software systems like Sage have highly optimized functions that implement common numerical operations like integration, solving ordinary differential equations, and solving systems of equations.

Sage is a collection of nearly 100 mathematical software packages, which are listed at `http://www.sagemath.org/links-components.html`. When possible, existing tools are integrated into Sage, rather than duplicating their functionality. The entire collection of tools can be downloaded and installed as a binary distribution or compiled from source code. The Python language provides a unified interface to all of the packages. Python is a high-level, interpreted, object-oriented programming language that is already well established in the research community. Users can interact with Sage through an interactive command-line interface or a graphical notebook interface. Sage can also be used as a Python library or embedded in LaTeX documents. Sage is "officially" available for recent versions of OS X, Linux, Solaris, and Open Solaris. It runs on Windows with the help of a virtual machine and it can be used on other platforms, with varying degrees of support. A current list of all the available platforms can be found at `http://wiki.sagemath.org/SupportedPlatforms`.

The mission statement of the Sage project is:

> *Creating a viable, free, open source alternative to Magma, Maple, Mathematica, and Matlab.*

If you are familiar with any of these commercial mathematical software systems, then you already have a good idea what Sage does. Sage offers several advantages over its commercial competitors. Sage is free, open-source software, released under the GNU Public License version 2 or higher (GPLv2+). There is no cost to download and install Sage, whether you want to put it on your personal computer, install it in a university teaching lab, or deploy it on every workstation in a company. This advantage is especially important in developing countries. The GPL license also means that Sage is free, as in "freedom." There are no restrictions on how or where you use the software, the license can never be revoked, and there is no annual maintenance fee. Another advantage is that you have access to every line of source code, so you can see how every calculation is performed, and track exactly what changes are made from one version to the next. Unlike commercial software, the bug list for Sage is public, and it can be accessed at `http://trac.sagemath.org/`. Users are encouraged to participate in the development of Sage by reporting and fixing bugs, and contributing new capabilities. With bugs and source code open for public review, you can have a high degree of confidence that Sage will produce correct results.

This book is written for people who are new to Sage, and perhaps new to mathematical software altogether. For this reason, the examples in the book emphasize undergraduate-level mathematics such as calculus, linear algebra, and ordinary differential equations. However, Sage is capable of performing advanced mathematics, and it has been cited in over 80 mathematical publications. A full list can be found at `http://www.sagemath.org/library-publications.html`. To benefit from this book, you should have some fundamental knowledge of computer programming, but the Python language will be introduced as needed throughout the book. The next chapter will take you through some examples that showcase a small subset of Sage's capabilities.

What this book covers

Chapter 1, What can You do with Sage? covers how Sage can be used for: making simple numerical calculations; performing symbolic calculations, solving systems of equations and ordinary differential equations; making plots in two and three dimensions; and analyzing experimental data and fitting models.

Chapter 2, Installing Sage covers how to install a binary version of Sage on Windows and install a binary version of Sage on OS X; install a binary version of Sage on GNU/Linux; compile Sage from source.

Chapter 3, Getting Started with Sage covers using the interactive shell; using the notebook interface; learning more about operators and variables; defining and using callable symbolic expressions; calling functions and making simple plots; defining your own functions; and working with objects in Sage.

Chapter 4, Introducing Python and Sage covers how to: use lists and tuples to store sequential data; iterate with loops; construct logical tests with "if" statements; read and write data files; and store heterogeneous data in dictionaries.

Chapter 5, Vectors, Matrices, and Linear Algebra covers how to create and manipulate vector and matrix objects; how Sage can take the tedious work out of linear algebra; learning about matrix methods for computing eigenvalues, inverses, and decompositions; and getting started with NumPy arrays and matrices for numerical calculations.

Chapter 6, Plotting with Sage covers how to plot functions of one variable; making various types of specialized 2D plots such as polar plots and scatter plots; using matplotlib to precisely format 2D plots and charts; and making interactive 3D plots of functions of two variables.

Chapter 7, Making Symbolic Mathematics Easy covers how to create symbolic functions and expressions, and learn to manipulate them; solve equations and systems of equations exactly, and find symbolic roots; automate calculus operations like limits, derivatives, and integrals; create infinite series and summations to approximate functions; perform Laplace transforms; and find exact solutions to ordinary differential equations.

Chapter 8, Solving Problems Numerically covers how to find the roots of an equation; compute integrals and derivatives numerically; find minima and maxima of functions; compute discrete Fourier transforms, and apply window functions; numerically solve an ordinary differential equation (ODE), and systems of ODEs; use optimization techniques to fit curves and find minima; and explore the probability tools in Sage.

Chapter 9, Learning Advanced Python Programming covers how to define your own classes; use inheritance to expand the usefulness of your classes; organize your class definitions in module files; bundle module files into packages; handle errors gracefully with exceptions; define your own exceptions for custom error handling; and use unit tests to make sure your package is working correctly.

Chapter 10, Where to go from here covers how to export equations as PNG and PDF files; export vector graphics and typeset mathematical expressions for inclusion in LaTeX documents; use LaTeX to document Sage worksheets; speed up collision detection using NumPy vector operations; create a Python script that uses Sage functionality; and create interactive graphical examples in the notebook interface.

What you need for this book

Required:

- Sage
- If using Windows, VMWare Player or VirtualBox is also required.
- Recommended, but not strictly necessary: LaTeX
- Optional, for building Sage from source on Linux: GCC, g++, make, m4, perl, ranlib, readline, and tar
- Optional, for building Sage from source on OS X: XCode
- A web browser is required to use the notebook interface

Who this book is for

If you are an engineer, scientist, mathematician, or student, this book is for you. To get the most from Sage by using the Python programming language, we'll give you the basics of the language to get you started. For this, it will be helpful if you have some experience with basic programming concepts.

Conventions

In this book, you will find several headings appearing frequently.

To give clear instructions of how to complete a procedure or task, we use:

Time for action – heading

1. Action 1
2. Action 2
3. Action 3

Instructions often need some extra explanation so that they make sense, so they are followed with:

What just happened?

This heading explains the working of tasks or instructions that you have just completed.

You will also find some other learning aids in the book, including:

Pop quiz – heading

These are short multiple choice questions intended to help you test your own understanding.

Have a go hero – heading

These set practical challenges and give you ideas for experimenting with what you have learned.

You will also find a number of styles of text that distinguish between different kinds of information. Here are some examples of these styles, and an explanation of their meaning.

Code words in text are shown as follows: "We can use the `help` function to learn more about it."

A block of code is set as follows:

```
print('This is a string')
print(1.0)
print(sqrt)
```

Any command-line input or output is written as follows:

```
sage: R = 250e3
sage: C = 4e-6
sage: tau = R * C
sage: tau
```

New terms and **important words** are shown in bold. Words that you see on the screen, in menus or dialog boxes for example, appear in the text like this: "clicking the **Next** button moves you to the next screen".

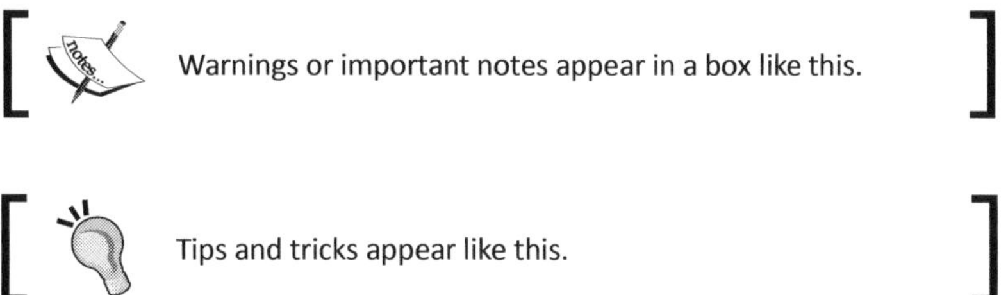

Warnings or important notes appear in a box like this.

Tips and tricks appear like this.

Reader feedback

Feedback from our readers is always welcome. Let us know what you think about this book—what you liked or may have disliked. Reader feedback is important for us to develop titles that you really get the most out of.

To send us general feedback, simply send an e-mail to `feedback@packtpub.com`, and mention the book title via the subject of your message.

If there is a book that you need and would like to see us publish, please send us a note in the **SUGGEST A TITLE** form on `www.packtpub.com` or e-mail `suggest@packtpub.com`.

If there is a topic that you have expertise in and you are interested in either writing or contributing to a book, see our author guide on `www.packtpub.com/authors`.

Customer support

Now that you are the proud owner of a Packt book, we have a number of things to help you to get the most from your purchase.

Downloading the example code

You can download the example code files for all Packt books you have purchased from your account at `http://www.PacktPub.com`. If you purchased this book elsewhere, you can visit `http://www.PacktPub.com/support` and register to have the files e-mailed directly to you.

Errata

Although we have taken every care to ensure the accuracy of our content, mistakes do happen. If you find a mistake in one of our books—maybe a mistake in the text or the code—we would be grateful if you would report this to us. By doing so, you can save other readers from frustration and help us improve subsequent versions of this book. If you find any errata, please report them by visiting `http://www.packtpub.com/support`, selecting your book, clicking on the **errata submission form** link, and entering the details of your errata. Once your errata are verified, your submission will be accepted and the errata will be uploaded on our website, or added to any list of existing errata, under the Errata section of that title. Any existing errata can be viewed by selecting your title from `http://www.packtpub.com/support`.

Piracy

Piracy of copyright material on the Internet is an ongoing problem across all media. At Packt, we take the protection of our copyright and licenses very seriously. If you come across any illegal copies of our works, in any form, on the Internet, please provide us with the location address or website name immediately so that we can pursue a remedy.

Please contact us at `copyright@packtpub.com` with a link to the suspected pirated material.

We appreciate your help in protecting our authors, and our ability to bring you valuable content.

Questions

You can contact us at `questions@packtpub.com` if you are having a problem with any aspect of the book, and we will do our best to address it.

1

What Can You Do with Sage?

Sage is a powerful tool—but you don't have to take my word for it. This chapter will showcase a few of the things that Sage can do to enhance your work. At this point, don't expect to understand every aspect of the examples presented in this chapter. Everything will be explained in more detail in the later chapters. Look at the things Sage can do, and start to think about how Sage might be useful to you. In this chapter, you will see how Sage can be used for:

- Making simple numerical calculations
- Performing symbolic calculations
- Solving systems of equations and ordinary differential equations
- Making plots in two and three dimensions
- Analysing experimental data and fitting models

Getting started

You don't have to install Sage to try it out! In this chapter, we will use the notebook interface to showcase some of the basics of Sage so that you can follow along using a public notebook server. These examples can also be run from an interactive session if you have installed Sage.

Go to `http://www.sagenb.org/` and sign up for a free account. You can also browse worksheets created and shared by others. If you have already installed Sage, launch the notebook interface by following the instructions in *Chapter 3*. The notebook interface should look like this:

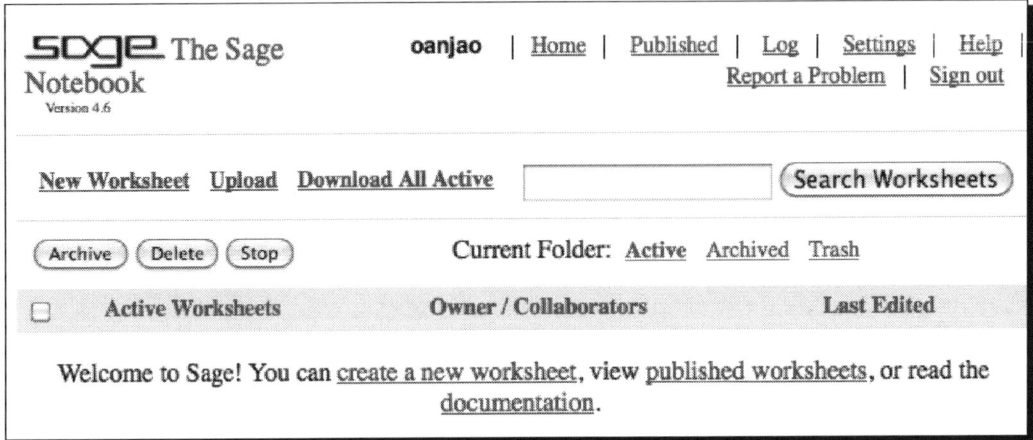

Create a new worksheet by clicking on the link called **New Worksheet**:

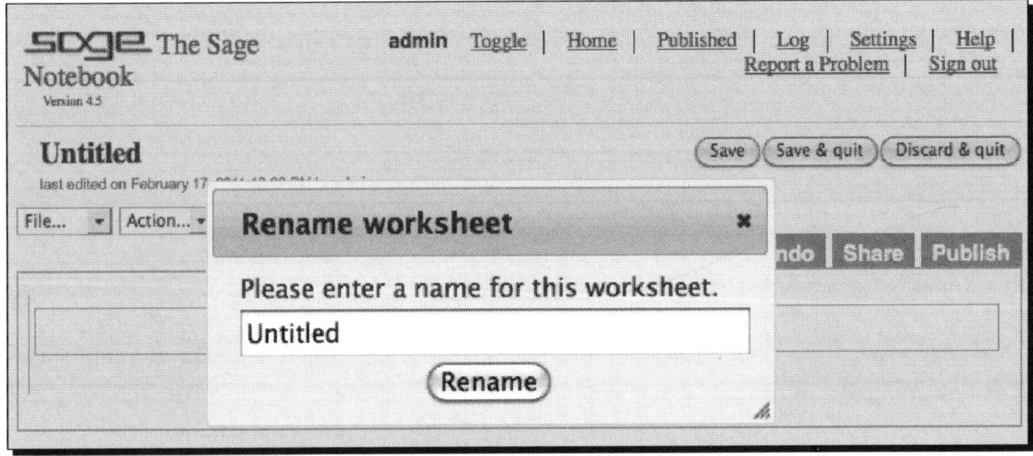

Type in a name when prompted, and click **Rename**. The new worksheet will look like this:

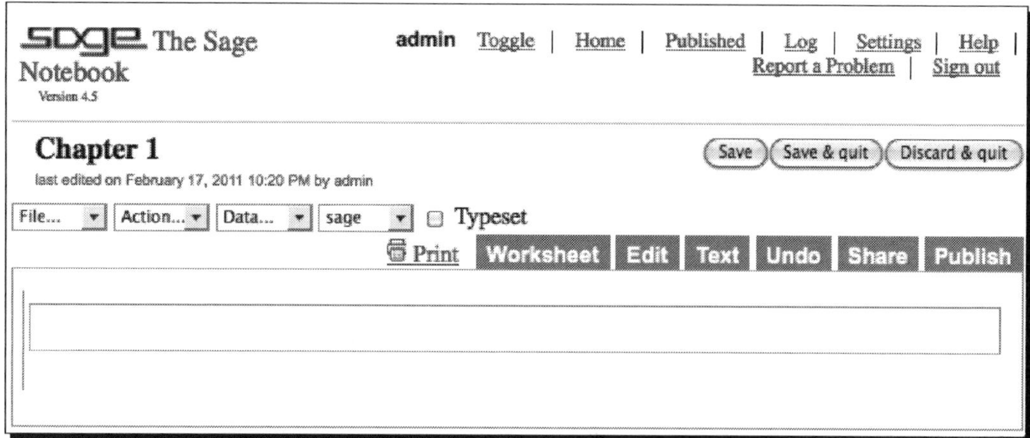

Enter an expression by clicking in an input cell and typing or pasting in an expression:

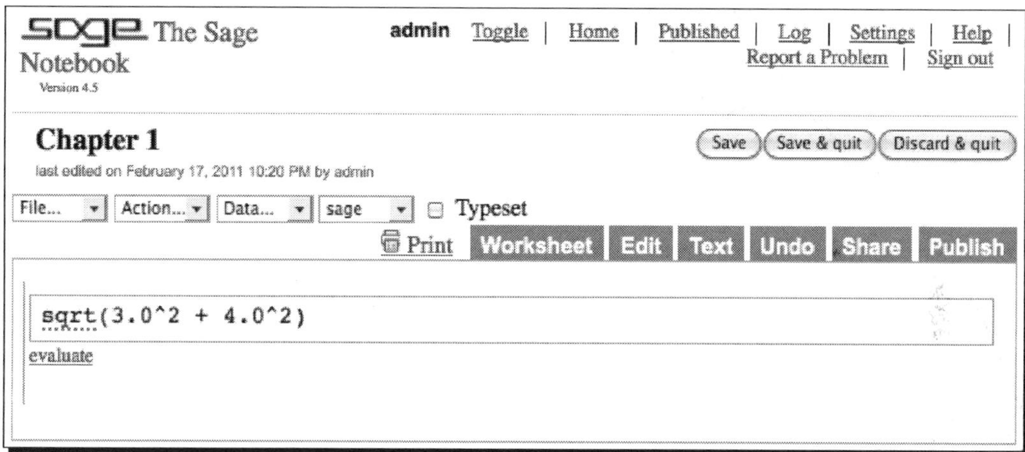

Click the **evaluate** link or press *Shift-Enter* to evaluate the contents of the cell.

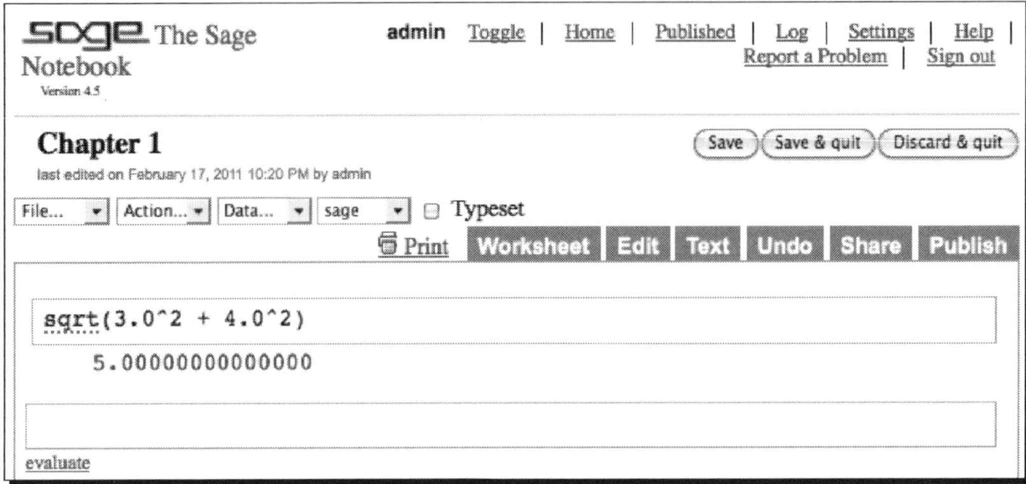

A new input cell will automatically open below the results of the calculation. You can also create a new input cell by clicking in the blank space just above an existing input cell. In *Chapter 3*, we'll cover the notebook interface in more detail.

Using Sage as a powerful calculator

Sage has all the features of a scientific calculator—and more. If you have been trying to perform mathematical calculations with a spreadsheet or the built-in calculator in your operating system, it's time to upgrade. Sage offers all the built-in functions you would expect. Here are a few examples:

```
sqrt(3.0^2 + 4.0^2)
    5.00000000000000

sin(3.14159 / 4)
    0.707106312093558

cosh(6.4)^2 - sinh(6.4)^2
    1.00000000000000

sqrt(-4.0)
    2.00000000000000*I
```

If you have to make a calculation repeatedly, you can define a function and variables to make your life easier. For example, let's say that you need to calculate the Reynolds number, which is used in fluid mechanics:

$$Re = \frac{L\,v}{\nu}$$

You can define a function and variables like this:

```
Re(velocity, length, kinematic_viscosity) = velocity * length /
kinematic_viscosity

v = 0.01
L = 1e-3
nu = 1e-6
Re(v, L, nu)
```

When you type the code into an input cell and evaluate the cell, your screen will look like this:

```
Re(velocity, length, kinematic_viscosity) = velocity * length /
kinematic_viscosity
v = 0.01
L = 1e-3
nu = 1e-6
Re(v, L, nu)
    10.0000000000000
```

Now, you can change the value of one or more variables and re-run the calculation:

```
v = 0.05
L = 8.4e-4
Re(v, L, nu)
    42.0000000000000
```

Sage can also perform exact calculations with integers and rational numbers. Using the predefined constant `pi` will result in exact values from trigonometric operations. Sage will even utilize complex numbers when needed. Here are some examples:

```
sin(pi / 4)
    1/2*sqrt(2)

print 1 / 2 + 1 / 4
    3/4

sqrt(-4)
    2*I
```

Symbolic mathematics

Much of the difficulty of higher mathematics actually lies in the extensive algebraic manipulations that are required to obtain a result. Sage can save you many hours, and many sheets of paper, by automating some tedious tasks in mathematics. We'll start with basic calculus. For example, let's compute the derivative of the following equation:

$$f(x) = \frac{x^2 - 1}{x^4 + 1}$$

The following code defines the equation and computes the derivative:

```
var('x')
f(x) = (x^2 - 1) / (x^4 + 1)
show(f)
show(derivative(f, x))
```

The results will look like this:

$$x \mapsto \frac{x^2 - 1}{x^4 + 1}$$

$$x \mapsto \frac{-4\,(x^2 - 1)x^3}{(x^4 + 1)^2} + \frac{2\,x}{x^4 + 1}$$

The first line defines a symbolic variable x (Sage automatically assumes that x is always a symbolic variable, but we will define it in each example for clarity). We then defined a function as a quotient of polynomials. Taking the derivative of f(x) would normally require the use of the quotient rule, which can be very tedious to calculate. Sage computes the derivative effortlessly.

Now, we'll move on to integration, which can be one of the most daunting tasks in calculus. Let's compute the following indefinite integral symbolically:

$$\int e^x cos(x)\, dx$$

The code to compute the integral is very simple:

```
f(x) = e^x * cos(x)
f_int(x) = integrate(f, x)
show(f_int)
```

The result is as follows:

$$x \mapsto \frac{1}{2}\,(\sin\,(x) + \cos\,(x))e^x$$

To perform this integration by hand, integration by parts would have to be done twice, which could be quite time consuming. If we want to better understand the function we just defined, we can graph it with the following code:

```
f(x) = e^x * cos(x)
plot(f, (x, -2, 8))
```

Sage will produce the following plot:

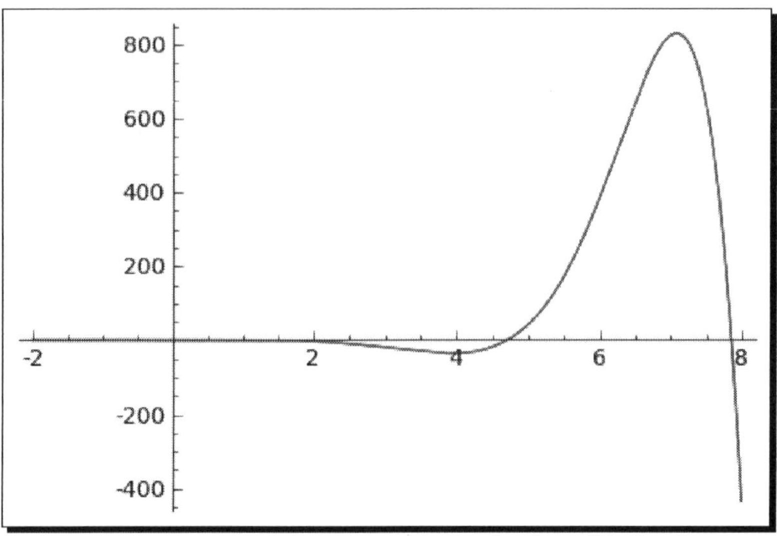

Sage can also compute definite integrals symbolically:

$$\int_{0}^{1} \sqrt{1 - x^2}\, dx$$

To compute a definite integral, we simply have to tell Sage the limits of integration:

```
f(x) = sqrt(1 - x^2)
f_integral = integrate(f, (x, 0, 1))
show(f_integral)
```

The result is:

$$x \mapsto \frac{1}{4}\pi$$

This would have required the use of a substitution if computed by hand.

Have a go hero

There is actually a clever way to evaluate the integral from the previous problem without doing any calculus. If it isn't immediately apparent, plot the function f(x) from 0 to 1 and see if you recognize it. Note that the aspect ratio of the plot may not be square.

The partial fraction decomposition is another technique that Sage can do a lot faster than you. The solution to the following example covers two full pages in a calculus textbook — assuming that you don't make any mistakes in the algebra!

```
f(x) = (3 * x^4 + 4 * x^3 + 16 * x^2 + 20 * x + 9) / ((x + 2) * (x^2 +
3)^2)
g(x) = f.partial_fraction(x)
show(g)
```

The result is as follows:

$$x \mapsto \frac{2x}{x^2+3} + \frac{1}{x+2} + \frac{4x}{(x^2+3)^2}$$

We'll use partial fractions again when we talk about solving ordinary differential equations symbolically.

Linear algebra

Linear algebra is one of the most fundamental tasks in numerical computing. Sage has many facilities for performing linear algebra, both numerical and symbolic. One fundamental operation is solving a system of linear equations:

$$\begin{pmatrix} 0 & -1 & -1 & 1 \\ 1 & 1 & 1 & 1 \\ 2 & 4 & 1 & -2 \\ 3 & 1 & -2 & 2 \end{pmatrix} \begin{pmatrix} x_1 \\ x_2 \\ x_3 \\ x_4 \end{pmatrix} = \begin{pmatrix} 0 \\ 6 \\ -1 \\ 3 \end{pmatrix}$$

Although this is a tedious problem to solve by hand, it only requires a few lines of code in Sage:

```
A = Matrix(QQ, [[0, -1, -1, 1], [1, 1, 1, 1], [2, 4, 1, -2],
    [3, 1, -2, 2]])
B = vector([0, 6, -1, 3])
A.solve_right(B)
```

The answer is as follows:

```
(2, -1, 3, 2)
```

Notice that Sage provided an exact answer with integer values. When we created matrix A, the argument `QQ` specified that the matrix was to contain rational values. Therefore, the result contains only rational values (which all happen to be integers for this problem). *Chapter 5* describes in detail how to do linear algebra with Sage.

Solving an ordinary differential equation

Solving ordinary differential equations by hand can be time consuming. Although many differential equations can be handled with standard techniques such as the Laplace transform, other equations require special methods of solution. For example, let's try to solve the following equation:

$$x^2 \frac{d^2y}{dx^2} + x\frac{dy}{dx} + (x^2 - v^2)\, y = 0$$

The following code will solve the equation:

```
var('x, y, v')
y=function('y', x)
assume(v, 'integer')
f = desolve(x^2 * diff(y,x,2) + x*diff(y,x) + (x^2 - v^2) * y == 0,
    y, ivar=x)
show(f)
```

The answer is defined in terms of Bessel functions:

$$k_1 \text{bessel}_j(v,x) + k_2 \text{bessel}_y(v,x)$$

It turns out that the equation we solved is known as Bessel's equation. This example illustrates that Sage knows about special functions, such as Bessel and Legendre functions. It also shows that you can use the `assume` function to tell Sage to make specific assumptions when solving problems. In *Chapter 7*, we will explore Sage's powerful symbolic capabilities.

More advanced graphics

Sage has sophisticated plotting capabilities. By combining the power of the Python programming language with Sage's graphics functions, we can construct detailed illustrations. To demonstrate a few of Sage's advanced plotting features, we will solve a simple system of equations algebraically:

```
var('x')
f(x) = x^2
g(x) = x^3 - 2 * x^2 + 2

solutions=solve(f == g, x, solution_dict=True)

for s in solutions:
    show(s)
```

The result is as follows:

$$\left\{x : -\sqrt{3} + 1\right\}$$

$$\left\{x : \sqrt{3} + 1\right\}$$

$$\{x : 1\}$$

We used the keyword argument `solution_dict=True` to tell the solve function to return the solutions in the form of a Python list of Python dictionaries. We then used a `for` loop to iterate over the list and display the three solution dictionaries. We'll go into more detail about lists and dictionaries in *Chapter 4*. Let's illustrate our answers with a detailed plot:

```
p1 = plot(f, (x, -1, 3), color='blue', axes_labels=['x', 'y'])
p2 = plot(g, (x, -1, 3), color='red')

labels = []
lines = []
markers = []
for s in solutions:
    x_value = s[x].n(digits=3)
    y_value = f(x_value).n(digits=3)
    labels.append(text('y=' + str(y_value), (x_value+0.5,
```

```
        y_value+0.5), color='black'))
    lines.append(line([(x_value, 0), (x_value, y_value)],
        color='black', linestyle='--'))
    markers.append(point((x_value,y_value), color='black', size=30))

show(p1+p2+sum(labels) + sum(lines) + sum(markers))
```

The plot looks like this:

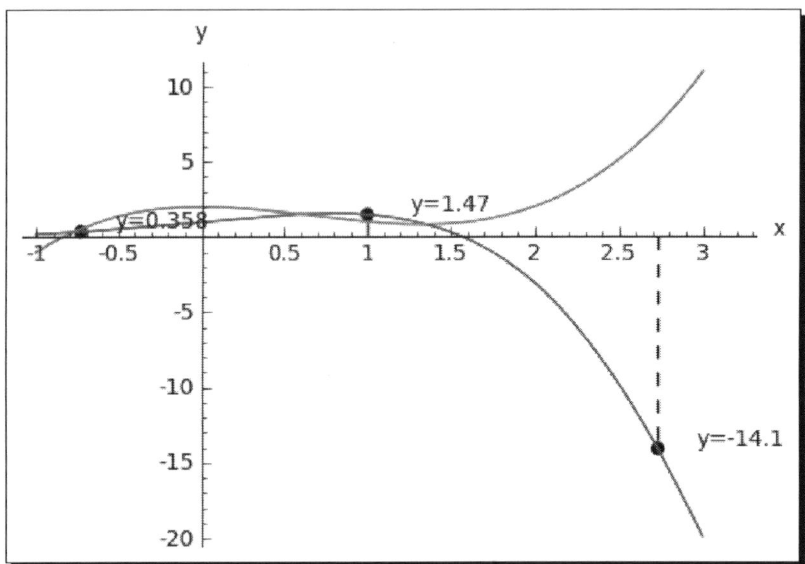

We created a plot of each function in a different colour, and labelled the axes. We then used another `for` loop to iterate through the list of solutions and annotate each one. Plotting will be covered in detail in *Chapter 6*.

Visualising a three-dimensional surface

Sage does not restrict you to making plots in two dimensions. To demonstrate the 3D capabilities of Sage, we will create a parametric plot of a mathematical surface known as the "figure 8" immersion of the Klein bottle. You will need to have Java enabled in your web browser to see the 3D plot.

```
var('u,v')
r = 2.0
f_x = (r + cos(u / 2) * sin(v) - sin(u / 2)
    * sin(2 * v)) * cos(u)
f_y = (r + cos(u / 2) * sin(v) - sin(u / 2)
    * sin(2 * v)) * sin(u)
```

```
f_z = sin(u / 2) * sin(v) + cos(u / 2) * sin(2 * v)
parametric_plot3d([f_x, f_y, f_z], (u, 0, 2 * pi),
    (v, 0, 2 * pi), color="red")
```

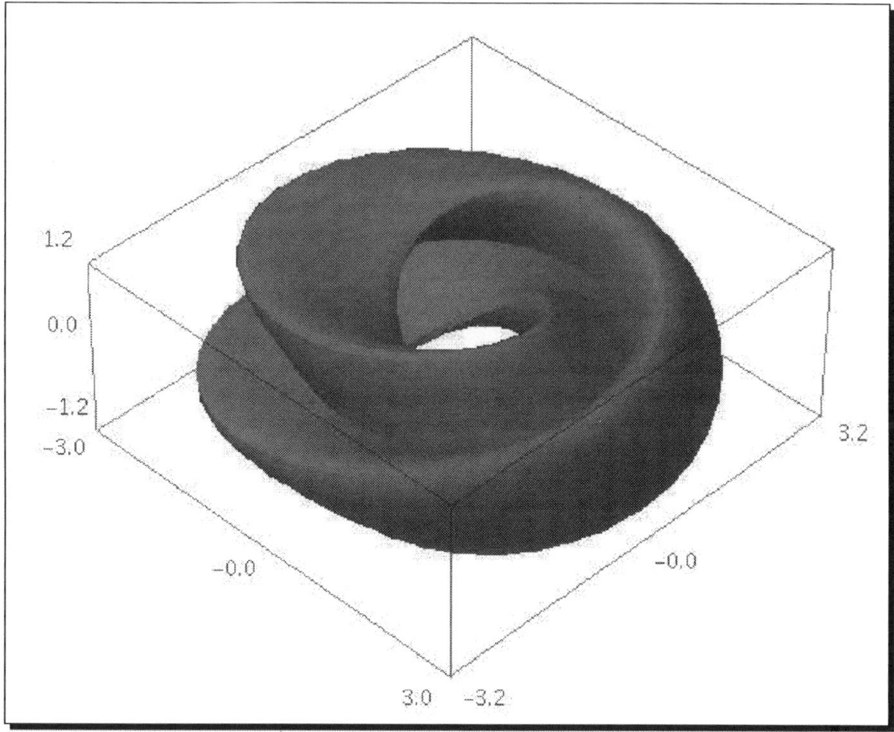

In the Sage notebook interface, the 3D plot is fully interactive. Clicking and dragging with the mouse over the image changes the viewpoint. The scroll wheel zooms in and out, and right-clicking on the image brings up a menu with further options.

Typesetting mathematical expressions

Sage can be used in conjunction with the LaTeX typesetting system to create publication-quality typeset mathematical expressions. In fact, all of the mathematical expressions in this chapter were typeset using Sage and exported as graphics. *Chapter 10* explains how to use LaTeX and Sage together.

A practical example: analysing experimental data

One of the most common tasks for an engineer or scientist is analysing data from an experiment. Sage provides a set of tools for loading, exploring, and plotting data. The following series of examples shows how a scientist might analyse data from a population of bacteria that are growing in a fermentation tank. Someone has measured the optical density (abbreviated OD) of the liquid in the tank over time as the bacteria are multiplying. We want to analyse the data to see how the size of the population of bacteria varies over time. Please note that the examples in this section must be run in order, since the later examples depend upon results from the earlier ones.

Time for action – fitting the standard curve

The optical density is correlated to the concentration of bacteria in the liquid. To quantify this correlation, someone has measured the optical density of a number of calibration standards of known concentration. In this example, we will fit a "standard curve" to the calibration data that we can use to determine the concentration of bacteria from optical density readings:

```
import numpy
var('OD, slope, intercept')
def standard_curve(OD, slope, intercept):
    """Apply a linear standard curve to optical density data"""
    return OD * slope + intercept
# Enter data to define standard curve
CFU = numpy.array([2.60E+08, 3.14E+08, 3.70E+08, 4.62E+08,
    8.56E+08, 1.39E+09, 1.84E+09])
optical_density = numpy.array([0.083, 0.125, 0.213, 0.234,
    0.604, 1.092, 1.141])
OD_vs_CFU = zip(optical_density, CFU)
# Fit linear standard
std_params = find_fit(OD_vs_CFU, standard_curve,
    parameters=[slope, intercept],
    variables=[OD], initial_guess=[1e9, 3e8],
    solution_dict = True)
for param, value in std_params.iteritems():
    print(str(param) + ' = %e' % value)
# Plot
data_plot = scatter_plot(OD_vs_CFU, markersize=20,
    facecolor='red', axes_labels=['OD at 600nm', 'CFU/ml'])
fit_plot = plot(standard_curve(OD, std_params[slope],
    std_params[intercept]), (OD, 0, 1.2))
show(data_plot+fit_plot)
```

The results are as follows:

```
slope = 1.324714e+09
intercept = 1.237283e+08
```

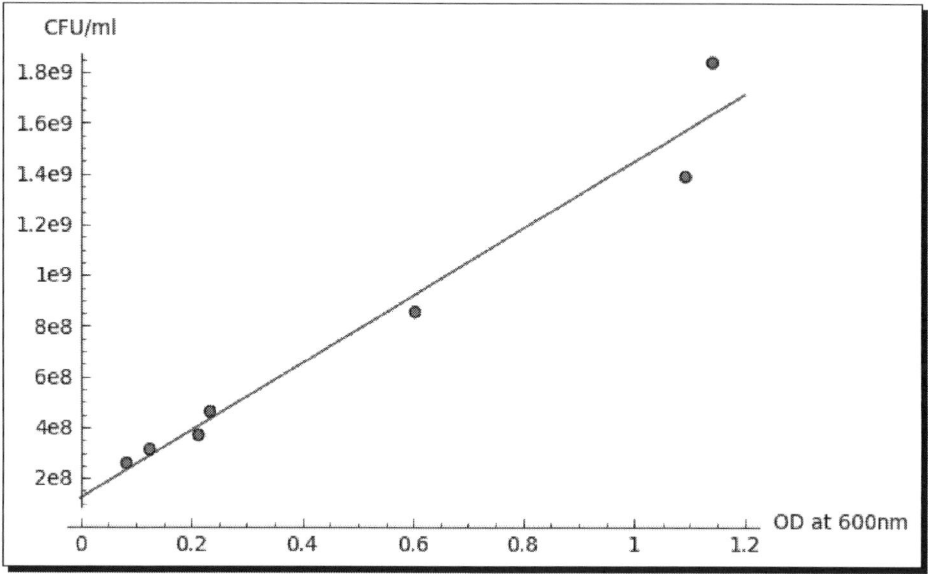

What just happened?

We introduced some new concepts in this example. On the first line, the statement `import numpy` allows us to access functions and classes from a module called NumPy. NumPy is based upon a fast, efficient array class, which we will use to store our data. We created a NumPy array and hard-coded the data values for OD, and created another array to store values of concentration (in practice, we would read these values from a file) We then defined a Python function called `standard_curve`, which we will use to convert optical density values to concentrations. We used the `find_fit` function to fit the slope and intercept parameters to the experimental data points. Finally, we plotted the data points with the `scatter_plot` function and the plotted the fitted line with the `plot` function. Note that we had to use a function called `zip` to combine the two NumPy arrays into a single list of points before we could plot them with `scatter_plot`. We'll learn all about Python functions in *Chapter 4*, and *Chapter 8* will explain more about fitting routines and other numerical methods in Sage.

Time for action – plotting experimental data

Now that we've defined the relationship between the optical density and the concentration of bacteria, let's look at a series of data points taken over the span of an hour. We will convert from optical density to concentration units, and plot the data.

```
sample_times = numpy.array([0, 20, 40, 60, 80, 100, 120,
    140, 160, 180, 200, 220, 240, 280, 360, 380, 400, 420,
    440, 460, 500, 520, 540, 560, 580, 600, 620, 640, 660,
    680, 700, 720, 760, 1240, 1440, 1460, 1500, 1560])

OD_readings = numpy.array([0.083, 0.087, 0.116, 0.119, 0.122,
    0.123, 0.125, 0.131, 0.138, 0.142, 0.158, 0.177, 0.213,
    0.234, 0.424, 0.604, 0.674, 0.726, 0.758, 0.828, 0.919,
    0.996, 1.024, 1.066, 1.092, 1.107, 1.113, 1.116, 1.12,
    1.129, 1.132, 1.135, 1.141, 1.109, 1.004, 0.984, 0.972, 0.952])

concentrations = standard_curve(OD_readings, std_params[slope],
     std_params[intercept])
exp_data = zip(sample_times, concentrations)

data_plot = scatter_plot(exp_data, markersize=20, facecolor='red',
    axes_labels=['time (sec)', 'CFU/ml'])
show(data_plot)
```

The scatter plot looks like this:

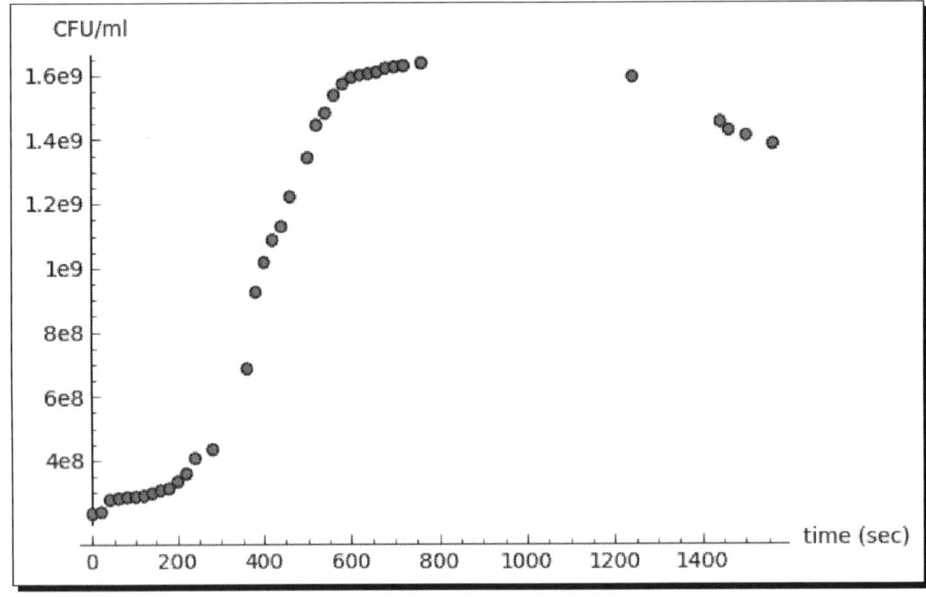

What just happened?

We defined one NumPy array of sample times, and another NumPy array of optical density values. As in the previous example, these values could easily be read from a file. We used the `standard_curve` function and the fitted parameter values from the previous example to convert the optical density to concentration. We then plotted the data points using the `scatter_plot` function.

Time for action – fitting a growth model

Now, let's fit a growth model to this data. The model we will use is based on the Gompertz function, and it has four parameters:

```
var('t, max_rate, lag_time, y_max, y0')

def gompertz(t, max_rate, lag_time, y_max, y0):
    """Define a growth model based upon the Gompertz growth curve"""
    return y0 + (y_max - y0) * numpy.exp(-numpy.exp(1.0 +
    max_rate * numpy.exp(1) * (lag_time - t) / (y_max - y0)))

# Estimated parameter values for initial guess
max_rate_est = (1.4e9 - 5e8)/200.0
lag_time_est = 100
y_max_est = 1.7e9
y0_est = 2e8

gompertz_params = find_fit(exp_data, gompertz,
    parameters=[max_rate, lag_time, y_max, y0],
    variables=[t],
    initial_guess=[max_rate_est, lag_time_est, y_max_est, y0_est],
    solution_dict = True)

for param,value in gompertz_params.iteritems():
    print(str(param) + ' = %e' % value)
```

The fitted parameter values are displayed:

```
lag_time = 2.950639e+02
y_max = 1.563822e+09
max_rate = 6.606311e+06
y0 = 3.051120e+08
```

Finally, let's plot the fitted model and the experimental data points on the same axes:

```
gompertz_model_plot = plot(gompertz(t, gompertz_params[max_rate],
    gompertz_params[lag_time], gompertz_params[y_max],
    gompertz_params[y0]), (t, 0, sample_times.max()))

show(gompertz_model_plot + data_plot)
```

The plot looks like this:

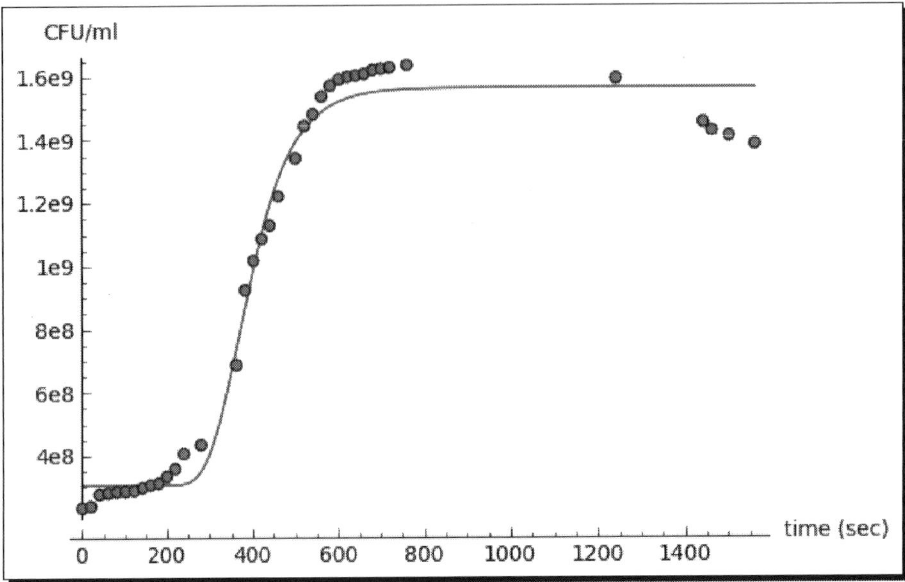

What just happened?

We defined another Python function called `gompertz` to model the growth of bacteria in the presence of limited resources. Based on the data plot from the previous example, we estimated values for the parameters of the model to use an initial guess for the fitting routine. We used the `find_fit` function again to fit the model to the experimental data, and displayed the fitted values. Finally, we plotted the fitted model and the experimental data on the same axes.

Summary

This chapter has given you a quick, high-level overview of some of the many things that Sage can do for you. Don't worry if you feel a little lost, or if you had trouble trying to modify the examples. Everything you need to know will be covered in detail in later chapters.

Specifically, we looked at:

- Using Sage as a sophisticated scientific and graphing calculator
- Speeding up tedious tasks in symbolic mathematics
- Solving a system of linear equations, a system of algebraic equations, and an ordinary differential equation

- Making publication-quality plots in two and three dimensions
- Using Sage for data analysis and model fitting in a practical setting

Hopefully, you are convinced that Sage will be the right tool to assist you in your work, and you are ready to install Sage on your computer. In the next chapter, you will learn how to install Sage on various platforms.

2
Installing Sage

Remember that you don't actually have to install Sage to start using it. You can start learning Sage by utilizing one of the free public notebook servers that can be found at `http://www.sagenb.org/`. However, if you find that Sage suits your needs, you will want to install a copy on your own computer. This will guarantee that Sage is always available to you, and it will reduce the load on the public servers so that others can experiment with Sage. In addition, your data will be more secure, and you can utilize more computing power to solve larger problems. This chapter will take you through the process of installing Sage on various platforms.

In this chapter we shall:

- Install a binary version of Sage on Windows and install a binary version of Sage on OS X
- Install a binary version of Sage on GNU/Linux
- Compile Sage from source

Before you begin

At the moment, Sage is fully supported on certain versions of the following platforms: some Linux distributions (Fedora, openSUSE, Red Hat, and Ubuntu), Mac OS X, OpenSolaris, and Solaris. Sage is tested on all of these platforms before each release, and binaries are always available for these platforms. The latest list of supported platforms is available at `http://wiki.sagemath.org/SupportedPlatforms`. The page also contains information about platforms that Sage will probably run on, and the status of efforts to port Sage to various platforms.

When downloading Sage, the website attempts to detect which operating system you are using, and directs you to the appropriate download page. If it sends you to the wrong download page, use the "Download" menu at the top of the page to choose the correct platform. If you get stuck at any point, the official Sage installation guide is available at `http://www.sagemath.org/doc/installation/`.

Installing a binary version of Sage on Windows

Installing Sage on Windows is slightly more involved than installing a typical Windows program. Sage is a collection of over 90 different tools. Many of these tools are developed within a UNIX-like environment, and some have not been successfully ported to Windows. Porting programs from UNIX-like environments to Windows requires the installation of Cygwin (`http://www.cygwin.com/`), which provides many of the tools that are standard on a Linux system. Rather than attempting to port all of the necessary tools to Cygwin on Windows, the developers of Sage have chosen to distribute Sage as a virtual machine that can run on Windows with the use of the free VMWare Player. A port to Cygwin is in progress, and more information can be found at `http://trac.sagemath.org/sage_trac/wiki/CygwinPort`.

Downloading VMware Player

The VMWare Player can be found at `http://www.vmware.com/products/player/`. Clicking the **Download** link will direct you to a registration form. Fill out and submit the form. You will receive a confirmation email that contains a link that must be clicked to complete the registration process and take you to the download page. Choose **Start Download Manager**, which downloads and runs a small application that performs the actual download and saves the file to a location of your choice.

Installing VMWare Player

After downloading VMWare Player, double-click the saved file to start the installation wizard. Follow the instructions in the wizard to install the Player. You will have to reboot the computer when instructed.

Downloading and extracting Sage

Download Sage by following the **Download** link from `http://www.sagemath.org`. The site should automatically detect that you are using Windows, and direct you to the right download page. Choose the closest mirror and download the compressed virtual machine. Be aware that the file is nearly 1GB in size. Once the download is complete, right-click the compressed file and choose **Extract all** from the pop-up menu.

Launching the virtual machine

Launch VMware Player and accept the license terms. When the Player has started, click **Open a Virtual Machine** and select the Sage virtual machine, which is called `sage-vmware.vmx`. Click **Play virtual machine** to run Sage. If you have run Sage before, it should appear in the list of virtual machines on the left side of the dialog box, and you can double-click to run it.

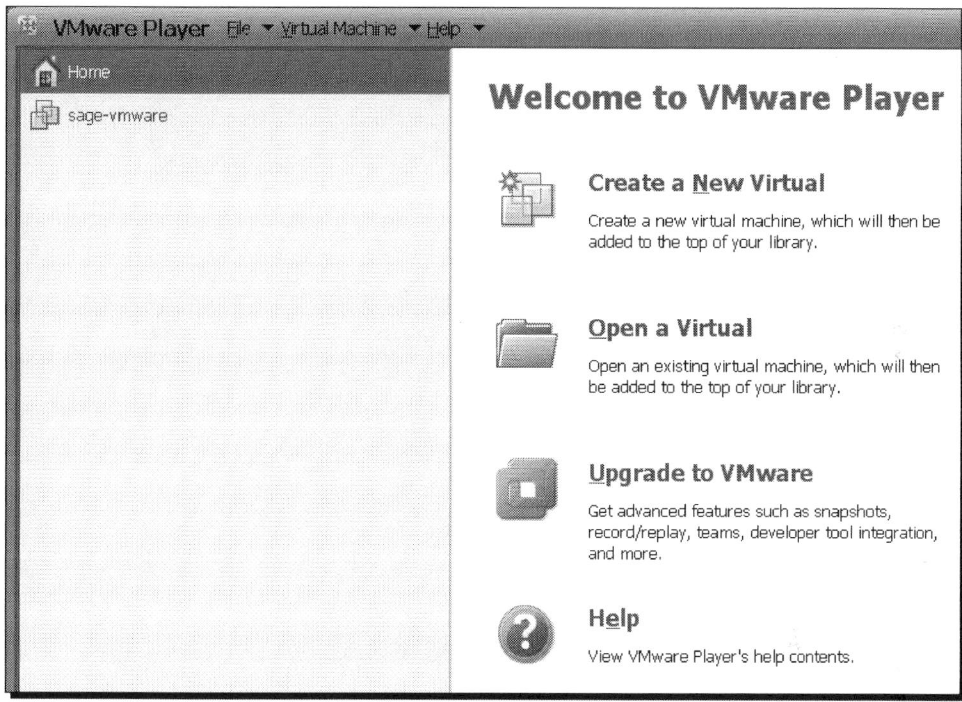

When the virtual machine launches, you may receive one or more warnings about various devices (such as Bluetooth adapters) that the virtual machine cannot connect to. Don't worry about this, since Sage doesn't need these devices.

Start Sage

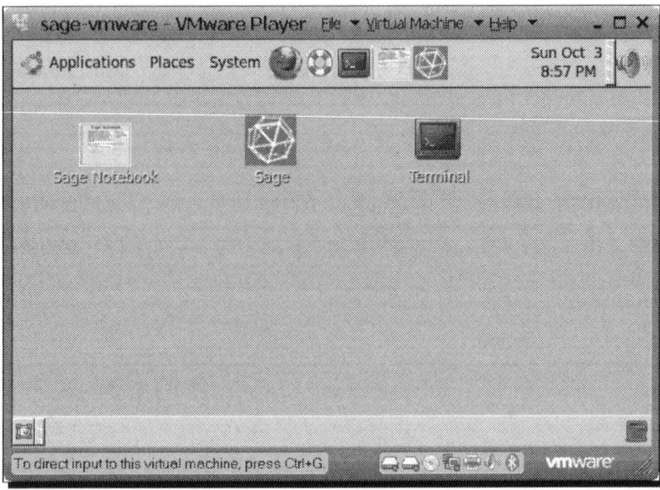

Once the virtual machine is running, you will see three icons. Double-clicking the **Sage Notebook** icon starts the Sage notebook interface, while the **Sage** icon starts the command-line interface. The first time you run Sage, you will have to wait while it regenerates files. When it finishes, you are ready to go.

You may get the warning "External network not set up" when launching the notebook interface. This does not cause any problems.

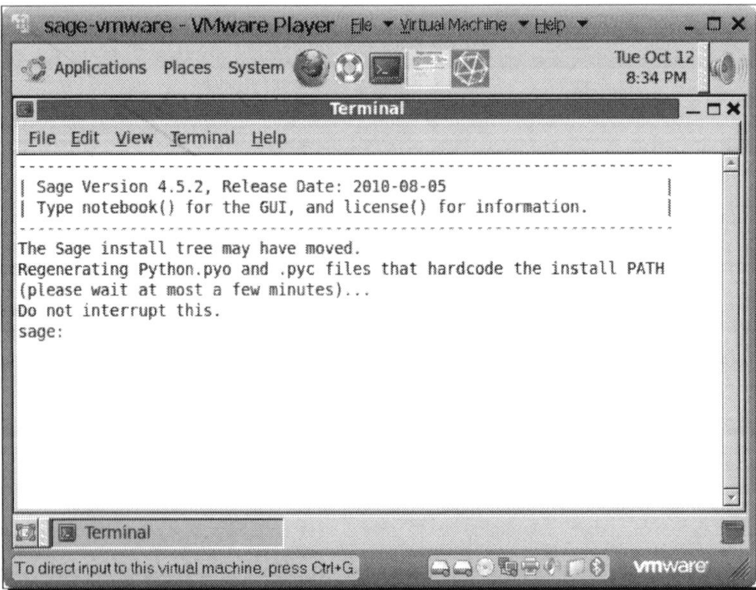

When you are done using Sage, choose **Shut Down...** from the System menu at the top of the window, and a dialog will appear. Click the **Shut Down** button to close the virtual machine.

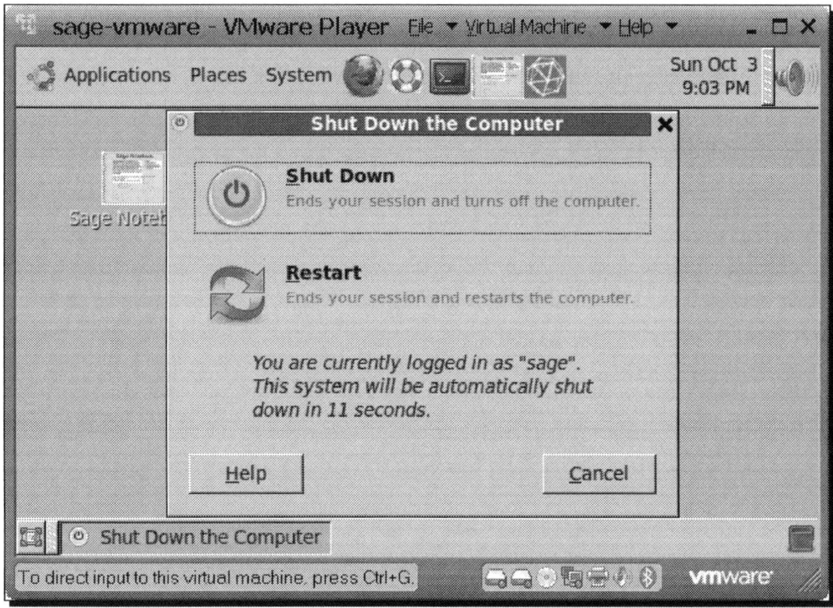

Installing a binary version of Sage on OS X

On Mac OS X, you have the option of installing a pre-built binary application, or downloading the source code and compiling Sage yourself. One advantage of the pre-built binary is that it is very easy to install, because it contains everything you need to run Sage. Another advantage of the binary is that building Sage from source requires a lot of computational resources, and may take a long time on older machines. However, there are a number of disadvantages to prebuilt binaries. The binary download is quite large, and the installed files take up a lot of disk space. Many of the tools in the binary may be duplicates of tools you already have on your system. Pre-built binaries cannot be tuned to take advantage of the hardware features of a particular platform, so building Sage from source is preferred if you are looking for the best performance on CPU-intensive tasks. You will have to choose which method is right for you.

Downloading Sage

Download Sage by following the **Download** link from `http://www.sagemath.org`. The site should automatically detect that you are using OS X, and direct you to the right download page. Choose a mirror site close to you. Select your architecture (Intel for new Macs, or PowerPC for older G4 and G5 macs). Then, click the link for the correct `.dmg` file for you version of Mac OS X. If you aren't sure, click the Apple menu on the far left side of the menu bar and choose **About This Mac**.

Installing Sage

Once the download is complete, double-click the `.dmg` file to mount the disk image. Drag the Sage folder from the disk image to the desired location on your hard drive (such as the `Apps` folder).

If the copy procedure fails, you will need to do it from the command line. Open the Terminal application and enter the following commands. Be sure to change the name `sage-4.5-OSX-64bit-10.6-i386-Darwin.dmg` to the name of the file you just downloaded:

```
$ cd /Applications
$ cp -R -P /Volumes/sage-4.5-OSX-64bit-10.6-i386-Darwin.dmg /sage .
```

After the copy process is complete, right-click on the icon for the disk image, and choose **Eject**.

Starting Sage

Use the Finder to visit the Sage folder that you just created. Double-click on the icon called **Sage**. It should open with the Terminal application. If it doesn't start, right-click on the icon, go to the **Open With** submenu and choose `Terminal.app`. The Sage command line will now be running in a Terminal window. The first time you run Sage, you will have to wait while it regenerates files. When it finishes, you are ready to go.

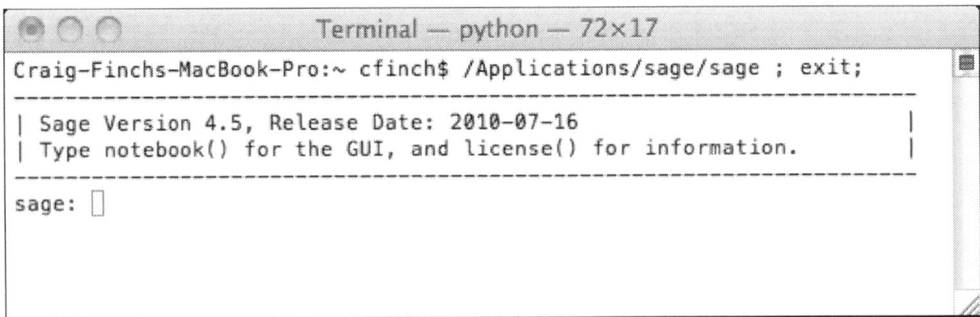

There are three ways to exit Sage: type `exit` or `quit` at the Sage command prompt, or press *Ctrl-D* in the Terminal window. You can then quit the Terminal application.

Installing a binary version of Sage on GNU/Linux

As with Mac OS X, you have the option of installing a pre-built binary application for your version of Linux, or downloading the source code and compiling Sage yourself. The same trade-offs apply to Linux. Keep in mind that the Sage team only distributes pre-build binaries for a few popular distributions. If you are using a different distribution, you'll have to compile Sage from source anyway. The following instructions will assume you are downloading a binary application. I will use Ubuntu as an example, but other versions of Linux should be very similar.

Most modern Linux distributions use a package manager to install and remove software. Sage is not available as an officially supported package for any Linux distribution at this time. "Unofficial" packages have been created for Debian, Mandriva, Ubuntu, and possibly others, but they are unlikely to be up to date and may not work properly. An effort to integrate Sage with Gentoo Linux can be found at `https://github.com/cschwan/sage-on-gentoo`.

Downloading and decompressing Sage

Download the appropriate pre-built binary from `http://www.sagemath.org/download-linux.html`. Choose the closest mirror, and then choose the appropriate architecture for your operating system. If you're not sure whether your operating system is built for 32 or 64 bit operation, open a terminal and type the following on the command line:

```
$ uname -m
```

If the output contains 64, then your system is probably a 64-bit system. If not, it's a 32-bit. An alternative way to check is with the following command:

```
$ file /usr/bin/bin
```

If the file type contains 64, your kernel probably supports 64 bit applications. If not, you need the 32 bit version. Select the appropriate prebuilt binary and save it to your computer.

Once the download is done, uncompress the archive. You can use the graphical archiving tool for your version of Linux (the Ubuntu archiver is shown in the following screenshot). If you prefer the command line, type the following:

```
tar --lzma -xvf sage-*...tar.lzma
```

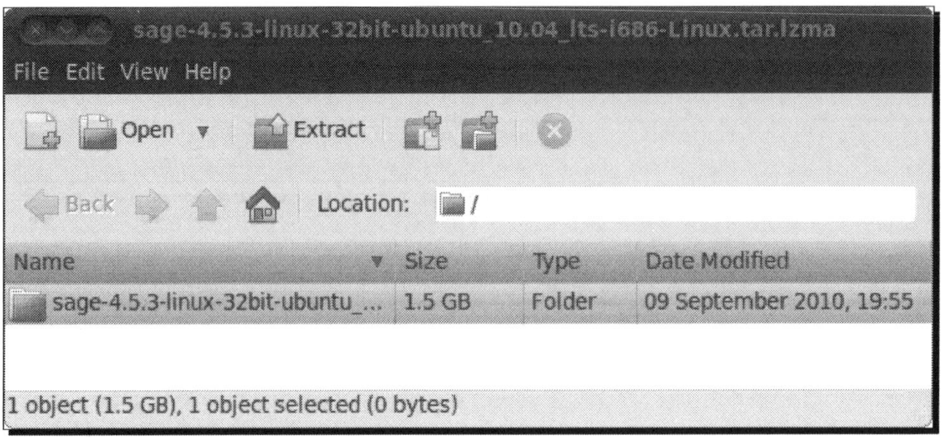

Running Sage from your user account

After decompression, you will have a single directory. This directory is self-contained, so no further installation is necessary. You can simply move it to a convenient location within your home directory. This is a good option if you don't have administrator privileges on the system, or if you are the only person who uses the system. To run Sage, open a terminal and change to the Sage directory (you will have to modify the command below, depending on the version you installed and where you installed it):

```
cfinch@ubuntu:$ cd sage-4.5.3-linux-32bit-ubuntu_10.04_lts-i686-Linux
```

Run Sage by typing the following:

```
cfinch@ubuntu:$ ./sage
```

Don't forget the period before the slash! The first time you run Sage, you will have to wait while it regenerates files, as shown in the following screenshot. When it finishes, you are ready to go.

```
File Edit View Terminal Help
----------------------------------------------------------------------
| Sage Version 4.5.3, Release Date: 2010-09-04                       |
| Type notebook() for the GUI, and license() for information.        |
----------------------------------------------------------------------
The Sage install tree may have moved.
Regenerating Python.pyo and .pyc files that hardcode the install PATH
(please wait at most a few minutes)...
Do not interrupt this.
sage:
```

There are three ways to exit Sage: type `exit` or `quit` at the Sage command prompt, or press *Ctrl-D* in the terminal window.

Installing for multiple users

If you are the administrator of a shared system, you may want to install Sage so that everyone can use it. Since Sage consists of one self-contained directory, I suggest moving it to the `/opt` directory:

```
sudo mv sage-4.5.3-linux-32bit-ubuntu_10.04_lts-i686-Linux /opt
[sudo] password for cfinch:
```

To make it easy for everyone to run Sage, make a symbolic link from `/usr/bin` to the actual location:

```
cfinch@ubuntu:/usr/bin$ sudo ln -s /opt/sage-4.5.3-linux-32bit-
ubuntu_10.04_lts-i686-Linux/sage sage
[sudo] password for cfinch:
```

As before, Sage will have to regenerate its internal files the first time it runs after moving. You should run Sage once as a user with administrative privileges, because other users won't have the necessary write permissions to save the files. Once this is completed, any user will be able to use Sage by typing Sage at the command prompt.

Building Sage from source

This section will describe how to build Sage from source code on OS X or Linux. Although Sage consists of nearly 100 packages, the build process hides much of the complexity. It is impossible to provide instructions for all of the platforms that can build Sage, but the following guidelines should cover most cases. The official documentation for building Sage from source is available at `http://sagemath.org/doc/installation/source.html`.

Prerequisites

In order to compile Sage, you will need about 2.5GB of free disk space, and the following tools must be installed:

- GCC
- g++
- gfortran
- make
- m4
- perl
- ranlib
- tar
- readline and its development headers
- ssh-keygen (only needed to run the notebook in secure mode)
- latex (highly recommended, though not strictly required)

If you are running OS X (version 10.4 or later), install XCode to get all of these tools. XCode is available for free when you sign up as a developer at `http://developer.apple.com/`. Make sure that you have XCode version 2.4 or later.

If you are running Linux, use your package manager to install any missing tools. For example, on a Debian-based system like Ubuntu, run the following on the command line:

```
$ sudo apt-get install build-essential m4 gfortran
$ sudo apt-get install readline-common libreadline-dev
```

To install LaTeX (optional):

```
$ sudo apt-get install texlive xpdf evince xdvi
```

Downloading and decompressing source tarball

Download the latest source tarball from `http://sagemath.org/download-source.html`. Open a terminal, change to the directory where you saved the tarball, and decompress it with the following command:

```
$ tar -xvf sage-*.tar
```

Building Sage

If you have a multi-core or multi-processor machine, you can speed up the build process by performing a parallel compilation. You can control this by setting the `MAKE` environment variable. For example, using Bash syntax, you can set the `MAKE` variable to use four cores:

```
$ export MAKE="make -j4"
```

Change to the Sage directory:

```
$ cd sage-*
```

Build Sage:

```
$ make
```

Sage may take a long time (1 hour to several days) to compile, depending on the speed of the machine.

Installation

When the compilation process is done, you should be able to run Sage from the build directory. If you want to move the Sage installation or make it available to other users on a shared Linux system, follow the directions in the previous sections.

Summary

At this point, you should have a functioning Sage installation on your machine. In the next chapter, you'll learn the basics of using Sage.

3
Getting Started with Sage

In this chapter, you will learn the basic ideas that will be the foundation for using all the features of Sage. We will start by learning how to use the command line and notebook interfaces efficiently. Then, we'll look at basic concepts like variables, operators, functions, and objects. By the end of the chapter, you should be able to use Sage like a sophisticated scientific graphing calculator.

- Using the interactive shell
- Using the notebook interface
- Learning more about operators and variables
- Defining and using callable symbolic expressions
- Calling functions and making simple plots
- Defining your own functions
- Working with objects in Sage

How to get help with Sage

The Sage documentation is accessible from the interactive shell and the notebook interface. Further help is available on the Web. The main Sage documentation page at `http://www.sagemath.org/help.html` provides links to dozens of resources. A few of these links are especially useful:

- The official Sage tutorial can be found at `http://www.sagemath.org/doc/tutorial/`, and it is also accessible from the **Help** link in the notebook interface. The Python language tutorial at `http://docs.python.org/tutorial/` will also be helpful.
- The reference manual at `http://www.sagemath.org/doc/reference/` provides the full API documentation, along with many examples.

- Thematic tutorials at `http://www.sagemath.org/doc/thematic_tutorials/index.html` focus on specific topics.
- The "Constructions" document at `http://www.sagemath.org/doc/constructions/index.html` describes how to do specific things with Sage.

Interactive resources, including mailing lists, an IRC channel, and a discussion forum are available if you get stuck. A complete list of these resources can be found at `http://www.sagemath.org/development.html`. The mailing lists sage-support and sage-devel are intended for general questions. Other lists are available to discuss more specific topics.

Starting Sage from the command line

In the previous chapter, we learned how to start Sage. If you want to pass options to Sage when it starts, you can do so with command line arguments.

1. On OS X or a UNIX-like platform, start by opening a terminal window. On Windows, start the virtual machine and double-click the **Terminal** icon.
2. If you have added the Sage application directory to the PATH environment variable, you can just type **sage** at the command prompt. If not, you will need to enter the full path to the Sage binary.
3. Add command line arguments, separated by spaces, and press *Enter*. For example, type the following at the command prompt to start Sage and automatically launch the notebook interface:

   ```
   $ /Applications/sage/sage -notebook
   ```

There are many command line arguments, but you probably won't need them right away. Three of the most useful arguments are as follows:

Argument	Description
`-help`	Describe the most widely used command line arguments
`-advanced`	Describe more advanced command line arguments
`-notebook`	Start Sage and launch the notebook interface

Using the interactive shell

The interactive shell provides a command-line interface to Sage. When you are done using Sage, remember to type `quit` or `exit` at the Sage prompt, or press *Ctrl-D*, to exit the interactive shell. In the following examples, lines which start with the Sage command prompt **sage:** indicate commands that you need to type in. Lines without the prompt indicate output from Sage. Although most of the examples in this book utilize the notebook interface, they will work in the interactive shell, unless noted otherwise.

Time for action – doing calculations on the command line

Let's say that you need to make some quick calculations to design a simple electrical circuit. We will use the example of a series RC circuit, which consists of a resistor and a capacitor connected in series:

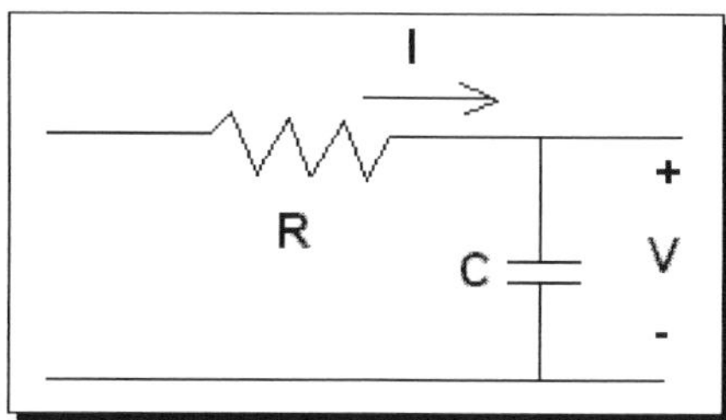

The voltage across the capacitor can be described by a linear, first-order differential equation. Eventually we will learn to solve differential equations with Sage, but for now we will just use the solution, which is well known:

$$V(t) = V_0 \, e^{-t/tau}$$

1. Define variables.

   First, we'll define some variables to work with. Type in the following text at the command prompt, and press *Enter* after every line:

```
sage: R = 250e3
sage: C = 4e-6
sage: tau = R * C
sage: tau
1.00000000000000
```

Sage doesn't give any output from variable definitions. You can type the variable name and press *Enter* to see what it contains.

2. Perform a calculation.

   The voltage across the capacitor is a function of time. Let's set an initial voltage v0 and compute the voltage after one second:

   ```
   sage: v0 = 100.0
   sage: t = tau
   sage: v0 * exp(-t / tau)
   36.7879441171442
   ```

   Here, we utilized the built-in function `exp(x)`, which computes the value of e to the power x. After a period of time equal to the time constant has elapsed, the voltage is about 36% of its original value.

3. Change some values.

   How does the voltage decay as time advances?

   ```
   sage: t = 4 * tau
   sage: v0 * exp(-t / tau)
   1.83156388887342
   ```

After a length of time equal to four time constants, the voltage is less than two per cent of its original value. Now, let's see how the value of tau impacts the voltage at a fixed time. Pressing the Up arrow allows you to scroll through the commands that you recently entered, in reverse order. To scroll the other way, press the Down arrow. Use the Up and Down arrows to get `v = v0 * exp(-t / tau)` on the command line, and edit it to match the following. Press *Enter* to see the result.

```
sage: t = tau
sage: v0 * exp(-t / (2 * tau))
60.6530659712633
```

Now, let's see what happens if tau gets smaller. Press the Up arrow to edit the previous command:

```
sage: v0 * exp(-t / (tau / 4))
1.83156388887342
```

The time constant controls how quickly the voltage decays. If you are going to work on something else, but might want to come back to this calculation, you can save your session with this command:

```
sage: save_session('RC_circuit')
```

This will save your variables in a file called **RC_circuit.sobj** in the top level of your home directory. You can enter an absolute or relative path to save the file in other locations. You can load these variables at any time in the future using the following command:

```
sage: load_session('RC_circuit')
sage: who
C   t   tau   v   v0
```

The `who` command lists the variables that you have already defined. This is very handy if you have a lot of variables and don't remember one of the names.

What just happened?

This example demonstrated some basic principles of command-line interaction with Sage. To perform a calculation, type an expression on the command line, and press *Enter* to see the result. If the result of a calculation is stored in a variable, it won't be shown. Typing the name of a variable and pressing *Enter* shows its value. You can use the Up and Down arrow keys to scroll through previous commands, edit a command, and run it again.

Getting help

There are three ways to get help from the Sage command line. To see the documentation for a command or function, type a `?` on the command line after the command. For example, to learn about the `exp` function type following:

```
sage: exp?
```

When you use any of the help commands, the normal contents of the terminal will be replaced by a help screen, which looks like this:

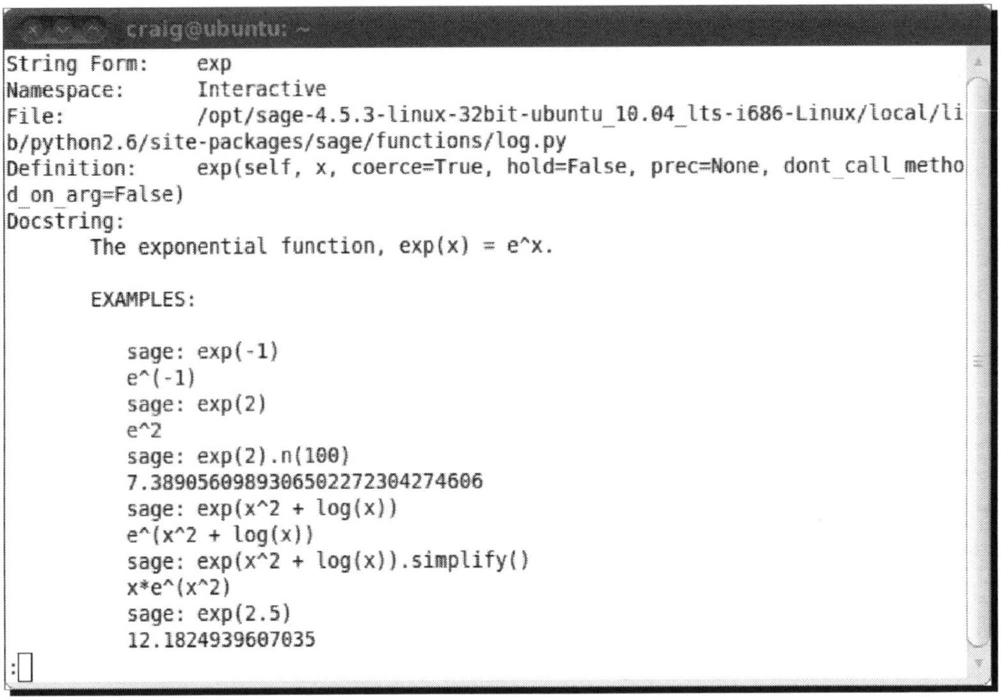

```
craig@ubuntu: ~
String Form:    exp
Namespace:      Interactive
File:           /opt/sage-4.5.3-linux-32bit-ubuntu_10.04_lts-i686-Linux/local/li
b/python2.6/site-packages/sage/functions/log.py
Definition:     exp(self, x, coerce=True, hold=False, prec=None, dont_call_metho
d_on_arg=False)
Docstring:
       The exponential function, exp(x) = e^x.

       EXAMPLES:

          sage: exp(-1)
          e^(-1)
          sage: exp(2)
          e^2
          sage: exp(2).n(100)
          7.3890560989306502272304274606
          sage: exp(x^2 + log(x))
          e^(x^2 + log(x))
          sage: exp(x^2 + log(x)).simplify()
          x*e^(x^2)
          sage: exp(2.5)
          12.1824939607035
:
```

Use the arrows to scroll up and down. Use the *Spacebar* to page down, and the *b* key to page up. Press *q* to leave the help screen and return to the command line. If you want to see the documentation and the source code for the function (if the code is available), type two question marks after the function name:

```
sage: exp??
```

Finally, to see the complete class documentation, use the `help` function:

```
sage: help(exp)
```

Command history

The Sage command line has a number of built-in shortcuts that help you work more efficiently. Most of these will be familiar to people who have worked with UNIX-like command line interfaces. We have already seen that you can use the Up arrow on your keyboard to scroll through commands that you have previously entered. To see a list of everything you have typed in this session, type `%hist` at the command prompt.

We can use the %macro command, in conjunction with the %hist command, to define macros. Let's say we frequently need to define some physical constants, so we want to save those commands as a macro. First, enter the following commands and then display them with the %hist command:

```
sage: epsilon_zero = 8.85418782e-12
sage: mu_zero = 1.25663706e-6
sage: NA = 6.0221415e23
sage: %hist
1: epsilon_zero = RealNumber('8.85418782e-12')
2: NA = RealNumber('6.0221415e23')
3: mu_zero = RealNumber('1.25663706e-6')
4: _ip.magic("hist ")
```

Note that the results of the %hist command will be different on your screen, because the command history for your session is not the same as the history for the session used to create this example. Look at the output from %hist and note the number to the left of each command. Now, use the %macro command to define a macro called constants using commands 1-3. You will have to replace the numbers 1 and 3 with the appropriate numbers from your command line history.

```
sage: %macro constants 1-3
Macro `constants` created. To execute, type its name (without quotes).
Macro contents:
epsilon_zero = RealNumber('8.85418782e-12')
NA = RealNumber('6.0221415e23')
mu_zero = RealNumber('1.25663706e-6')
```

We can now use the command constants to quickly define some variables that contain physical constants. For more information about the %macro command, type the following:

```
sage: %macro?
```

Tab completion

Tab completion can also make your life easier. Type the first letter (or first few letters) of a command at the prompt, and press *Tab* to see a list of possible completions. For example, type pl and press *Tab*:

```
sage: pl
plot                  plot_step_function    plotkin_bound_asymp
plot3d                plot_vector_field     plotkin_upper_bound
plot_slope_field      plot_vector_field3d
```

Interactively tracing execution

Only the interactive shell allows you to trace the execution of a command interactively. Use the `trace` function, which accepts a string that contains a Sage command. For example, to trace the execution of the following `exp` function:

```
sage: trace("exp(1.0)")
```

This command starts the Python debugger, which gives you the **ipdb>** prompt. To step through execution of the function, type `step` (or just `s`) at the prompt and press *Enter*. Type `?` to get help on other commands you can use in the debugger. Type `quit` (or just `q`) to quit the debugger and return to the Sage command line. A typical session looks like this:

```
sage: trace("exp(1.0)")
> <string>(1)<module>()

ipdb> step
--Call--
> /opt/sage-4.5.3-linux-32bit-ubuntu_10.04_lts-i686-Linux/local/lib/python2.6/sit
e-packages/sage/functions/log.py(86)__call__()
     85
---> 86     def __call__(self, x, coerce=True, hold=False, prec=None,
     87             dont_call_method_on_arg=False):

ipdb> step
> /opt/sage-4.5.3-linux-32bit-ubuntu_10.04_lts-i686-Linux/local/lib/python2.6/sit
e-packages/sage/functions/log.py(105)__call__()
    104         """
--> 105         if prec is not None:
    106             from sage.misc.misc import deprecation

ipdb> quit
sage: 
```

Using the notebook interface

The notebook interface is a more flexible way to work with Sage. Your calculations and the resulting numbers and plots can be saved together in a worksheet. You can add headings and text to document what you've done. In Chapter 10, we'll learn how to use LaTeX to typeset mathematical expressions right in a worksheet.

Starting the notebook interface

There are several ways to start the notebook interface. If you are running Sage in a virtual machine on Windows, double-click on the icon labelled **Sage Notebook**. If you are starting Sage from the command line, you can use the **–notebook** option to start Sage and launch the notebook interface. If you already have the Sage interactive shell running, use the `notebook()` function to start the notebook interface:

```
sage: notebook()
```

If a web browser doesn't open automatically, manually start the web browser and go to `http://localhost:8000`.

If this is your first time running the notebook interface, follow the prompts in the terminal to enter a password for the administrative account.

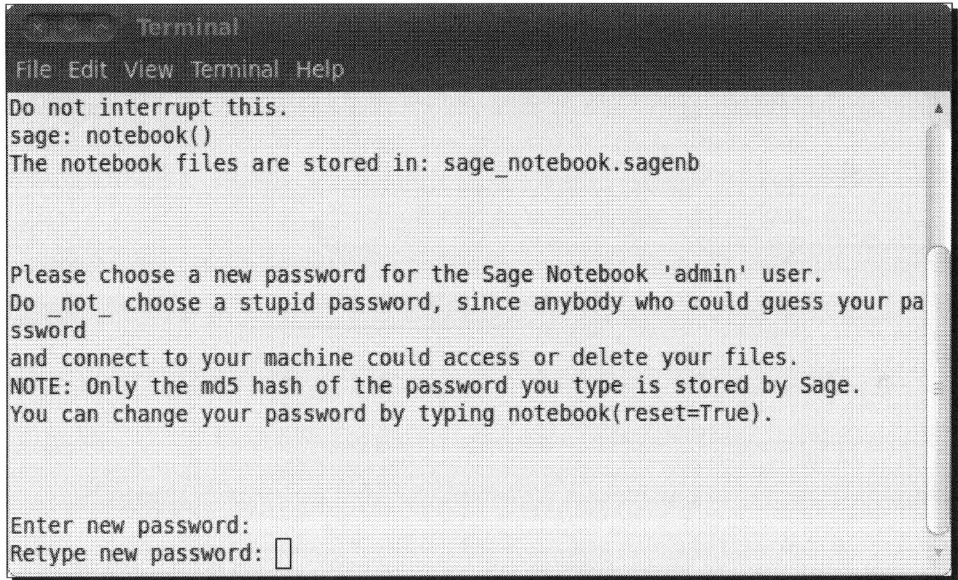

When you have entered a password, you will see a screen that allows you to log in. Log in using the name and password you just created.

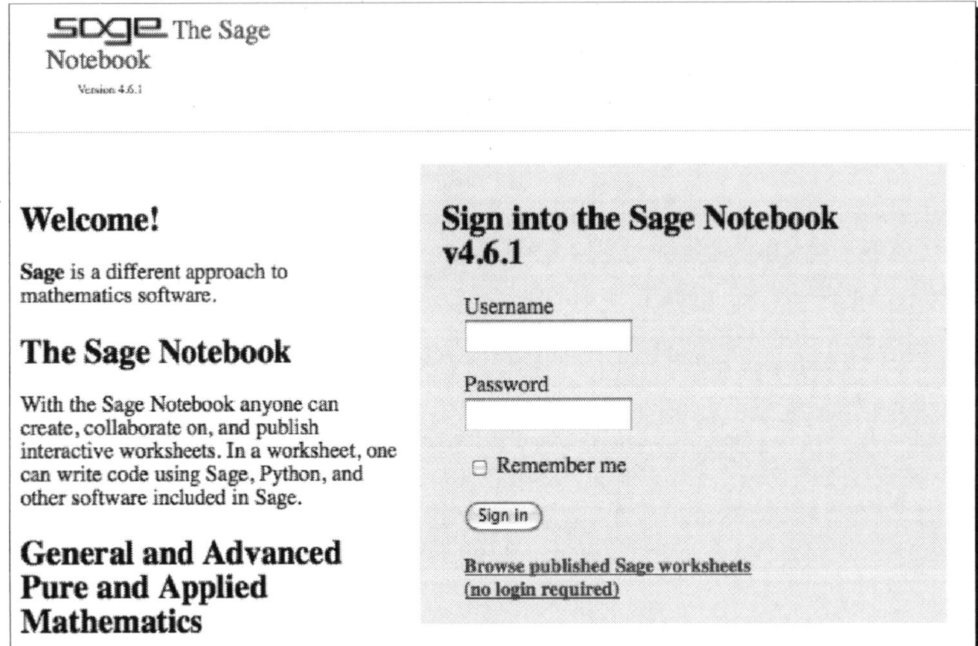

Once you have logged in, you will see the home page for the notebook interface:

You can create a new worksheet by clicking the **New Worksheet** link. When prompted, enter a name in the dialog box. The blank worksheet should look like this:

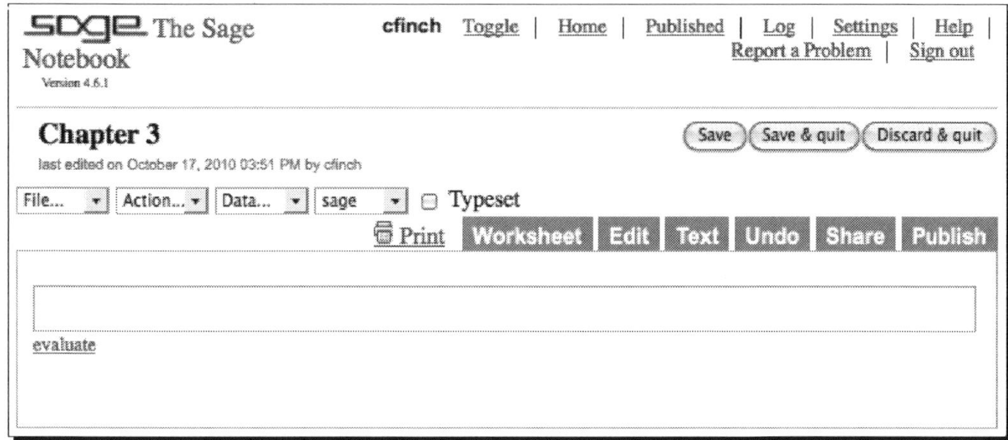

You can access many powerful features of the notebook interface from this page:

- The **File** menu allows you to perform operations such as saving, renaming, and deleting worksheets
- The **Action** menu allows you to control the evaluation of cells, such as interrupting a calculation that is taking too long
- The **Data** menu allows you to attach a data file to a worksheet
- The **sage** menu allows you to choose which tool evaluates the code in a cell

The six tabs towards the right side of the screen allow you to perform other operations:

- The **Worksheet** tab shows the default view of the worksheet
- The **Edit** tab allows you to edit a text representation of the worksheet
- The **Text** tab shows you a read-only text representation of the worksheet
- The **Undo** tab shows a revision history of the worksheet, and allows you to go back to a previous version
- The **Share** tab allows you to give other Sage users the ability to edit your worksheets
- The **Publish** tab allows you to make your worksheet available on the Web, where it can be viewed by anyone who can access the web server on your computer

Time for action – doing calculations with the notebook interface

Now, we will use the Notebook interface to repeat the calculations that we did with the interactive shell. We will add some text to document what we've done.

1. Define variables.

   The empty white box in the middle of the worksheet is an input cell. Click in the input cell and type in the following text:

   ```
   R = 250e3      # ohms
   C = 4e-6       # Farads
   tau = R * C
   tau
   ```

   To evaluate the cell, press *Shift-Enter* or click the **evaluate** link, which is found just below the bottom-left corner of the input cell. As soon as the code executes, an empty input cell appears on the screen below the previous cell. The screen will look like this:

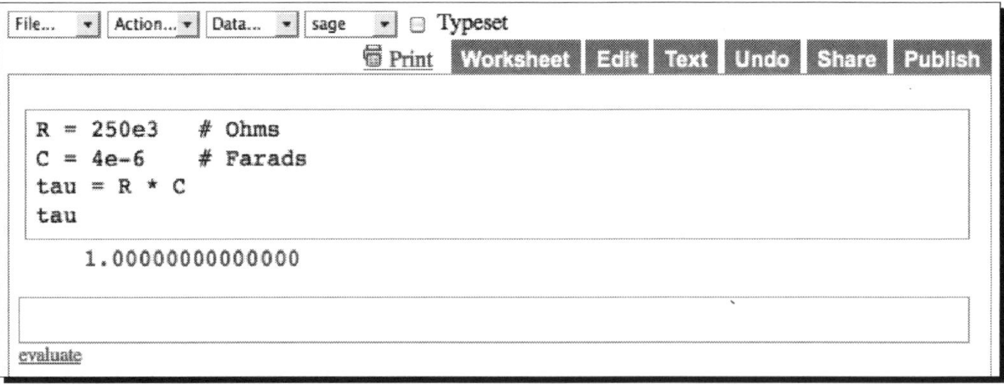

2. Perform a calculation.

   You can also insert an empty input cell by moving the cursor into the blank space above or below an existing cell. When a thin, solid bar appears in the blank space, click to insert a new input cell. Enter the following code in the next input cell:

   ```
   v0 = 20.0      # Volts
   t = 1.0        # seconds
   v0 * exp(-t / tau)
   ```

   Click the **evaluate** link or press *Shift-Enter* to execute the code. The result will appear below the input box.

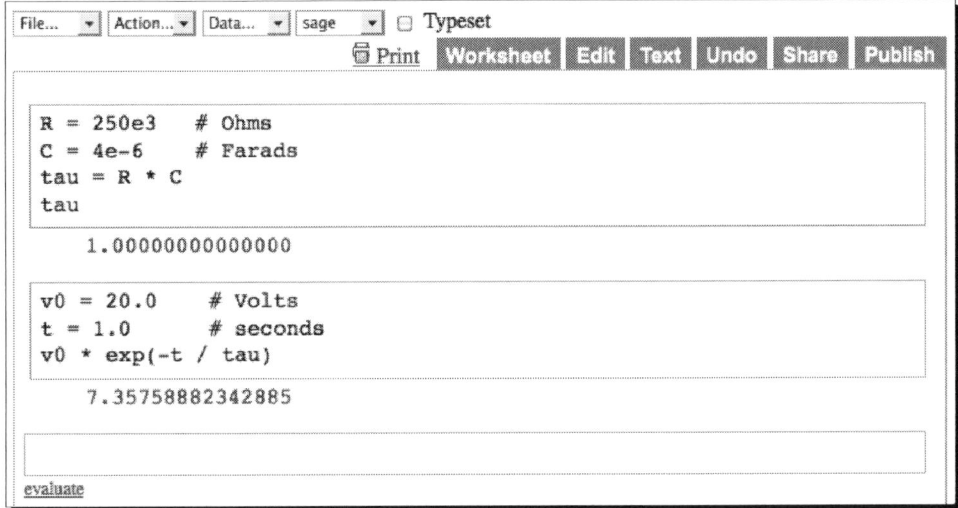

3. Add documentation.

Let's add a text field to document what we've done. Move the mouse cursor to the empty space just above the first input box. As your mouse enters this area, a thin, solid bar will appear. Hold down the *Shift* key and click on this rectangle to insert a new text cell. The text cell will include a graphical editor that allows you to enter text and apply HTML formatting. Choose **Heading 1** from the menu at the upper left corner of the editor, and type **RC Circuit Analysis** into the box. Click the **Save Changes** button to exit the editor.

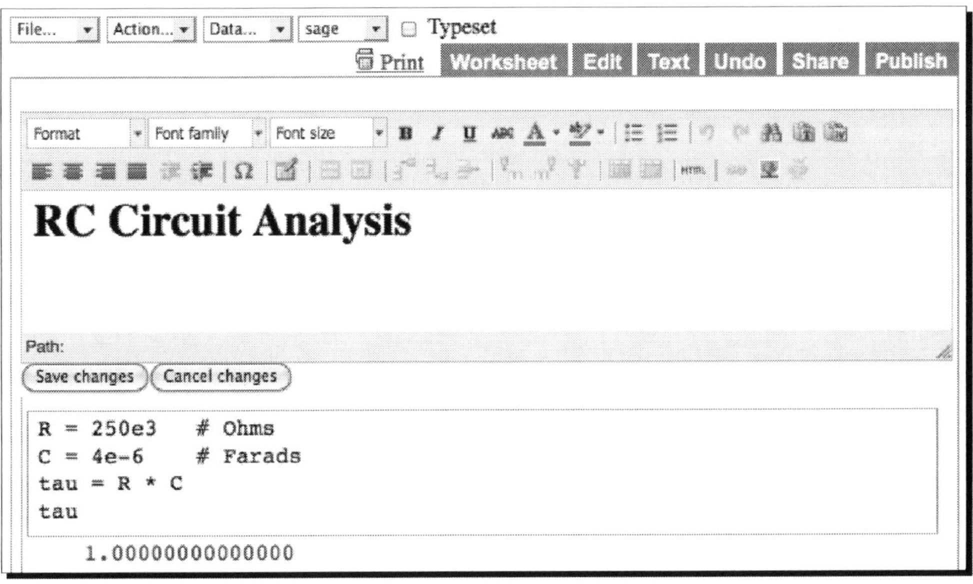

4. Save your work.

   Click the **Save** button at the top-right corner of the worksheet. If you are done with this notebook, click **Save & quit**.

What just happened?

We repeated the calculation that we performed earlier. This time, we were able to create a single document that contains calculations, results, and documentation. We made use of comments in the input cells to note the units for each value (you can also use comments on the command line). A `#` sign indicates the beginning of a comment. Sage ignores anything on the line after the `#`. Get in the habit of using comments to remind yourself how the code works. As in the interactive shell, no output is displayed when a value is assigned to a variable. Only the last line of an input cell will produce output on the screen. We'll see how to produce more output in the next section.

Getting help in the notebook interface

To get help with the notebook interface, click the **Help** link in the upper-right corner of the notebook window. To get help on a command or function, type the command name in an empty input cell, followed by a `?`. Press *Tab*, or evaluate the cell, to see the documentation. You can also type the command name followed by `??` to see the source code. Another option is to type `help(command)`, which will result in a link that you can click to open the documentation in a new tab or window. To search the documentation, type `search_doc("my query")` in an empty input cell and evaluate the cell. You can also search the source code by using `search_src("my query")`.

Working with cells

The example showed some of the basic commands that can be used to edit worksheets. The following shortcuts are useful for working with cells:

Evaluate cell	With cursor in cell, hold *Shift* and press *Enter*
Insert new input cell	Move cursor between cells and click when solid bar appears
Insert new text cell	Move cursor between cells and *Shift*-click when solid bar appears
Delete cell	Delete cell contents, and then press *Backspace*
Split cell at cursor	Press *Ctrl-;*
Join two cells	Click in the lower cell and press *Ctrl-backspace*

Working with code

The notebook interface also provides some shortcuts to make it easier to edit code in input cells:

Tab completion	Start typing the name of a command, function, or object and press *Tab* to see possible completions.
Indent block of text	Highlight block and press > to indent or < to unindent. In Firefox, highlight block and press *Tab* to indent or *Shift-Tab* to unindent.
Comment a block of code	Highlight code and press *Ctrl-.*
Uncomment a block of code	Highlight code and press *Ctrl-,*
Close parenthesis	Press *Ctrl-0* to automatically insert a closing parenthesis (if needed). Press *Ctrl-0* multiple times to close multiple parentheses.

Closing the notebook interface

When you are done with your worksheet, click **Save & quit** at the upper-right corner of the window. This will return you to the main screen of the notebook interface. Click **Sign out** (in the upper-right hand corner of the window) to exit. To return to the command line interface, click in the terminal window and press *Ctrl-C* to terminate the web server and resume using the command line.

Have a go hero – using the notebook interface

We have just touched on a few aspects of the analysis of RC circuits. Using the Wikipedia article as a reference, add more text boxes to explain more about the calculations we just performed.

`http://en.wikipedia.org/wiki/RC_circuit`

Displaying results of calculations

Before we go any further, we need to learn about the `print` function. `print` takes one argument, which is enclosed in parenthesis. `print` evaluates its argument and writes the result to either the interactive shell or an output cell in a worksheet. If the argument is a string, `print` simply prints the string. If the argument is another type, it will be converted to a string before being printed. By default, each call to the `print` function will result in a new line of output. For example, enter the following code in an input cell to see how `print` works in a worksheet:

```
print('This is a string')
print(1.0)
print(sqrt)
```

The result looks like this:

```
This is a string
1.00000000000000
<function sqrt at 0x1004c4b18>
```

We'll use `print` extensively to display the output from Sage calculations. In older Python code, you will often see `print` used as a statement instead of a function:

```
print 'This is a string'
```

Python versions 2.6 and later support using `print` as either a statement or a function. However, in Python 3 and later only the function syntax will be supported. Therefore, we will use `print` as a function in order to make our code compatible with future versions of Python.

Operators and variables

Operators and variables are two fundamental elements of numerical computing. Sage uses the Python programming language as the interface for all of its components, so writing code for Sage is very similar to writing Python code. Sage extends the Python language with additional types that are well suited for mathematical calculations. In this section, we'll learn more about how operators and variables work in Sage.

Arithmetic operators

The following table lists the operators that are available in Sage:

Operator	Function	Operator	Function
=	Assignment	==	Equality
+	Addition	>	Greater than
-	Subtraction	>=	Greater than or equal to
*	Multiplication	<	Less than
/	Division	<=	Less than or equal to
** or ^	Power	!=	Not equal to
%	Modulo (remainder)		
//	Integer quotient		

Note that the assignment operator is a single equal sign, while the test for equality is a double equal sign. The following example illustrates the difference between the two:

```
sage: a = 4    # assigns the value 4 to a
sage: a == 5   # tests whether a is equal to 5
False
```

When performing arithmetic, it is important to know which operations take precedence over others. Operations with higher precedence will be done first. The following table lists the operators in order from lowest to highest precedence:

or
and
not
in, not in
is, is not
>, <=, >, >=, ==, !=, <>
+, -
*, /, %
**, ^

If there is any ambiguity, use parenthesis to make it clear which operations should be done first. This will also make your code easier to read.

Pop quiz – working with operators

Try to figure out what answer Sage will give to the following math problems, and check your answers with Sage:

```
2 + 3^2
4 + 2 * 5
3 * 2 == 2 * 10
5 * 2 > 7 + 1
2 + 1 == 3 * 1 and 5 < 6
True and not False or True
```

Numerical types

Variables in Sage, like Python, are dynamically typed. Unlike traditional languages such as C or FORTRAN, Sage does not require you to declare variables before using them. A variable can be assigned a real number in one line of code, an integer in another line, and a string in the next. However, mathematical operations require numerical types to be defined with more accuracy. The results of a calculation can change, depending on the types of variables involved. In the following examples, we will use the `type` function to determine the type of any variable in Sage.

Integers and rational numbers

When you define a variable without using a decimal point or exponential notation, Sage assumes the variable is an integer. Operations on integers can result in integers, rational numbers, or symbolic expressions. Evaluate the following code in an input cell:

```
a = 10
print(a)
print(type(a))
print(a / 3)
print(type(a / 3))
print(sqrt(a))
print(type(sqrt(a)))
```

The result should look like this:

```
10
<type 'sage.rings.integer.Integer'>
10/3
<type 'sage.rings.rational.Rational'>
sqrt(10)
<type 'sage.symbolic.expression.Expression'>
```

Real numbers

A real number is any decimal number. Sage creates a real number when you define a variable using a decimal point or exponential notation. You can use the notation "1e9" to represent "one times ten to the power nine."

```
b = 10.0
print(b)
print(type(b))
print(b / 3)
print(type(b / 3))
print(sqrt(b))
print(type(sqrt(b)))
```

The result should look like this:

```
10.0000000000000
<type 'sage.rings.real_mpfr.RealLiteral'>
3.33333333333333
<type 'sage.rings.real_mpfr.RealNumber'>
3.16227766016838
<type 'sage.rings.real_mpfr.RealNumber'>
```

Most operations in Sage can return real numbers with arbitrary precision. Later in the chapter, we'll see how to find out how many bits of precision are available for a real number. Note that the results of a floating-point calculation depend on how the floating-point operations are implemented on a particular type of processor. Therefore, floating-point numbers shown here may be slightly different when the calculations are repeated on different platforms.

Complex numbers

Complex numbers consist of a real part and an imaginary part. Sage represents a complex number with a complex number type or a symbolic type, depending on how you define the number. If you define a complex number on the command line using the built-in constant `I` (or `i`) to represent the square root of -1, then the number is stored as a symbolic expression. Operations on integers and rational numbers will also return a symbolic expression. In contrast, the square root of a negative real number is stored as a complex number type.

```
c1 = sqrt(-1.0)
print(c1)
print(type(c1))

c2 = sqrt(-1)
print(c2)
print(type(c2))

c3 = 1.0 + i*sqrt(2.0)
print(c3)
print(type(c3))
```

The result should look like this:

```
1.00000000000000*I
<type 'sage.rings.complex_number.ComplexNumber'>
I
<type 'sage.symbolic.expression.Expression'>
1.00000000000000 + 1.41421356237310*I
<type 'sage.symbolic.expression.Expression'>
```

Symbolic expressions

In addition to numerical calculations, Sage has extensive capabilities to perform symbolic mathematics. We'll cover this subject in detail in Chapter 7. For now, we'll use the `var` function to declare symbolic variables.

```
var('x, y, z')
print(x)
print(type(x))
z = x + y
print(z)
```

The result should look like this:

```
x
<type 'sage.symbolic.expression.Expression'>
x + y
```

`var` accepts a string argument with variable names separated by commas (we'll cover strings in a bit). It makes the code more readable if you use a space after each comma.

Defining variables on rings

For engineering and scientific computation, you will generally use real or complex numbers and ignore the other types. However, when working with symbolic mathematics or doing theoretical work, it may be very important to specify the correct ring for a variable. Sage allows you to specify the ring over which a number is defined. Four commonly used rings are as follows:

Ring	Constructor in Sage
Integers	ZZ
Rational numbers	QQ
Real numbers	RR
Complex numbers	CC

You can use rings to specify the type of a variable, as shown in this example:

```
integer_var = ZZ(4)
rational_var = QQ(4/3)
real_var = RR(4/3)
complex_var = CC(sqrt(-1))
print(integer_var)
print(rational_var)
print(real_var)
print(complex_var)
```

The result should look like this:

```
4
4/3
1.33333333333333
1.00000000000000*I
```

Notice that the expression `QQ(4/3)` returns an exact rational number, but `RR(4/3)` returns a floating-point approximation. A useful trick is to use `I` to define a complex number, and then use `CC` to force the result to have a complex number type rather than a symbolic expression type.

Combining types in expressions

It often happens that integers, rational numbers, real numbers, and complex numbers need to be combined in a mathematical expression. Most of the time, you don't need to worry about this because Sage will automatically choose the best type for the result of the calculation, so that no information will be lost. For example, adding an integer to a real number results in a real number, to avoid losing the non-integer part of the result.

Pop quiz – understanding types

What type will result from the following Sage commands? Check your answers with the `type` function in Sage.

```
3/2
2/3.0
sin(pi/3)
sqrt(-1)
sqrt(-1.0)
CC(7 + 3 * i)
```

Strings

Strings are another fundamental type in Python and Sage. We will use strings extensively, in conjunction with the `print` function, to display results from our calculations. We will also use strings to document functions that we define.

Time for action – using strings

Let's practice with strings:

```
string_1 = 'Single quoted string'
string_2 = "Sometimes it's good to use double quotes"

multiline_string = """    This string
    contains single quotes ' and double quotes "
    and spans multiple lines"""

print(string_1)
print(string_2)
print(multiline_string)
```

```
numerical_value = 1.616233
print('The value is ' + str(numerical_value))
```

The result should look like this:

```
Single quoted string
Sometimes it's good to use double quotes
    This string
    contains single quotes ' and double quotes "
    and spans multiple lines
The value is 1.61623300000000
```

What just happened?

A string literal is an arbitrary sequence of characters enclosed in quotation marks, such as `'Single quoted string'` in the example above. String literals can be assigned to variables, like any other type. Single or double quotes can be used. If you need to use a single quote within the string, you need to enclose the string in double quotes, as we did with the string literal assigned to the variable `string_2`. Enclosing a string in triple quotes (either single or double) allows you to include newlines and quotation marks in the string. We used triple quotes to assign a string value to the variable `multiline_string`.

The last two lines of the example show how we can use strings to improve the output from our calculations. The `str` function returns a string representation of its argument, which is a real number in this example. Every object in Sage, including functions, has a string representation, although it's not necessarily useful. We then used the `+` operator to concatenate (join) the two strings. This operator performs addition if used with numerical types, and concatenation if used with strings. This is known as operator overloading. We'll use `print`, `str`, and the `+` operator extensively to improve the output from our calculations.

Callable symbolic expressions

The definition of the word "function" is a potential source of confusion in Sage because there are two types of constructs that are commonly referred to as functions. Mathematicians define a function as a relation that associates each element of a given set (called the domain) with an element of another set (the range). In computer programming, a function is a block of code within a larger program that performs a specific task. Sage supports both types of functions. In order to avoid confusion, we will use the term "callable symbolic expression" to refer to a function in the mathematical sense. The word "function" will refer to a function definition using the Python programming language, which we will learn about in the next section.

Time for action – defining callable symbolic expressions

Let's say we want to define this mathematical function and perform some calculations with it:

$$f(x) = a\,x^3$$

Evaluate the following code to define the function:

```
var('a, x')
f(x) = a * x^3

print(type(f))
print(f)
show(f)

print(f(2, a=5))
print type(f(2, a=5))
```

The result should look like this:

```
<type 'sage.symbolic.expression.Expression'>
x |--> a*x^3
```

$$x \mapsto ax^3$$

```
40
<type 'sage.symbolic.expression.Expression'>
```

Now, let's define another function, which is the derivative of f(x):

$$g(x) = \frac{d}{dx}f(x)$$

Evaluate the following code to define `g(x)`:

```
g(x) = derivative(f, x)
show(g)
g(x=2, a=3)
```

The result should look like this:

$x \mapsto 3\,ax^2$

36

What just happened?

We started out using the `var` function to define some symbolic variables. Technically, we didn't need to explicitly define `x` as a symbolic variable, because Sage assumes that `x` is symbolic by default. We then used the notation `f(x) = a * x^3` to define a callable symbolic expression called `f`, and we confirmed that `f` was symbolic by using the `type` function. We used the `print` function to display `f`, and then introduced a new function called `show` to display a typeset representation of `f`. Finally, we called `f` with specific values for `x` and `a`. When we evaluate `f`, the result always has a symbolic type, even when the result is a numerical value.

In the next section, we created a new callable symbolic expression called `g` that is defined as the derivative of `f` with respect to `x`. `derivative` is a Sage function for computing symbolic derivatives, which we'll cover in Chapter 7. We then computed the value of `g` for specific numerical values of `a` and `x` to verify that `g` is also a callable symbolic expression.

Automatically typesetting expressions

Near the top of every worksheet is a check box with the label **Typeset**. When it's not checked, symbolic expressions are displayed on a single line:

```
f(x) = a * x^3
f
```

```
x |--> a*x^3
```

When the box is checked, expressions are typeset:

```
f(x) = a * x^3
f
```

$x \mapsto ax^3$

The Typeset check box has no effect on the `print` or `show` functions; `print` always displays an expression as text, and `show` always typesets expressions.

Functions

Functions are a way to encapsulate and modularize data processing. Data can be passed to a function using arguments. The function performs some kind of operation, and (optionally) returns a result.

Time for action – calling functions

We've already seen many simple examples of calling functions. Now, we'll use the `plot` function to illustrate more advanced ways to call functions. Evaluate the following code:

```
var('x')
sinc(x) = sin(x) / x

plot(sinc, (x, -10, 10))
```

The result should look like this:

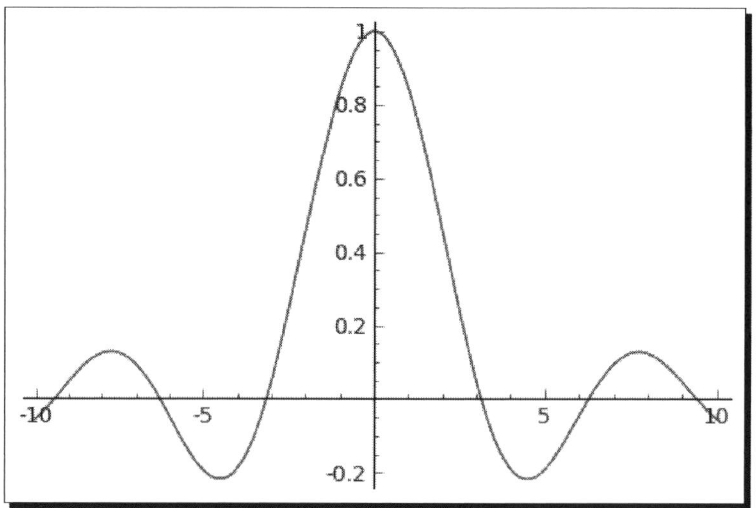

Now, let's customize our plot:

```
plot(sinc, x, xmin=-15, xmax=15, thickness=2, color='red',
    legend_label='sinc')
```

The customized plot should look like this:

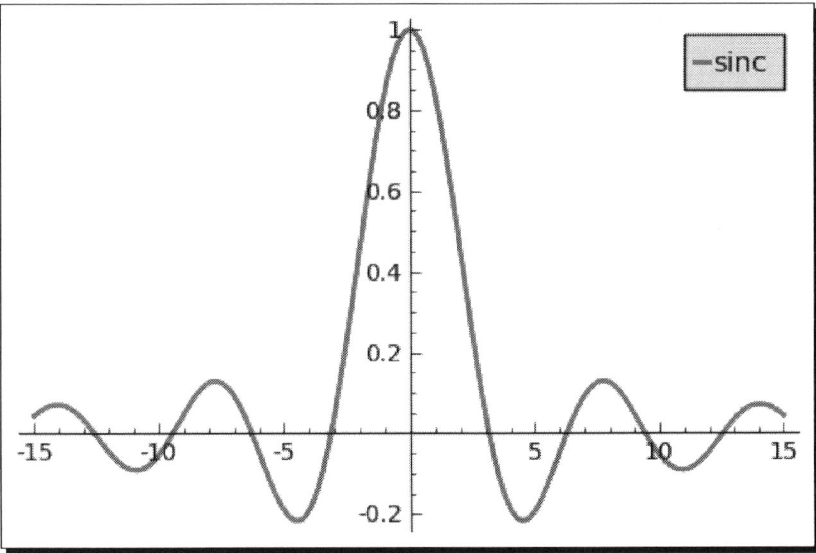

What just happened?

In the first part of the example, we defined a callable symbolic expression that represents the sinc function. This function has important applications in signal processing and information theory. We plotted the function using a simple call to the `plot` function. When calling a function with multiple arguments, it is important to put the arguments in the right order. The first argument to plot is the callable symbolic expression. The second argument is known as a tuple, which we'll learn about in the next chapter. The tuple contains the independent variable, the minimum value of the plotting domain, and the maximum value of the domain.

In the second part of the example, we used keyword arguments to customize the plot. The arguments we used in previous examples are called positional arguments. Positional arguments are required, and they must occur in the correct order. A keyword argument is optional—if a keyword argument is not specified in the function call, it takes on a default value. If keywords are used, the arguments can be placed in any order. However, keyword arguments must come after all the positional arguments. In general, a function is called using the syntax:

```
result = function_name(argument_1, argument_2, … , argument_n,
keyword=value)
```

The number of positional arguments in the function call must match the number in the definition. The function does not have to return a value, and you don't have to assign its return value to a variable. In simple cases, it's possible to pass optional arguments without keywords by passing the optional arguments in the right order. However, this is discouraged, because it makes the code less readable and more prone to bugs.

Sage has very sophisticated plotting capabilities, which we will cover in Chapter 6. If you are interested in learning more now, evaluate the command `plot?` in a worksheet cell or in the interactive shell to get help on the `plot` function.

Have a go hero – make some more plots

Use the plot command to make plots of some of the built-in mathematical functions listed in the next section. Practice using keyword arguments to customize the plots. Then, use the built-in functions to define a callable symbolic expression, and plot it.

Built-in functions

A vast number of functions are pre-defined in Sage. Even more are available through Python modules, which we will learn about in the next chapter. For now, here is a brief summary of the most commonly used mathematical functions, and how to access them in Sage:

Function	Sage	Function	Sage
sine	sin(x)	square root	sqrt(x)
cosine	cos(x)	ex	exp(x)
tangent	tan(x)	natural logarithm	log(x)
arcsine	arcsin(x)	absolute value	abs(x)
arccosine	arccos(x)	complex conjugate	conjugate(x)
arctangent	arctan(x)		

Numerical approximations

Any numerical type in Sage can be converted to a real number with the `numerical_approx` function (this function can also be abbreviated as `n` or `N`). For example:

```
print(pi)
print(numerical_approx(pi))
print(type(numerical_approx(pi)))
print(numerical_approx(pi, prec=16))
print(numerical_approx(pi, digits=5))
```

The result should look like this:

```
pi
3.14159265358979
<type 'sage.rings.real_mpfr.RealNumber'>
3.142
3.1416
```

The `numerical_approx` function accepts three arguments. The first argument, which is mandatory, is the item to be converted to a real number. The keyword argument `prec` can be used to specify the number of bits of precision for the real number. Alternately, the keyword argument `digits` can be used to specify the number of digits of precision.

The reset and restore functions

It's possible to accidentally re-define a built-in function or constant. For example, the letters `i` and `n` are commonly used as names for counting variables in loops. Fortunately, the `restore` function can be used to restore predefined global variables (such as `i` and `n`) to their default values. Here's a short example:

```
print(e + i * 5)

i = 10
e = 5
print(e + i * 5)

restore('e i')
print(e + i * 5)
```

The result should look like this:

```
e + 5*I
55
e + 5*I
```

If you call `restore` without any arguments, it will restore all the predefined variables to their default values. Another useful function is called `reset`. This function deletes all the variables you have defined, restores all global variables to their default values, and resets the interfaces to other computer algebra systems.

If you start getting strange results from your calculations, you may have accidentally re-defined a built-in function or constant. Try calling the `reset()` function and running the calculation again. Remember that `reset` will delete any variables or functions that you may have defined, so your calculation will have to start over from the beginning.

Defining your own functions

Sage allows you to define your own functions using Python syntax. This will be very useful for keeping your code organized, especially as we move into writing longer programs.

Time for action – defining and using your own functions

Let's return to the series RC circuit that we have been using as an example. We will now define a function that computes the voltage across the capacitor. You can enter the following code in an input cell in a worksheet, or on the command line. When you type the colon at the end of the first line and press *Enter*, the cursor will automatically indent the lines that follow. *Make sure that you consistently indent each line inside the function.*

```
def RC_voltage(v0, R, C, t):
    """
    Calculate the voltage at time t for an R-C circuit
    with initial voltage v0.
    """
    tau = R * C
    return v0 * exp(-t / tau)

R = 250e3    # Ohms
C = 4e-6     # Farads
v0 = 100.0     # Volts
t = 1.0       # seconds

v = RC_voltage(v0, R, C, t)
print('Voltage at t=' + str(n(t, digits=4)) + 's is ' +
    str(n(v, digits=4)) + 'V')
```

This block of code produces the following output:

Voltage at t=1.000s is 36.79V

If you are using the interactive shell, pressing *Enter* after the first line will create a blank line so that you can enter the next line of the function, instead of executing the code. To return to the command prompt, press *Enter* on a blank line. Defining a function on the command line looks like this:

```
sage: def RC_voltage(v0, R, C, t,):
....:     """
....:     Calculate the voltage at time t for a series R-C circuit
....:     with initial voltage v0.
....:     """
....:     tau = R * C
....:     return v0 * exp(-t / tau)
....:
```

Our function even has documentation like a built-in function. Executing the following command displays the documentation:

```
RC_voltage?
```

Having trouble getting the code running?

Python, like most programming languages, is very picky about how you type in the code. This is often frustrating for new programmers, but you'll quickly get used to it. Go over what you typed in and look for these common mistakes. Did you forget the colon after the parenthesis when defining the function? Did you uniformly indent each line within the function? Did you use three double quotes on each end of the documentation string? Also, pay attention to the error messages that are produced, particularly the last one.

What just happened?

We defined a function and found that it can be used just like the built-in functions in Sage. Sage functions are defined using the general form:

```
def function_name(argument_1, argument_2, … , argument_n):
    """
Documentation string here
"""
    statement one
    statement two
    ...
    return some_value
```

The first line declares the name of the function and the argument list. Don't forget the colon after the argument list! It's also valid to define a function without any arguments, in which case the parenthesis must be empty.

The body of the function is a block of code that is uniformly indented. A unique feature of the Python language is that indentation is used to delimit blocks of code, rather than using symbols like curly braces. That is why it is so important to indent each line in the body of the function by the same amount. The first item within the function body is called the docstring. While this is optional, it's good to get in the habit of including it. Sage displays the docstring when the user asks for help on the function. The docstring is triple-quoted, which means that Sage will display its contents exactly as you format them. Next, the function can have any number of statements. Note that our function has its own local variable, tau. You can also define functions within functions. The final line of the function definition is the `return` keyword, followed by one or more variables whose values will be returned. If the function doesn't return anything, the `return` keyword can be used without any variable names, or `return` can be omitted.

If you find a block of code occurring more than once in your program, stop and move that block of code to a function. Duplicate blocks of code will make your programs harder to read and more prone to bugs.

Functions with keyword arguments

There are two good reasons to use keyword arguments when defining a function. One reason is to allow the user to omit arguments that are seldom changed from their default value. The other is to reduce confusion when calling the function. In the example above, it might be easy to accidentally interchange the resistance and capacitance values when calling the function, resulting in a bug that's hard to track down.

Time for action – defining a function with keyword arguments

Let's re-define our function with keyword arguments:

```
def RC_voltage(t, v0=100, R=1000, C=1e-9):
    """
    Calculate the voltage at time t for an R-C circuit
    with initial voltage v0.
    """
    tau = R * C
    return v0 * exp(-t / tau)
res = 250e3    # Ohms
cap = 4e-6     # Farads
```

```
v0 = 100.0      # Volts
t = 1.0         # seconds

v = RC_voltage(t, v0=v0, R=res, C=cap)
print('Voltage at t=' + str(n(t, digits=4)) + 's is ' +
    str(n(v, digits=4)) + 'V')
```

The output is the same as the previous example.

What just happened?

Declaring keyword arguments is very similar to declaring positional arguments. If there are keyword arguments, they must be defined after the positional arguments. The default value of each keyword argument must be given. The following is the general form of a function definition with positional and keyword arguments:

```
def function_name(argument_1, argument_2, … , argument_n,
   keyword_arg_1=default_value,… , keyword_arg_n=default_value ):
   """
   Documentation string here
   """
   statement one
   statement two
   ...
   return some_value
```

In our function definition, we used keyword arguments for the initial voltage, resistance, and capacitance. We had to move the time argument `t` so that it came before the keyword arguments. When we called the function, we used the keywords v0, R, and C to specify the initial voltage, resistance, and capacitance. In this case, it doesn't really make sense to use a keyword argument for `t`, since it's the only positional argument and there is no chance of confusing it with the keyword arguments.

Objects

Over the past three decades, object-oriented programming (OOP) has created a fundamental shift in the way that programmers approach problems. In the early days of OOP, people involved in scientific computing could largely ignore object-oriented principles. Today, that is no longer the case. While the algorithms of scientific computing are still fundamentally procedural, the software packages are increasingly constructed in an object-oriented fashion. OOP allows scientific software to be more organized, easier to use, and more maintainable. In this section, you will learn how to use pre-defined objects in Sage. In Chapter 9, you will learn how to create custom objects.

Time for action – working with objects

If you are already familiar with objects from another programming language (such as Java or C++), then you will immediately be familiar with objects in Sage. If not, this example should help you understand the concept:

```
real_number = RR(10/3)
print(type(real_number))
print('Value: ' + real_number.str())
print(real_number.n(digits=5))
print('Precision: ' + str(real_number.precision()))
print(real_number.ceil())
```

The result should look like this:

```
<type 'sage.rings.real_mpfr.RealNumber'>
Value: 3.33333333333333
3.3333
Precision: 53
4
```

What just happened?

We've already been using objects without knowing it—every number in Sage is actually an object! An object is a construct that consists of data (called attributes) and behaviours (called methods). An object's attributes and methods are defined by a class. We say that an object is an instance of a particular class. In our example, the object called `real_number` is an instance of a class called `RR`. We create an object using syntax that is just like a function call:

```
new_object = Class_Name(arg1, arg2, …)
```

The number and type of arguments (positional vs. keyword) will depend upon the class definition.

The object called `real_number` has an attribute that stores a representation of the floating-point number 1.4372. It has another attribute that stores the precision of the floating-point number. Objects can have other objects as attributes, leading to very complicated structures. An object's attributes can be interrogated and manipulated using methods. Methods are functions that are associated with an object. For example, the `precision` method returns the number of bits of precision for the real number:

```
real_number.precision()
```

We can use the `str` method to obtain a string representation of a real number:

```
real_number.str()
```

Methods are called with the syntax:

```
result = object_name.method_name(argument_1, argument_2, ... ,
argument_n)
```

One of the strengths of object-oriented programming is that the design of the object limits the ways that we can manipulate its data. For example, it wouldn't make any sense if we were allowed to change the value of a floating-point number without updating the number of bits of precision.

> As you start using objects, you may be frustrated by the lack of direct access to the data. You may find yourself tempted to avoid using the methods, and directly manipulate the data in an object. This defeats the purpose of using objects! If the methods seem to be hindering your use of the object, you probably aren't using them right. Take another look at the documentation and examples, and re-think your approach.

Getting help with objects

If you know an object's class, you can use the `help` function to see its architecture. In the previous example, we used the `type` function to determine that a real number's class is `sage.rings.real_mpfr.RealNumber`. We can use the `help` function to learn more about it. In the interactive shell, the class documentation looks like this:

```
sage: help(sage.rings.real_mpfr.RealLiteral)


Help on class RealNumber in module sage.rings.real_mpfr:


class RealNumber(sage.structure.element.RingElement)
 |  File: sage/rings/real_mpfr.pyx (starting at line 1034)
 |
 |  A floating point approximation to a real number using any specified
 |  precision. Answers derived from calculations with such
 |  approximations may differ from what they would be if those
 |  calculations were performed with true real numbers. This is due to
 |  the rounding errors inherent to finite precision calculations.
 |
 |  The approximation is printed to slightly fewer digits than its
 |  internal precision, in order to avoid confusing roundoff issues
 |  that occur because numbers are stored internally in binary.
 |
```

```
|  Method resolution order:
|      RealNumber
|      sage.structure.element.RingElement
|      sage.structure.element.ModuleElement
|      sage.structure.element.Element
|      sage.structure.sage_object.SageObject
|      __builtin__.object
|
...
```

The same information is available from the notebook interface, but the formatting will differ. You can view the source code for a class by typing its name, followed by two question marks:

```
RR??
```

You can quickly access a list of methods by typing the name of an object followed by a period and pressing *Tab*. If the object has many methods and you are using the interactive shell, Sage will give you fair warning:

```
sage: real_number.
Display all 105 possibilities? (y or n)
```

If you are using the notebook interface, a table of methods will appear:

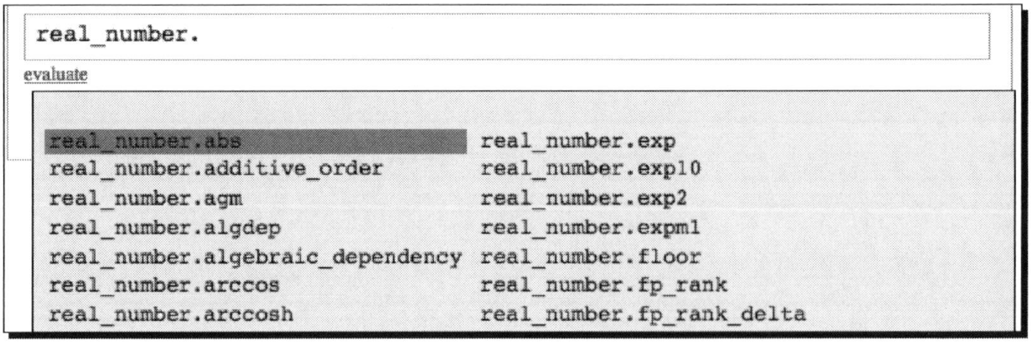

```
real_number.
evaluate

real_number.abs                       real_number.exp
real_number.additive_order            real_number.exp10
real_number.agm                       real_number.exp2
real_number.algdep                    real_number.expm1
real_number.algebraic_dependency      real_number.floor
real_number.arccos                    real_number.fp_rank
real_number.arccosh                   real_number.fp_rank_delta
```

To find out more about a particular method, type the name of the object, a period, and the method name, followed by a question mark. Here is an example of how this looks in the interactive shell (it will also work in the notebook interface):

```
sage: real_number.cos?
Type:        builtin_function_or_method
Base Class:    <type 'builtin_function_or_method'>
```

```
String Form:  <built-in method cos of sage.rings.real_mpfr.RealLiteral
object at 0x100478c08>
Namespace:    Interactive
Definition:    real_number.cos(self)
Docstring:


       Returns the cosine of this number


       ...
```

As with classes and functions, typing two question marks after the method name will display its source code.

Learning object-oriented programming for the first time can be confusing, but it will pay off. For now, we've only talked about how to use pre-defined types of objects. In Chapter 9, you will learn how to define your own classes for creating custom objects.

Summary

In this chapter, we learned the basics of interacting with Sage. Specifically, we covered:

- How to use the interactive shell
- How to use the notebook interface to perform calculations and add documentation to worksheets
- Operators and variables
- Calling functions
- Making simple plots
- Defining our own functions
- Working with objects

We have only started to unlock the power and flexibility of Sage. In the next chapter, we will learn more about the programming features of Python that are available in Sage.

4

Introducing Python and Sage

By now, you have learned the basic principles of interacting with Sage. We will now unlock the power of the Python programming language. The programmatic features of Python complement the mathematical features of Sage.

In this chapter, we shall learn how to:

- Use lists and tuples to store sequential data
- Iterate with loops
- Construct logical tests with "if" statements
- Read and write data files
- Store heterogeneous data in dictionaries

So, let's start programming...

Python 2 and Python 3

It is important to understand that two stable versions of Python are available. Python 2 was first released in October 2000, and version 2.7 is the latest in a long line of evolutionary upgrades. The Python developers realized that certain aspects of the Python language could not be improved without breaking compatibility with existing code. The result was Python 3, which is the first release of Python that is intentionally backwards-*incompatible*. In other words, some code written for Python 2 will have to be modified to run on a Python 3 interpreter. For this reason, the migration from Python 2 to Python 3 has been rather slow, even though Python 3 is mature and stable. Version 2.7 is the final release of Python 2, and new features are being added only to Python 3. Sage uses Python 2.7 (as of Sage version 4.6), so the code in this book is written for Python 2.7. Whenever possible, the examples have been written so that they will continue to run when Sage eventually switches to Python 3. When looking at Python documentation and examples online, make sure that you are reading about Python 2, rather than Python 3.

Writing code for Sage

In this chapter, we'll be writing longer blocks of code. While all of the examples can be entered and run using the notebook interface, it is often easier to edit large sections of code with a text editor that is specifically designed for programming. These text editors have special features, such as syntax highlighting and automatic indentation that can help you write code more easily and avoid some common bugs. Unlike word processors or rich-text editors, programmer's text editors save pure text files that do not contain hidden formatting information that can confuse the Python interpreter. Many good text editors are available; the following editors are some popular free and open-source options. GNU Emacs and vim are two popular editors for Linux systems, although Windows, OS X, and Solaris versions are also available. If you are used to the Windows or Mac user interface, it will take some time to get comfortable with the user interface for Emacs or vim. Kate (KDE) and gedit (GNOME) are available for Linux users who prefer a more conventional user interface. Notepad++ is a free, open-source programmer's text editor for Windows, with a familiar installation process and a friendly user interface. TextWrangler is a free text editor for OS X (although it is not open source). jEdit is a Java-based cross-platform editor that will run on any platform that supports Java. To find out more and download the software, use the following links:

- `http://www.gnu.org/software/emacs/`
- `http://www.vim.org/`
- `http://projects.gnome.org/gedit/`
- `http://kate-editor.org/`
- `http://notepad-plus-plus.org/`
- `http://www.barebones.com/products/textwrangler/`
- `http://www.jedit.org/`

Since Sage uses the Python programming language, Sage code follows the same conventions as Python code. These conventions are described in the Style Guide for Python (`http://www.python.org/dev/peps/pep-0008/`). It is a good idea to familiarize yourself with these conventions and follow them, so that your code can be easily read by other members of the Sage and Python communities. Since Python uses indentation to denote blocks of code, one of the most important rules is to never mix tabs and spaces. If you use an external text editor, configure the editor so that it inserts four spaces (rather than an invisible tab character) every time you press the *Tab* key.

Long lines of code

The convention in the Python and Sage communities is to create scripts that are 80 characters wide. If a line of code is longer than 80 characters, it will have to be continued on the next line. If a line needs to be continued, add a backslash \ as the last character on the line:

```
term1 = (v2 * cos(n * float(pi)) - v1) / n \
    * sin(n * float(pi) * x_val/l) \
    * exp(-k * n**2 * float(pi)**2 * t / l**2)
```

This is called "explicit line joining." Expressions contained within parentheses, square brackets, or curly braces can be split over more than one line without using a backslash, which is called "implicit line joining." Implicitly joined lines can even contain comments:

```
parameters = {'diffusion coefficient' : k,     # m^2/sec
    'length' : l,     # m
    'left_BC' : v1,     # m
    'right_BC' :v2,     # m
    'time' : t,     # sec
    'num_x_steps' : num_x_steps}
```

In pure Python code, the indentation of the continuation lines is not important, although they are usually indented for clarity. Sage occasionally has a problem with extra whitespace in continuation lines, which is why certain examples in this book have continuation lines that are not indented.

Running scripts

If you have entered code into a text editor, save the file with a **.sage** extension. Files with a **.sage** extension may contain code that is specific to Sage, and a standard Python interpreter may not be able to run them. Sage can also run files that have a **.py** extension. Files with a **.py** extension should contain only Python code, so that they can be run with a standard Python interpreter.

A file containing Sage source code can be loaded and run in Sage with the `load` command:

```
load("/Users/cfinch/Documents/Articles/Sage Math/Chapters/Chapter 4/
example1.py")
```

This works with either the Notebook or command-line interface. `attach` is another handy command:

```
attach("/Users/cfinch/Documents/Articles/Sage Math/Chapters/Chapter 4/
example1.py")
```

`attach` is similar to `load`, but it continues to monitor the text file for changes. Once you make changes in the text editor and save them, all you have to do is press *Enter* on the Sage command line, and Sage will automatically reload and re-run the file.

Sequence types: lists, tuples, and strings

Python has seven compound data types that are known as sequence types because they are used to represent sequences of items. In this section, we will learn about three of the most commonly used sequence types. We'll start with lists, and learn many ways to create and manipulate them. The concepts we learn will then be applied to tuples and strings.

Lists in Python are similar in concept to arrays in C and Fortran, and equivalent to lists in Mathematica and vectors in MATLAB. Python lists are much more powerful and flexible than arrays in lower-level programming languages like C.

Time for action – creating lists

Enter the following code into an input cell in a Sage notebook. Alternatively, you can create a new text file containing the code, save it with a **.sage** extension, and use the `load` command to run it in Sage.

```
# Creating lists with Python
list1 = ['a', 'b', 'c', 'd', 'e']
print("A list of characters: " + str(list1))

list2 = []
print("\nAn empty list: " + str(list2))
list2.append('f')
list2.append('g')
print("After appending items: " + str(list2))

list3 = list()
list3.extend(list1)
print("\nList 3 after extending: " + str(list3))
list3.append(list2)
print("List 3 after appending a list:" + str(list3))

list_of_ints = range(1, 11, 2)
print("\nA list of integers: " + str(list_of_ints))

# Sage-specific list creation
list_of_floats = srange(0.0, 2*n(pi), step=n(pi)/2, universe=RDF)
print("A list of real numbers:")
print(list_of_floats)
print("A list of symbols:")
print(srange(0, 2*pi, pi/4))
```

```
list_of_ints_2 = [1..11, step=2]
print("Another list of integers: " + str(list_of_ints_2))
```

The output should look like this:

```
A list of characters: ['a', 'b', 'c', 'd', 'e']
list1[0] = a
list1[1:4] = ['b', 'c', 'd']
list1[1:] = ['b', 'c', 'd', 'e']
list1[:4] = ['a', 'b', 'c', 'd']
list1[-1] = e
list1[-3:] = ['c', 'd', 'e']

A list of integers: [1, 3, 5, 7, 9]

An empty list: []
After appending items: ['f', 'g']

List 3 after extending: [1, 3, 5, 7, 9]
List 3 after appending a list:[1, 3, 5, 7, 9, [11, 13]]
```

What just happened?

We demonstrated several ways to create lists. We started by using standard Python syntax to create lists. A list can be defined with square brackets. The list can be empty, or you can initialize the list with any number of items separated by commas:

```
new_list_object = [element_1, element_2, element_3]
empty_list = []
```

If you create an empty list, you can populate the list by using the `append` method to add a new item to the end of the list:

```
empty_list.append(new_item)
```

You can use the `extend` method to add multiple elements to the end of the list:

```
empty_list.append([list_of_items])
```

You can also use `append` to add a list of items to an existing list, but the results will be different from `extend`:

```
List 3 after extending: [1, 3, 5, 7, 9]
List 3 after appending a list:[1, 3, 5, 7, 9, [11, 13]]
```

extend adds each item to the list, while append adds the entire list as a single item. This example also demonstrates that you can nest lists, and that a single list can contain items of different types.

The items in a list usually have the same type. Technically, it is possible to mix types in a list, but this is generally not a good idea for keeping your code organized and readable. If the need arises to use items of different types, it may be better to use a dictionary, which is described later in this chapter.

Certain built-in functions also return lists, such as the function list. If list is called with a sequence type argument, it returns a list that contains the items of the sequence type; if called with no argument, it returns an empty list. The range function creates a list of integers. In its most basic form, it returns a list of integers that starts at zero and increments by one until it reaches (but does not include) the specified value:

```
sage: range(10)
[0, 1, 2, 3, 4, 5, 6, 7, 8, 9]
```

If two arguments are provided, range returns a list that starts at the first argument and increments by one until it reaches (but does not include) the second argument:

```
sage: range(5,10)
[5, 6, 7, 8, 9]
```

If a third argument is present, it is used as the increment from one value to the next:

```
sage: range(2,10,3)
[2, 5, 8]
```

Sage provides some additional ways to create lists that complement the standard ways of creating lists in Python. The srange function is a more flexible version of range that can create lists composed of any Sage numerical type. In the example, we used srange to create a list of double-precision floating point numbers, as well as a list of symbolic values. srange accepts the following optional arguments:

Keyword	Default value	Description
end	None	Endpoint for sequence
step	1	Step
universe	None	Force all items to lie in the same universe (such as a particular field or ring)
check	True	Ensure all elements lie in the same universe

Keyword	Default value	Description
include_endpoint	False	Include endpoint in sequence
endpoint_ tolerance	1.0e-05	For inexact rings, used to determine whether endpoint has been reached

Sage has another shortcut for creating a list of integers that is similar to the `range` function:

```
[start_value..endpoint, step=1]
```

The start value and endpoint are enclosed in square brackets and separated by two decimal points. The step can be specified with the `step` keyword (the default step is one).

Getting and setting items in lists

Now that we know how to create lists, we will learn how to get and set items in the list.

Time for action – accessing items in a list

Evaluate the following code:

```
list1 = ['a', 'b', 'c', 'd', 'e']
print("A list of characters: " + str(list1))

# Getting elements with indices and slices
print("list1[0] = " + str(list1[0]))
print("list1[1:4] = " + str(list1[1:4]))
print("list1[1:] = " + str(list1[1:]))
print("list1[:4] = " + str(list1[:4]))
print("list1[-1] = " + str(list1[-1]))
print("list1[-3:] = " + str(list1[-3:]))
```

The results should look like this:

```
A list of characters: ['a', 'b', 'c', 'd', 'e']
list1[0] = a
list1[1:4] = ['b', 'c', 'd']
list1[1:] = ['b', 'c', 'd', 'e']
list1[:4] = ['a', 'b', 'c', 'd']
list1[-1] = e
list1[-3:] = ['c', 'd', 'e']
```

What just happened?

The items in a list can be accessed using an integer value, which is known as an index. The index is placed in a square bracket like this:

```
sage: list1[0]
'a'
```

The index of the first item is zero, the index of the next element is one, and so on. It's also possible to select elements from the end of the list instead of the beginning. The last element is -1, the second-to-last is -2, etc.

Multiple elements can be selected at once using slice notation. The colon is the slice operator. The slice starts at the index corresponding to the number before the colon and goes up to (but does not include) the index corresponding to the number after the slice.

```
list1[start_index:stop_index]
```

If the first number is omitted, the slice starts at the beginning of the list.

```
list1[:stop_index]
```

If the number after the colon is missing, the slice goes all the way to the end of the list.

```
list2[start_index:]
```

The value of an item in a list can be changed using indices. You can also change multiple items at the same time with slices. You can replace a slice of a list with a different number of elements, and even delete the slice altogether. Slicing is a very powerful technique—and a source of bugs until you understand it thoroughly!

Pop quiz – lists and indexing

Test your understanding of lists with the following examples. Try to predict what the result will be, and check your answers using Sage.

```
a = [1,3,5,7,9,11]
b = [0,2,4,6,8,10]
print(a[1])
print(a[0:4])
print(a[-1])
print(a[-4:-1])
print(a[-4:])

a[0] = 3.7324
print(a)
a[0:3] = b[0:3]
```

```
print(a)
b[-2:] = []
print(b)
```

List functions and methods

Like everything in Sage, lists are objects. Every list has methods for manipulating the data in the list. We've already used the `append` method to add items to the end of a list.

```
mylist.append(value)     # Appends an item to end of list
```

In the next section, we will use the `append` method in conjunction with a `for` loop to create a list of values.

The `len` function is used so often with lists that it's worth mentioning on its own. This function returns the number of items in the list.

Python lists have many advanced features. It will be worth your time to browse the Python documentation at:

`http://docs.python.org/tutorial/datastructures.html#more-on-lists`

`http://docs.python.org/library/stdtypes.html#sequence-types-str-unicode-list-tuple-buffer-xrange`

Tuples: read-only lists

Lists are one example of a Python sequence type. A closely related type of sequence is called a tuple. Tuples behave a lot like lists, but the data in a tuple is immutable. That means that the data is essentially read-only—the elements in a tuple cannot be modified. Tuples are less flexible than lists, and therefore less widely used.

Time for action – returning multiple values from a function

Tuples are often used to return multiple values from a Python function. Let's create a simple function that takes the x, y, and z components of a Euclidean vector and returns the unit vector that points in the same direction.

```
def get_unit_vector(x, y, z):
    """
    Returns the unit vector that is codirectional with
    the vector with given x, y, z components.
    This function uses a tuple to return multiple values.
    """
```

```
        norm = sqrt(x**2 + y**2 + z**2)
        return x / norm, y / norm, z / norm

    x = 3.434
    y = -2.1
    z = 7.991

    unit_x, unit_y, unit_z = get_unit_vector(x, y, z)

    print("Unit vector:")
    print("x: " + str(unit_x) + " y: " + str(unit_y) +
        " z: " + str(unit_z))
    print("Norm: " + str(sqrt(unit_x**2 + unit_y**2 + unit_z**2)))
```

Execute the code. The results should look like this:

```
Unit vector:
x: 0.383792724228756 y: -0.234701432987882 z: 0.893094833812460
Norm: 1.00000000000000
```

What just happened?

This example demonstrated how to return multiple values from a function. The function definition should be familiar to you by now. The only new feature occurs in the last line of the function:

```
        return x / norm, y / norm, z / norm
```

All you have to do to create a tuple is string together multiple values with commas in between. This is called "tuple packing." Optionally, you can put parenthesis around the tuple:

```
        return (x / norm, y / norm, z / norm)
```

The only thing that's a little tricky is when the tuple only has one element:

```
sage: tup = ('data',)
sage: tup = 'data',
```

You have to place a comma after the element, in order to distinguish the tuple from a simple variable. Alternatively, you can build up tuple by starting with an empty tuple and joining other tuples using the + sign:

```
sage: tup = ()
sage: tup = tup + ('string data',)
sage: tup += (0.314,)
sage: tup
```

```
('string data', 0.314000000000000)
```

Note that Python allows you to replace the construct `var=var+value` with the shortcut `var+=value`. This shortcut can be used with any mathematical operator in Python.

In the example, the function returned a three-element tuple, and we assigned the three elements of the tuple to three variables using syntax similar to this:

```
sage: three_element_tuple = = ('a', 'b', 'c')
sage: v1, v2, v3 = three_element_tuple
```

This is the inverse of creating a tuple, so it is called "tuple unpacking." We can also access elements of a tuple using index and slice notation, just like we did with lists.

```
sage: tup = 0.9943, 'string data', -2
sage: tup[1]
'string data'
sage: tup[1:]
('string data', -2)
```

Note that slicing a tuple returns another tuple. Let's see what happens when we try to modify an element in a tuple:

```
sage: tup[1] = 'new data'
---------------------------------------------------------------------------
TypeError                                 Traceback (most recent call last)

/Users/cfinch/Documents/Articles/Sage Math/Chapters/Chapter 4/<ipython
console> in <module>()

TypeError: 'tuple' object does not support item assignment
```

That's what we mean when we say tuples are immutable!

Strings

In the previous chapter, you learned a little bit about strings. It turns out that strings in Python are very powerful because they have all the features of sequence types. Strings are immutable sequences, like tuples, and support indexing and slicing.

Time for action – working with strings

Let's see how we can apply the principles of sequence types to strings. We'll also see how to improve our output with the print function. Enter and run the following code:

```
first_name = 'John'
last_name = 'Smith'
full_name = first_name + ' ' + last_name
print(full_name)
print(len(full_name))
print(full_name[:len(first_name)])
print(full_name[-len(last_name):])
print(full_name.upper())
print('')

n_pi = float(pi)
n_e = float(e)

print(n_pi)
print("pi = " + str(n_pi))
print("pi = {0}    e = {1}".format(n_pi, n_e))
print("pi = {0:.3f}    e = {1:.4e}".format(n_pi, n_e))
```

The results should look like this:

```
John Smith
10
John
Smith
JOHN SMITH

3.14159265359
pi = 3.14159265359
pi = 3.14159265359    e = 2.71828182846
pi = 3.142    e = 2.7183e+00
```

What just happened?

We started out by defining two strings that represent a person's first name (given name) and last name (family name). We joined the strings using the + operator, and computed the length of the combined string with the `len` function. We then used some slice operations to extract the first and last name from the string containing the full name. Like everything else in Python, a string is an object, with a host of pre-defined methods. Because strings are immutable, methods that modify the string actually return a copy of the string which contains the modified data. For example, the `upper` method used in the example returned a new string containing an upper-case version of the existing string, rather than modifying the existing string. To get around this, we can assign the new string to the old variable:

```
sage: full_name = full_name.upper()
sage: full_name
'JOHN SMITH'
```

For a complete list of string methods in Python, check out `http://docs.python.org/library/stdtypes.html#string-methods`

In the second part of the example, we used the `float` function to obtain Python floating-point numbers that approximate `pi` and `e`. When we print the value of a number using the `print` function or the `str` function, we have no control over how that number is displayed. The `format` method of the string object gives us much more control over how the numbers are displayed. We created a special string literal using double quotes, and called the `format` method with one or more arguments. The first argument of the `format` method is used to replace `{0}`, the second argument is used to replace `{1}`, and so on. This is exactly equivalent to using the `str` function to convert the numbers to strings, and then joining them with the + operator. The final line of the example shows the real advantage of using `format`. By placing a format specification inside the curly braces, we can precisely control how numerical values are displayed. We displayed `pi` as a floating-point number with three decimal places, and we displayed `e` as an exponential with four decimal places. Format specifications are very powerful, and can be used to control the display of many types of data. A full description of format specifications can be found at `http://docs.python.org/library/string.html#format-string-syntax`.

The `format` method is relatively new in Python. A lot of code uses the older syntax:

```
print 'pi = %5.3f.' % n_pi
```

While the older syntax still works, it is deprecated and will eventually be removed from the language. Get in the habit of using the `format` method.

Other sequence types

The principles you have learned in this section also apply to four other sequence types: Unicode strings, byte arrays, buffers, and `xrange` objects. We will learn more about `xrange` in the next section. The `unicode` type is used to hold Unicode strings. Unicode is a system that is designed to represent almost all of the different types of characters used in the vast majority of the world's languages. In Python 2.x (currently used in Sage), built-in strings (the `str` type) do not support Unicode. In Python 3.x, the `str` class has been upgraded to support Unicode strings, and the `unicode` type is obsolete. The `bytearray` type is designed to store a sequence of bytes, and seems to be used mainly for working with encoded characters. The `buffer` type is rarely used, and has been eliminated from Python 3.

For loops

A Python `for` loop iterates over the items in a list. The `for` loop in Python is conceptually similar to the `foreach` loop in Perl, PHP, or Tcl, and the `for` loop in Ruby. The Python `for` loop can be used with a loop counter so that it works like the `for` loop in MATLAB or C, the `Do` loop in Mathematica, and the `do` loop in Fortran.

Time for action – iterating over lists

Let's say you have some data stored in a list, and you want to print the data in a particular format. We will use three variations of the `for` loop to display the data.

```
time_values = [0.0, 1.5, 2.6, 3.1]
sensor_voltage = [0.0, -0.10134, -0.27, -0.39]

print("Iterating over a single list:")
for value in sensor_voltage:
    print(str(value) + " V")

print("Iterating over multiple lists:")
for time, value in zip(time_values, sensor_voltage):
    print(str(time) + " sec    " + str(value) + " V")

print("Iterating with an index variable:")
for i in range(len(sensor_voltage)):
    print(str(time_values[i]) + " sec    " +
        str(sensor_voltage[i]) + " V")
```

The output should be:

```
Iterating over a single list:
0.00000000000000 V
-0.101340000000000 V
-0.27000000000000 V
-0.39000000000000 V
Iterating over multiple lists:
0.00000000000000 sec     0.00000000000000 V
1.5000000000000 sec     -0.101340000000000 V
2.6000000000000 sec     -0.27000000000000 V
3.1000000000000 sec     -0.39000000000000 V
Iterating with an index variable:
0.00000000000000 sec     0.00000000000000 V
1.5000000000000 sec     -0.101340000000000 V
2.6000000000000 sec     -0.27000000000000 V
3.1000000000000 sec     -0.39000000000000 V
```

What just happened?

We started by creating two lists: one to hold time values, and one to hold the measured value at each time point. In the first `for` loop, we iterated over the data list and printed each value. We iterated over the list with the syntax:

```
for loop_variable in list_name:
    statement 1
    statement 2
```

On the first iteration, the loop variable takes on the value of the first item in the list, and the statements in the loop body are executed. On each subsequent iteration, the loop variable takes on the value of the next item in the list, and the statements in the loop body are repeated for each item in the list.

The second `for` loop demonstrated how to loop over multiple lists simultaneously with the `zip` function. `zip` accepts one or more sequence types (with the same number of elements) as arguments and returns a list of tuples, where each tuple is composed of the one element from each sequence. The syntax `time,value` was used to unpack each tuple, so that we could access the values through the variables `time` and `value`. Iterating over both lists allowed us to print out both the time and the corresponding measured value, which is much more useful.

The third loop in the example demonstrated a different way to iterate over lists with the syntax:

```
for loop_counter in range(len(list_name)):
    statement 1
    statement 2
```

The `range` and `len` functions were used to generate a list of indices for the given list, and the `for` loop iterated over the list of indices. The loop variable `i` was used as an index to access the elements of the lists. This technique allows the Python `for` loop to be used in a way that is conceptually similar to the `for` loop in MATLAB or C, the `Do` loop in Mathematica, and the `do` loop in Fortran.

The Python function `xrange` can be used in place of the `range` function in a `for` loop to conserve memory. The `range` function creates a list of integers, and the `for` loop iterates over the list. This list of integers can waste a lot of memory if the loop has to iterate millions of times. The `xrange` function returns an `xrange` object, that generates each integer only when it is required. The `xrange` function accepts the same arguments as `range`. There is also a Sage function called `xsrange`, which as before is analogous to `srange`.

Don't forget to put a colon at the end of the `for` statement!

Remember to consistently indent every statement in the loop body.

Although the variable `i` is often used as a loop counter, the default value of `i` in Sage is the square root of negative one. Remember that you can use the command `restore('i')` to restore `i` to its default value.

Time for action – computing a solution to the diffusion equation

It's time for a more involved example that illustrates the use of `for` loops and lists in numerical computing. The analytical solution to a partial differential equation often includes a summation of an infinite series. In this example, we are going to write a short program that computes a solution to the diffusion equation in one dimension on a finite interval of length l. The diffusion equation is defined by:

$$\frac{\partial v}{\partial t} = D\frac{\partial^2 v}{\partial x^2}$$

The diffusion equation can be used to model physical problems such as the diffusion of heat in a solid, or the diffusion of molecules through a gas or liquid. The value of v(x,t) can represent the temperature or concentration at a point x and time t. The value of v is fixed at each end of the interval:

$$v\,(x = 0, t) = v_1$$
$$v\,(x = l, t) = v_2$$

The initial condition is that v is equal to an arbitrary function f(x):

$$v\,(x, t = 0) = f(x)$$

The solution to this boundary value problem can be found in a textbook such as *The Conduction of Heat in Solids* by H. S. Carslaw and J. C. Jaeger:

$$v = v_1 + (v_2 - v_1)\frac{x}{l} + \frac{2}{\pi}\sum_{n-1}^{\infty}\frac{v_2\,cos(n\pi - v_1)}{n}\sin\left(\frac{n\pi x}{l}\right)e^{-kn^2pi^2t/l^2}$$
$$+\frac{2}{l}\sum_{n-1}^{\infty}\sin\left(\frac{n\pi x}{l}\right)e^{-kn^2pi^2t/l^2}\int_0^l f(x')\sin\left(\frac{n\pi x'}{l}\right)dx'$$

This formula is quite complicated, and it's difficult to understand its physical meaning just by looking at it. Let's use Sage to visualize the solution to this boundary value problem. Create a plain text file using the editor of your choice, and enter the following code. Save the file with a **.sage** extension, such as **example1.sage**. If you are going to use the command line to run the program, note the path to the location where you saved the file.

```
from matplotlib import pyplot as plt
def diffusion_profile(x,t,v1,v2,k,l):
    """
    Compute the value at each point in space for a range of
    x values at a single time point.
    Arguments:
    x   list of x values
    t   time value (real number)
    v1  concentration at left boundary
    v2  concentration at right boundary
    k   diffusion coefficient
    l   length of interval
    Returns a list of values at each point in space.
    """
    pi_n = pi.numerical_approx()
    v = []
    for x_val in x:
        sum1 = 0.0
```

```
        sum2 = 0.0
        for n in xrange(1,100):
            term1 = (v2 * cos(n * float(pi)) - v1) / n \
                * sin(n * float(pi) * x_val/l) \
                * exp(-k * n**2 * float(pi)**2 * t / l**2)
            sum1 += term1
            term2 = sin(n * float(pi) * x_val / l) \
                * exp(-k * n**2 * float(pi)**2 * t / l**2) \
                * l / (float(pi) * n) * (1 - cos(n * float(pi)))
            sum2 += term2
        v.append(v1 + ((v2 - v1) * x_val / l
        + 2 / float(pi) * sum1 + 2 / l * sum2))
    return v

# Define coefficients
k = 0.1
l = 1.0
v1 = 0.0
v2 = 1.0
t = 1.0
x_max = 1.0
num_x_steps = 10
# Create a list of x values
dx = x_max/num_x_steps
x = srange(0.0, x_max + dx, dx)
# Set up plotting
plt.figure(figsize=(6,4))  # open new plotting window
plt.hold(True)     # keep old plots
# Plot
profile = diffusion_profile(x,t,v1,v2,k,l)
plt.plot(x, profile)  # plot the profile
# Finalize plot
plt.xlabel('x')    # label the x axis
plt.ylabel('v')    # label the y axis
plt.title('t='+str(t))     # add a title above plot
plt.axis([0.0, x_max, 0.0, 1.0]) # set xmin, xmax, ymin, ymax
plt.savefig('series_solution.png')    # save a picture
```

Run the source code from the Sage command line or notebook interface using the load command:

load example1.py

The program saves the plot as an image. If you ran the program from the Sage command line, you will have to open the file in an image viewer. If you ran the program from the Notebook interface, Sage will automatically open the image file in a cell in your worksheet.

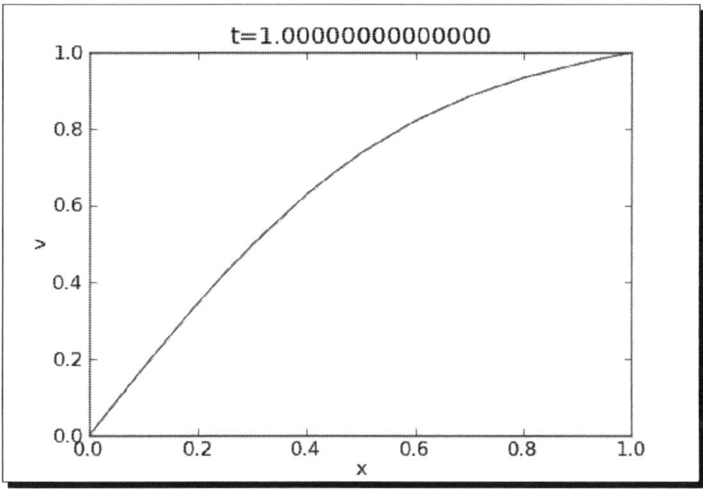

What just happened?

We defined a function that computes the temperature (or concentration) for a range of x values at a particular time. We then defined parameters for the problem, and used the function to solve the problem. We then used functions from `matplotlib` to plot the results. Let's go over each step of the example in more detail.

The function was defined as described in Chapter 3. We added a detailed docstring that documents the arguments and describes what the function does. The first statement in the function used the `numerical_approx` method to obtain a floating-point representation of the symbolic constant `pi`. The calculation consists of two nested `for` loops. The outer loop iterates over the list of x values. The inner loop is used to sum up the first 100 terms of the infinite series. The inner `for` loop uses the `xrange` function to obtain a list counter variable, which we need to compute the value of each term in the series. With only 100 terms, we could have used the `range` function in place of `xrange`. Note that we used the backslash / to explicitly join several long lines in the function. We also used implicit line joining in the statement:

```
v.append(v1 + ((v2 - v1) * x_val / l
        + 2 / float(pi) * sum1 + 2 / l * sum2))
```

A backslash is not required for this statement because the expression is enclosed in parenthesis.

Defining the parameters for the problem was straightforward. We used the Sage function `srange` to generate a list of x values. We then used the `pyplot` interface to `matplotlib` to plot the results. The first line of the script makes functions and classes from `matplotlib` available to our program:

```
from matplotlib import pyplot as plt
```

Specifically, we are importing the module called `pyplot` from the package called `matplotlib`, and we are assigning `plt` as a shortcut to `pyplot`. To access these functions and classes, we use the syntax `plt.function_name`. This keeps `pyplot` names from getting mixed up with Sage names. Plotting with `pyplot` will be covered in detail in Chapter 6.

When loops are nested, the code in the innermost loop executes most often. When a calculation needs to run fast, you will get the greatest speed increase by optimizing the code in the innermost loop. We'll cover optimization in Chapter 10.

Pop quiz – lists and for loops

1. What is the value of the sum computed in the following loop?

   ```
   sum = 0
   for i in range(10):
       sum += i
   print(sum)
   ```

2. How many lines will be printed when the following loop runs?

   ```
   for i in range(3):
       for j in range(4):
           print("line printed")
   ```

   Enter the code in Sage to check your answers.

Have a go hero – adding another for loop

Try changing the value of the constant t to see the effect on the profile (suggested values: 0.01, 0.05, 0.1, and 1.0). This is a tedious process that can be automated with a `for` loop. Define a list containing time values, and add another `for` loop that repeats the calculation for various values of t.

To create a plot like the one shown below, these two plotting statements should be placed before the loop:

```
plt.figure(figsize=(6,4))  # open new plotting window
plt.hold(True)     # keep old plots
```

Your loop should include only one plotting statement in the loop body:

```
pylab.plot(x, profile)  # plot the profile
```

The rest of the plotting statements should come after the loop.

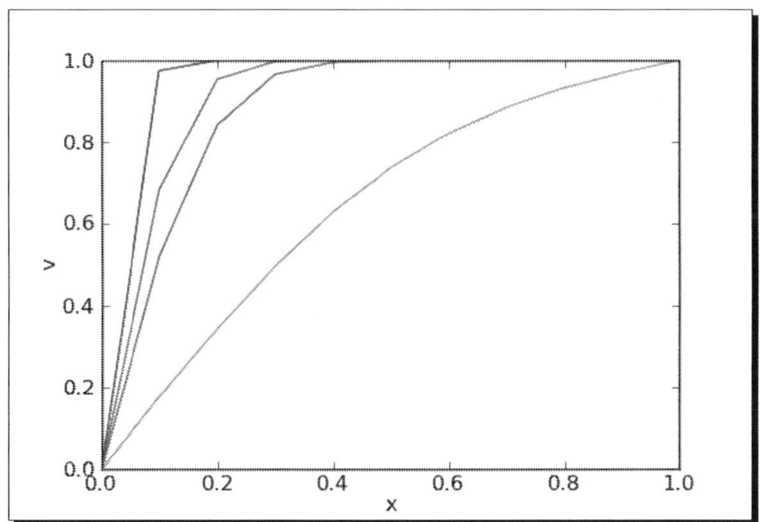

List comprehensions

A list comprehension is a way of creating a list that is similar to a `for` loop, but more compact.

Time for action – using a list comprehension

Let's see how list comprehensions work by comparing them to a `for` loop that performs a similar operation. Enter the following code in a text file or an input cell in a worksheet:

```
list1 = [' a  ', '    b   ', 'c    ']

list1_stripped = []
for s in list1:
    list1_stripped.append(s.strip())
print(list1_stripped)

list1_stripped_2 = [s.strip() for s in list1]
```

```
print(list1_stripped_2)

list2 = []
for val in srange(0.0, 10.0, 1.0):
    if val % 2 == 0:
        list2.append(numerical_approx(val**2, digits=3))
print(list2)

list3 = [numerical_approx(val**2, digits=3) for val in
    srange(0.0, 10.0, 1.0) if val % 2 == 0]
print(list3)
```

Run the example. You should get:

```
['a', 'b', 'c']
['a', 'b', 'c']
[0.000, 4.00, 16.0, 36.0, 64.0]
[0.000, 4.00, 16.0, 36.0, 64.0]
```

What just happened?

This example demonstrated how a list comprehension can be used in place of a `for` loop to create a list. In the first part of the example, we defined a list of strings, each of which contained whitespace before and/or after the character. First, we defined an empty list and used a `for` loop to iterate over the list of strings. The string method `strip` was used to remove the whitespace from each string, and we used the list method `append` to create a new list of stripped strings. We then used a list comprehension to perform the same operation. The general syntax for a list comprehension is:

```
new_list = [ operation_on_value for value in existing_list ]
```

If you are creating a new list, then the existing list can be generated by a function like `range` or `srange`. In the second part of the example, we used a `for` loop with the `srange` function to generate a list of even floating-point numbers. We used an `if` clause so that our list will contain only squares of even numbers. We did this to demonstrate how the `if` clause works—a better way to generate a list of even numbers would be to give `srange` a step size of two. We then repeated the operation with a list comprehension. We'll learn more about `if` statements soon. List comprehensions are somewhat more compact than an equivalent `for` loop. For more examples of list comprehensions, see `http://docs.python.org/tutorial/datastructures.html#list-comprehensions`

While loops and text file I/O

Lists and loops are the two basic tools we need to access data that is stored in a file. The problem with using a `for` loop to access a data file is that we don't necessarily know how many iterations will be needed, because we don't always know how many lines are in the file. The solution is to use a `while` loop.

Time for action – saving data in a text file

Let's save the results of a calculation to a text file. In the next example, we will get the data back into Sage. When you enter the following code, change the path to the data file so that it gets saved in a convenient location.

```
from matplotlib import pyplot as plt
import os

# Create some data
times = srange(0.0, 10.0, 0.1)
data = [sin(t) for t in times]

# Plot the data
plt.figure(figsize=(6,4))
plt.plot(times, data)
plt.savefig('example2a.png')
plt.close()

# Save data to a text file
path = '/Users/cfinch/Documents/Writing/Sage for Beginners/Chapters/
Chapter 4/'
fileName = 'data.txt'
text_file = open(os.path.join(path, fileName), 'w')
for i in range(len(data)):
    text_file.write('{0}, {1}{2}'.format(times[i], data[i],
        os.linesep))

text_file.close()
```

Run the script using one of the methods previously described. A plot of the data is saved to a PNG file, and the data is saved to a text file with two columns. The plot should look like this:

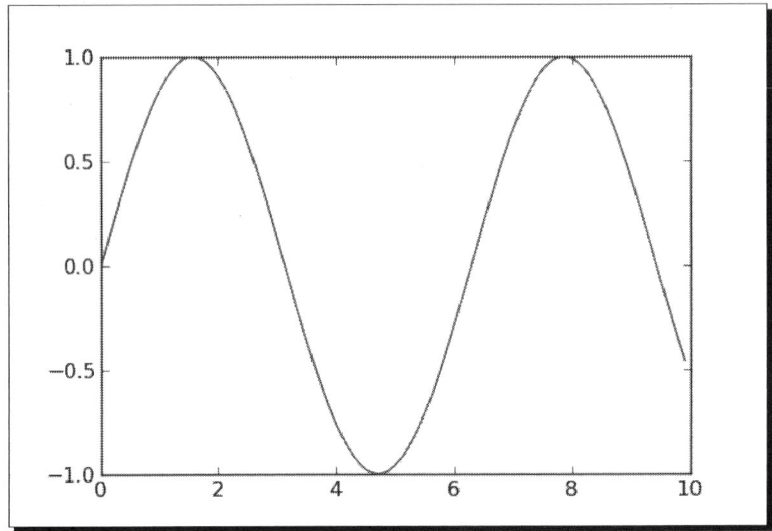

The first few lines of the text file should look like this:

```
0.000000000000000, 0.000000000000000
0.100000000000000, 0.0998334166468282
0.200000000000000, 0.198669330795061
```

What just happened?

We used the `srange` function to generate a list of time points, and then used a list comprehension to create a list containing the sine of each time point. We plotted the data, using the `pyplot` interface to `matplotlib`, like we did in a previous example. The data was then saved to a text file.

The file object is the key component in file operations. A file object is created using the `open` function:

```
text_file_object = open('data.txt', 'w')
```

The first argument to `open` is a string containing the name of the file. The second argument is a string that indicates in which mode the file should be opened. The first letter of the mode string chooses read, write, or append mode. The letter **b** can be appended to the mode string to indicate that the file should be opened in binary mode. If the mode string is omitted, the file is opened for reading in text mode.

Text mode string	Binary mode string	Result
r	rb	File is opened for reading. The file must already exist. Attempting to write to the file returns an error.
w	wb	File is opened for writing. If the file exists, it will be overwritten.
a	ab	File is opened for appending. Data that is written to the file will be appended at the end of the file.

If you open a file in text mode, the special character **\n** may be converted to the appropriate newline character for your platform. If you don't want this conversion to happen, add the letter 'b' to the end of the mode string to open the file in binary mode.

We used the `write` method of the file object to write data to the file:

```
text_file.write(my_string)
```

The `write` method accepts one argument, which is the string to be written to the file. When we were finished with the file, we used the `close` method to close it. It's very important to close a file, especially when the file is open for writing. Many operating systems buffer data, rather than writing every little piece of data to the file. Closing the file is the easiest way to ensure that all of the data actually gets written to the file.

We used a module called `os` from the Python standard library module to help us write code that can run on multiple platforms. A text file must have a special character to denote the end of each line in the file. Unfortunately, for historical reasons, each family of operating systems (Mac, Windows, and UNIX) uses a different end-of-line character. The `os` module has a constant called `linesep` that contains the correct character for the platform that the code is run on. We used the statement `import os` to make the module available, and accessed the constant using the syntax `os.linesep`. We also used the function `os.path.join` to join the path to the file name with the correct character for the current operating system.

Time for action – reading data from a text file

Now, we will read the data from the text file. This is a good place to demonstrate the `while` loop, since we won't always know in advance how many lines are in the file. Run the following code to load the data.

```
from matplotlib import pyplot as plt
import os

path = '/Users/cfinch/Documents/Writing/Sage for Beginners/Chapters/
Chapter 4/'
fileName = 'data.txt'
```

```
# Read in the data file
times = []
data = []
text_file = open(os.path.join(path, fileName), 'r')
line = text_file.readline()
while len(line) > 0:
    print(line)
    # split each line into a list of strings
    elements = line.split(',')

    # Strip newlines and convert strings to real numbers
    times.append(float(elements[0].strip()))
    data.append(float(elements[1].strip()))
    line = text_file.readline()
text_file.close()
# Plot the data
plt.figure()
plt.plot(times, data)
plt.savefig('example2b.png')
plt.close()
```

The data is plotted to another image file. This plot should be identical to the plot in the previous example. When you run this example in the Notebook interface, Sage will not print every line of the file. When text output gets too long, Sage will truncate the output and provide a link that you can click to see the rest of the output. The result will look like this:

```
WARNING: Output truncated!
full_output.txt



0.000000000000000, 0.000000000000000

0.100000000000000, 0.0998334166468282

0.200000000000000, 0.198669330795061

0.300000000000000, 0.295520206661340

0.400000000000000, 0.389418342308651
```

What just happened?

This script demonstrated how to open a text file for reading and read in one line at a time. The `open` function was used to create a file object as previously described. Since we are reading data, the `readline` method was used to read one line of data from the file and return the line as a string. Once again, we used the `os` module to handle operations involving paths and newlines.

While loops

A while loop is used when we don't know how many iterations will be required. The general syntax for a while loop is:

```
while conditional_expression:
    statement 1
    statement 2
    ...
```

The loop iterates as long as the conditional expression evaluates to the Boolean value `True`. The loop terminates as soon as the expression evaluates to `False`. In this example, the loop iterates as long as the string that is read from the file has one or more characters. The `readline` method returns a string for every line in the file. Even a blank line has a newline character, so the conditional expression will be `True` for every line in the file. The `readline` method returns an empty string after reading the last line of the file, which causes the conditional expression to evaluate to `False` and end the loop. There are two very important things to remember when using a `while` loop:

1. Make sure the conditional expression can be evaluated before the first iteration of the loop. In the example, the first line is read from the file *before* the `while` loop.
2. Make sure that the conditional expression will evaluate to `False` at some point. Otherwise, the loop will repeat endlessly. The last statement of the loop in the example loads another line from the file. When the end of the file is reached, the conditional expression will evaluate to `False`.

Parsing strings and extracting data

Since each line of the file was read as single string, we had to do some work to extract the numerical data. First, we used the `split` method of the `string` object to break the string at the comma:

```
elements = line.split(',')
```

The result was a list of strings called `elements`. The first element of this list is the string that contains the time value. Next, we used the `strip` method of the `string` object to remove any unnecessary white space, such as the invisible newline character that is found at the end of every line:

```
elements[0].strip()
```

Finally, we used the `float` function to convert the string to a Python floating-point number, and appended the result to a list. In the example, the parsing operations were combined like this:

```
times.append(float(elements[0].strip()))
data.append(float(elements[1].strip()))
```

Finally, the lists are ready to be plotted.

Alternative approach to reading from a text file

A Python file object is iterable, which means that you can iterate over a file object just like you can iterate over a list. This allows you to use the following syntax:

```
for line in text_file:
    # split each line into a list of strings
    elements = line.split(',')

    # Strip newlines and convert strings to real numbers
    times.append(float(elements[0].strip()))
```

When using this approach, you should *not* include a call to `text_file.readline()` in the loop body.

Have a go hero – define a function for reading the text file

It's good practice to organize your code as you're writing. In the previous example, we should separate the code that reads the data from the file from the code that does the plotting. Define a function that takes a file name as an argument and reads the data. Use a tuple to return a list of time values and a list of data values. Call the function to read the data, and to plot the data.

Have a go hero – replace a for loop with a while loop

In a previous example, we used a `for` loop to sum up the first 100 terms of an infinite series. The number 100 was chosen somewhat arbitrarily because it happened to work for this particular example. Some infinite series may require more than 100 terms to converge, while others may only require a few terms. We can improve this aspect of the program by replacing the `for` loop that performs the summation with a `while` loop. The summation should continue until the sum changes very little from one iteration to the next.

If statements and conditional expressions

We have already seen conditional expressions in the context of `while` loops. Conditional expressions can be used with `if` statements to allow a program to make decisions while it is running. There are numerous applications for `if` statements. For example, they can be used to detect invalid values and prevent errors:

```
input_value = 1e99
if input_value > 1e10:
    print("Warning: invalid parameter detected.")
else:
    print("--- Start of iteration ---")
```

The general syntax for an if statement is the following:

```
if conditional_expression:
    statements
else:
    statements
```

The `else` clause is optional. Python doesn't have a `switch` statement for choosing between multiple values. Instead, it has a special keyword called `elif`, which is a contraction of "else if." This can be used to emulate a `switch` statement. For example, we can use `if` with `elif` to choose an algorithm based on user input:

```
solution_type = "numerical"

if solution_type == "analytical":
    print('analytical')
elif solution_type == "numerical":
    print("numerical")
elif solution_type == "symbolic":
    print("symbolic")
else:
    print("ERROR: invalid solution type")
```

`if` statements are not ideal for catching runtime errors. In Chapter 9, we will learn about exceptions, which are a much more elegant way to deal with runtime errors.

Storing data in a dictionary

Dictionaries are another fundamental data structure in Python. A dictionary is similar to a list in that it is comprised of a series of data elements. One important difference is that a dictionary uses "keys" instead of indices to access elements. The keys can be strings or other data types. While a list is a sequence, the elements in a dictionary don't have any intrinsic order. A dictionary is a good choice to collect different types of data.

Time for action – defining and accessing dictionaries

Let's go back to our program that computes an analytical solution to a boundary value problem. Certain parameters are required to carry out the calculation. So far, we just stored the parameter as a collection of numbers. In a more complex program, this simplistic approach could introduce subtle bugs if we accidentally used one of the parameter variables for something else.

```
# Define parameters
k = 0.1
l = 1.0
v1 = 0.0
v2 = 1.0
t = 1.0
num_x_steps = 10

# Store parameters in a dictionary
parameters = { 'diffusion coefficient' : k,
    'length' : l,
    'left_BC' : v1,
    'right_BC' :v2,
    'time' : t,
    'num_x_steps' : num_x_steps
}

# Access the dictionary
print("Value of time is {0}".format(parameters['time']))
parameters['time'] = 2.0
print("New value of time is {0}".format(parameters['time']))
print('')
print("Dictionary contains {0} items:".format(len(parameters)))
```

```
for key, value in parameters.iteritems():
    print('{0} : {1}'.format(key, value))
```

Run the script and review the output, which should look like this:

```
Value of time is 1.0000000000000
New value of time is 2.0000000000000

Dictionary contains 6 items:
right_BC : 1.0000000000000
length : 1.0000000000000
time : 2.0000000000000
num_x_steps : 10
left_BC : 0.00000000000000
diffusion coefficient : 0.100000000000000
```

What just happened?

We have collected a variety of parameters into a single data structure using a dictionary. We used strings as keys to the dictionary to make it easy to recall parameter values. We defined the dictionary using curly brackets to enclose key-value pairs:

```
empty_dict = {}
my_dict = { key1:value1, key2:value2, …, keyN:valueN}
```

Many operations on dictionaries are analogous to operations on lists. We demonstrated how to get and set values of items in the dictionary using square brackets:

```
value = my_dict['key name']
```

Because the keys are not necessarily numbers, there is no equivalent of slices for dictionaries. The `len` function is also used to return the number of (key,value) pairs in a dictionary.

We then iterated over the dictionary to print the keys and values using the `iteritems` method:

```
for key, value in parameters.iteritems():
    print(key)
    print(value)
```

The method `iterkeys` iterates only over the keys, while `itervalues` iterates only over the values. A full list of dictionary methods can be found at `http://docs.python.org/library/stdtypes.html#dict`

Note that iterating over a dictionary won't necessarily print the items in the same order every time! An important distinction between dictionaries and lists is that the elements in a dictionary have no intrinsic order. You should not rely upon the elements of a dictionary being returned in any particular order.

Ordered dictionaries

Python 2.7 and versions above 3.1.3 contain a new class called OrderedDict, which works just like an ordinary dictionary except that it remembers the order in which items were inserted. This class is not available in Sage 4.6.1 because Sage is still using Python 2.6, but it should be available soon.

Lambda forms

Sometimes you need to define a short, simple Python function. You can always use the `def` keyword to define the function and give it a name. You can also use the `lambda` keyword to define an anonymous function that consists of a single expression.

Time for action – using lambda to create an anonymous function

Why would you want an anonymous function? Let's try sorting a list of dictionaries:

```
data = [{'Name':'Albert', 'age':32},
    {'Name':'Yuen', 'age':16},
    {'Name':'Priya', 'age':45}]
print(sorted(data))
print(sorted(data, key=lambda item : item['age']))
```

The results should look like this:

```
[{'age': 32, 'Name': 'Albert'}, {'age': 45, 'Name': 'Priya'}, {'age': 16, 'Name': 'Yuen'}]
[{'age': 16, 'Name': 'Yuen'}, {'age': 32, 'Name': 'Albert'}, {'age': 45, 'Name': 'Priya'}]
```

What just happened?

We defined a list of dictionaries, each of which contains data about a person. We then used the `sorted` function to sort the items in the list. The first time we called `sorted`, it appeared that the list had been sorted alphabetically, by the first letter of each name. This behaviour is unpredictable—if we added a last name to each dictionary, would the first or last name be used as the sorting key? To prevent this kind of problem, we can use the keyword `key` to specify a function that is called on each item before sorting takes place. In the second function call, we used `lambda` to define an anonymous function that returns the integer value of `'age'` from the dictionary. We can see that the list is now sorted by age.

The general syntax for declaring an anonymous function with `lambda` is:

```
lambda arg_1, arg_2, ... , arg_n : expression
```

There can be multiple arguments, but only one expression. Like nested functions, lambda forms can reference variables from their containing scope. Lambda forms are not used often in Python programming, but they do show up occasionally in Sage examples.

Summary

We learned about some key aspects of Python in this chapter. When combined with the information in Chapter 3, we now have all the tools we need to implement algorithms in Sage.

Specifically, we covered:

- How to create and run Sage scripts
- Basic principles of sequence types like lists, tuples, and strings
- How to store data more permanently in text files
- Repeating operations and iterating over lists with loops
- Using conditional expressions and logic to make decisions in a program
- How to use dictionaries to store data

This chapter provides a working knowledge of Python, but it is hardly complete. Refer to the Python documentation on the Web to learn more about the details of this powerful programming language. Now that we have been introduced to sequence types like lists, we can learn about specialized array and matrix types for performing mathematical calculations.

5

Vectors, Matrices, and Linear Algebra

Linear algebra is a fundamental task for mathematical software. Linear algebra is easily automated because it involves tedious computations that must be performed according to well-defined formulas and algorithms. Sage has extensive support for various types of calculations with vectors and matrices. Sage's vector and matrix objects build upon the basic mathematical types that we learned about in Chapter 3. We will also learn about a Python library called NumPy that is very useful for numerical calculations.

In this chapter we will:

- Learn how to create and manipulate vector and matrix objects
- See how Sage can take the tedious work out of linear algebra
- Learn about matrix methods for computing eigenvalues, inverses, and decompositions
- Get started with NumPy arrays and matrices for numerical calculations

There are many ways to do linear algebra in Sage. Sage is a collection of tools, each of which has its own way of representing vectors and matrices. Therefore, you will find that there are multiple ways to accomplish the same thing. We will focus on the high level constructs that are unique to Sage. Then, we will introduce the NumPy package, which provides a powerful set of tools for numerical computation. Let's get started!

Vectors and vector spaces

Vectors and matrices are so important that they are represented by special types of objects in Sage. We'll start with vectors.

Time for action – working with vectors

Vectors have important applications in physics and engineering. Vectors are used to represent position, velocity, angular momentum, electromagnetic fields, and so on. Let's see how to perform some basic operations with vectors in Sage. You can enter the following code in an input cell in a worksheet, or enter it line by line in the interactive shell. You can also enter the code into a plain text file, save it with a `.sage` extension, and run it from the Sage command line as described in the previous chapter:

```
R3 = VectorSpace(QQ, 3)
(b1, b2, b3) = R3.basis()
print("Basis for space:")
print b1
print b2
print b3

vector1 = R3([-1, 2, 7])    # define some vectors
vector2 = R3([4, -9, 2])

print("Linear combinations:")
var('a b')
print(a * vector1 + b * vector2)

print("Norm of vector 1:")
print(sqrt(vector1 * vector1))    # definition
print(vector1.norm())    # using norm method

print("Scalar multiplication:")
print(2 * vector1)

print("Scalar (dot) products:")
print(vector1 * vector2)                    # using operators
print(vector1.inner_product(vector2))   # using methods
print(b1 * b2)

print("Pairwise product:")
print(vector1.pairwise_product(vector2))

print("Vector (cross) product:")
print(vector1.cross_product(vector2))
```

Execute the code (remember that you can press *Shift-Enter* in an input cell to run the code from the Notebook interface). If you are using the notebook interface, the result should look like this:

```
Basis for space:
(1, 0, 0)
(0, 1, 0)
(0, 0, 1)
Linear combinations:
(-a + 4*b, 2*a - 9*b, 7*a + 2*b)
Norm of vector 1:
3*sqrt(6)
3*sqrt(6)
Scalar multiplication:
(-2, 4, 14)
Scalar (dot) products:
-8
-8
0
Pairwise product:
(-4, -18, 14)
Vector (cross) product:
(67, 30, 1)
```

What just happened?

This example demonstrated some of the most useful operations that Sage can perform on vectors. We started by defining a vector space that consists of three-element vectors with rational numbers as elements. While it's not strictly necessary to define the vector space, it does provide some helpful tools, such as access to the basis vectors of the space. We then defined a pair of vectors and demonstrated various operations, such as the cross product and dot product.

Creating a vector space

The `VectorSpace` class is used to create an object that represents a vector space.

```
my_vector_space = VectorSpace(base_field, dimension)
```

The first argument is the base field, such as the field of rational, real, or complex numbers, over which the vector space is defined. You can also define a vector space over the symbolic ring to perform symbolic calculations. The second argument is the dimension of the space, which is effectively the number of elements in each vector.

At this point, it is important to explain more about rings and fields. Rings were introduced in Chapter 3. Fields are a superset of rings; every field is a ring, but not every ring is a field. The following table summarizes the rings and fields that we have used so far:

Full name	Shortcut	Ring?	Field?	Description
`IntegerRing`	`ZZ`	Yes	No	Integers
`RationalField`	`QQ`	Yes	Yes	Rational numbers
`RealField`	`RR`	Yes	Yes	Real numbers
`ComplexField`	`CC`	Yes	Yes	Complex numbers

All of the rings we have used so far are also fields, with the exception of integers. Therefore, you cannot use integers as the base field for a vector. However, you can use the symbolic ring `SR` as a base field for a vector or vector space. The reason is that the symbolic ring is not a ring in the strict mathematical sense. The symbolic ring is simply a way of stating that a particular construct will contain symbols instead of numerical values.

Creating and manipulating vectors

There are two ways to create a vector object. In the example, we first defined a vector space, and used the vector space to create the vector. A list of elements (of the appropriate length) is used to define the elements of the new vector:

```
new_vector = my_vector_space([element_1, element_2, element_n])
```

The other way is to use the `vector` function, which automatically constructs a vector space over the specified field and returns a vector object:

```
new_vector = vector(base_field,[element_1, element_2, element_n])
```

The first argument is the base field, and the second is a list of elements. Both ways return equivalent vectors.

Time for action – manipulating elements of vectors

The elements of a vector can be manipulated like the elements of any other Python sequence type, such as lists and strings. That means individual elements are accessed using square brackets, as shown in the following example:

```
u = vector(QQ, [1, 2/7, 10/3])     # QQ is the field of rational
numbers
print("u=" + str(u))
print("Elements: {0}, {1}, {2}".format(u[0], u[1], u[2]))
print("The slice [0:2] is {0}".format(u[0:2]))
print("The last element is {0}".format(u[-1]))
```

```
u[len(u) - 1] = 3/2
print("The last element is now {0}".format(u[-1]))

print "Assigning a real value to an element:"
u[2] = numerical_approx(pi, digits=5)
print(u)
```

The output from this code will look like this if you are using the notebook interface:

```
u=(1, 2/7, 10/3)
Elements: 1, 2/7, 10/3
The slice [0:2] is (1, 2/7)
The last element is 10/3
The last element is now 3/2
Assigning a real value to an element:
(1, 2/7, 355/113)
```

What just happened?

We created a vector called u, defined over the field of rational numbers (remember that QQ is a short form of RationalField) and manipulated the elements of the vector just like elements in a list. We demonstrated that the usual tricks for accessing list elements work on vectors. When we accessed an individual element of the vector, the result had a numerical type. When we used slicing to extract one or more elements from a vector, the resulting elements were returned as a vector object. We also used indexing to change the value of an element in the vector.

Something interesting happened when we tried to assign a real value to an element of the vector. Rather than returning an error, Sage found a rational number to represent the real value. The lesson here is that it's important to choose the right base field in order to get the right results. In general, you can use the RealField (RR) for most numerical calculations, unless you are working with complex number, when you should use ComplexField (CC). For purely symbolic calculations, use the symbolic ring SR.

Vector operators and methods

Sage supports a wide variety of arithmetic operations on vectors. The operators + and – perform vector addition and subtraction, respectively. The * operator performs scalar multiplication if one variable is a vector and the other is a scalar. If both variables are vectors, the * operator returns the inner (or scalar) product. The inner product is also available as a method of the vector object, as shown in the example. Other vector methods include:

u.dot_product(v)	Same as the inner product u.v
u.cross_product(v)	Cross product u x v
u.inner_product(v)	Inner (scalar)product u.v
u.pairwise_product(v)	Returns the vector (u[0]*v[0], u[1]*v[1], ... , u[n-1]*v[n-1])
u.norm(p)	p-norm of vector u. p=0 is the Euclidean norm. p=1 is the sum of the elements, and p=Infinity is the maximum element in u.

Matrices and matrix spaces

We will now look at matrices and matrix spaces. Sage uses a different type of object to represent matrices.

Time for action – solving a system of linear equations

One of the most basic operations in mathematics is solving a system of linear equations. Many sophisticated numerical techniques, such as the finite element method, are designed to reduce a complicated problem to a system of linear algebraic equations that must be solved. Let's see how vectors and matrices in Sage can make this easier. We will repeat the example from Chapter 1, and explain it in more detail:

$$\begin{pmatrix} 0 & -1 & -1 & 1 \\ 1 & 1 & 1 & 1 \\ 2 & 4 & 1 & -2 \\ 3 & 1 & -2 & 2 \end{pmatrix} \begin{pmatrix} x_1 \\ x_2 \\ x_3 \\ x_4 \end{pmatrix} = \begin{pmatrix} 0 \\ 6 \\ -1 \\ 3 \end{pmatrix}$$

Enter the following code in a worksheet. If you are using the interactive shell, you will need to have LaTeX installed to use the `show` command. If you don't have LaTeX, replace `show` with `print` in this example and the ones that follow:

```
M4 = MatrixSpace(QQ, 4)     # Rational numbers
print("Identity matrix:")
show(M4.identity_matrix())
A = M4.matrix([[0, -1, -1, 1], [1, 1, 1, 1], [2, 4, 1, -2],
    [3, 1, -2, 2]])
print("Matrix A:")
show(A)
b = vector(QQ, [0, 6, -1, 3])     # Rational numbers
print("Vector b:")
show(b)
solution = A.solve_right(b)
print("Solution to A.x=b:")
show(solution)
```

Execute the code. The result will look like this:

```
Identity matrix:
```

$$\begin{pmatrix} 1 & 0 & 0 & 0 \\ 0 & 1 & 0 & 0 \\ 0 & 0 & 1 & 0 \\ 0 & 0 & 0 & 1 \end{pmatrix}$$

```
Matrix A:
```

$$\begin{pmatrix} 0 & -1 & -1 & 1 \\ 1 & 1 & 1 & 1 \\ 2 & 4 & 1 & -2 \\ 3 & 1 & -2 & 2 \end{pmatrix}$$

```
Vector b:
```

$$(0, 6, -1, 3)$$

```
Solution to A.x=b:
```

$$(2, -1, 3, 2)$$

What just happened?

We solved a system of linear equations in just a few lines of code. First, we created a space of 4x4 matrices, defined over the ring of rational numbers. We were able to get away with using rational numbers because this is a textbook example that was contrived to have an integer solution! In practice, it makes more sense to define a matrix over the ring of real or complex numbers. Defining the matrix space gave us access to the appropriate identity matrix. We used the `show` function to display the matrix as it would appear in a typeset document. You can also use the `print` function. We then created a matrix in this space, and filled it with integer elements. We also defined a vector of the appropriate length, and used the `solve_right` method to solve the matrix equation Ax=b. The backslash operator can be used as a shortcut for the `solve_right` method:

```
A\b    # equivalent to A.solve_right(b)
```

Creating matrices and matrix spaces

The MatrixSpace class is used to create an object that represents a matrix space. The first argument is the base ring. Note that MatrixSpace requires a ring as its first argument, while VectorSpace requires a field. The second argument is the number of rows in the matrix, and the third argument is the number of columns. If the third argument is omitted, the matrix is assumed to be square. The optional fourth argument can be used to indicate that the matrix is sparse, which can reduce memory usage.

```
my_matrix_space = MatrixSpace(base_ring , nrows [, ncols] [, sparse])
```

Creating new matrices is similar to creating new vectors. Each row of the matrix is defined as a list of elements. If you have already created a matrix space, a new matrix is created using the matrix method:

```
new_matrix = my_matrix_space.matrix([row1, row2, row3])
```

If you don't need to explicitly create a matrix space, use Matrix to create a matrix in a single step:

```
new_matrix = Matrix(base_ring,[row1, row2, row3])
```

Accessing and manipulating matrices

The elements of a matrix can be accessed using notation similar to the notation for vectors, lists, and other Python sequence types. However, two indices are required to specify the row and the column of each element.

Time for action – accessing elements and parts of a matrix

Let's experiment with different ways to access individual elements and parts of a matrix. Enter and evaluate the following code:

```
 A = Matrix(QQ, [[0, -1, -1, 1], [1, 1, 1, 1], [2, 4, 1, -2],
     [3, 1, -2, 2]])
print("Matrix A:")
show(A)

# Getting elements of a matrix
print("A[0] = {0}".format(A[0]))
print("A[1, 2] = {0}".format(A[1, 2]))
print("A[2, 1] = {0}".format(A[2, 1]))
print("A[0:2]")
show(A[0:2])
print("A[0, 2:4] = {0}".format(A[0, 2:4]))
print("A[:,0]:")
```

```
show(A[:,0])

# Getting parts of a matrix
print("Third row:")
print(A.row(2))
print("Second column:")
print(A.column(1))
print("Lower right submatrix:")
show(A.submatrix(2, 2, 2, 2))
```

The result should look like this:

```
Matrix A:
```

$$\begin{pmatrix} 0 & -1 & -1 & 1 \\ 1 & 1 & 1 & 1 \\ 2 & 4 & 1 & -2 \\ 3 & 1 & -2 & 2 \end{pmatrix}$$

```
A[0] = (0, -1, -1, 1)
A[1, 2] = 1
A[2, 1] = 4
A[0:2]
```

$$\begin{pmatrix} 0 & -1 & -1 & 1 \\ 1 & 1 & 1 & 1 \end{pmatrix}$$

```
A[0, 2:4] = [-1  1]
A[:,0]:
```

$$\begin{pmatrix} 0 \\ 1 \\ 2 \\ 3 \end{pmatrix}$$

```
Third row:
(2, 4, 1, -2)
Second column:
(-1, 1, 4, 1)
Lower right submatrix:
```

$$\begin{pmatrix} 1 & -2 \\ -2 & 2 \end{pmatrix}$$

What just happened?

The individual elements of a matrix are accessed using a pair of indices separated by a comma. The first index selects the row, and the second selects the column. Like all Python sequence types, the indices start at zero. When you access a single element, the result is a simple numeric type. Using a single index returns an entire row at once, as a vector object. Slicing is a little more complicated. Using a single slice argument returns one or more rows, in the form of a matrix object. If you give two arguments and one of them is a slice, the returned type might be a vector or a matrix. Here are some guidelines:

- Accessing a single element returns a simple numeric type
- Accessing a single row, or a slice of a single row, returns a vector type
- Accessing elements from more than one row (such as a column or sub-matrix) returns a matrix type

We also used the `row`, `column`, and `submatrix` methods of the Matrix object to get parts of the matrix. The types returned by these operations are also determined by the guidelines given above. Try using the `type` function to check the type returned from the operations in this example.

Manipulating matrices

The previous example showed how we can get parts of matrix. A Sage matrix object also has methods for performing elementary row operations on the matrix.

Time for action – manipulating matrices

Let's try some elementary row operations to see how they work. Evaluate the following code:

```
A = Matrix(QQ, [[1, 2, 3], [4, 5, 6], [7, 8, 9]])
print("Matrix A:")
show(A)

# Elementary row operations
print("Scaling second row by two:")
A.rescale_row(1, 2)
show(A)

print("Swapping first and second rows:")
A.swap_rows(0, 1)
show(A)

print("Adding 3*(row 1) to row 0:")
A.add_multiple_of_row(0, 1 ,3)
show(A)
```

```
print("A in echelon form:")
show(A.echelon_form())
```

The result will look like this:

```
Matrix A:
```

$$\begin{pmatrix} 1 & 2 & 3 \\ 4 & 5 & 6 \\ 7 & 8 & 9 \end{pmatrix}$$

```
Scaling second row by two:
```

$$\begin{pmatrix} 1 & 2 & 3 \\ 8 & 10 & 12 \\ 7 & 8 & 9 \end{pmatrix}$$

```
Swapping first and second rows:
```

$$\begin{pmatrix} 8 & 10 & 12 \\ 1 & 2 & 3 \\ 7 & 8 & 9 \end{pmatrix}$$

```
Adding 3*(row 1) to row 0:
```

$$\begin{pmatrix} 11 & 16 & 21 \\ 1 & 2 & 3 \\ 7 & 8 & 9 \end{pmatrix}$$

```
A in echelon form:
```

$$\begin{pmatrix} 1 & 0 & -1 \\ 0 & 1 & 2 \\ 0 & 0 & 0 \end{pmatrix}$$

What just happened?

We defined a matrix A and used its methods to perform some elementary row operations. You could use a sequence of these operations to reduce a matrix to echelon form. However, it's much easier to let Sage take care of that by using the `echelon_form` method.

Pop quiz – manipulating matrices

Test your understanding of selecting elements and parts of matrices. For the matrix defined below, what will the output be from each of these operations? Check your answers by entering the code in Sage:

```
A = Matrix(QQ, [[1, 2, 3], [4, 5, 6], [7, 8, 9]])
print(A[1])
print(type(A[1]))
print(A[1,2])
print(A[1:3,1:3])
print(type(A[1:3,1:3]))
print(A.column(2))
```

Matrix algebra

Sage defines standard operations for performing matrix algebra. A few are available through the standard operators, and the rest are available as matrix methods.

Time for action – matrix algebra

Let's try some basic matrix algebra. Enter and evaluate the following code:

```
M3 = MatrixSpace(QQ, 3, 2)

A = M3.matrix([[3, 2, 1], [4, 5, 6]])
B = M3.matrix([[2, 2, 2], [1, 2, 3]])
print("Matrix addition:")
show(A + B)

print("Scalar multiplication:")
show(1/2 * A)

var('a b c d e f')
C = Matrix(QQ, [[4, 2, 1], [5, 3, 7]])
D = Matrix(SR, [[a, b], [c, d], [e, f]])
print("Matrix multiplication:")
show(C * D)

var('x1 x2 x3')
X = vector([x1,x2,x3])
print("Multiplying a matrix and a vector:")
show(C * X)
```

The result should look like this:

```
Matrix addition:
```

$$\begin{pmatrix} 5 & 4 \\ 3 & 5 \\ 7 & 9 \end{pmatrix}$$

```
Scalar multiplication:
```

$$\begin{pmatrix} \frac{3}{2} & 1 \\ \frac{1}{2} & 2 \\ \frac{5}{2} & 3 \end{pmatrix}$$

```
Matrix multiplication:
```

$$\begin{pmatrix} 4a+2c+e & 4b+2d+f \\ 5a+3c+7e & 5b+3d+7f \end{pmatrix}$$

```
Multiplying a matrix and a vector:
```

$$(4x_1 + 2x_2 + x_3, 5x_1 + 3x_2 + 7x_3)$$

What just happened?

We performed some basic matrix algebra. The + and – operators perform element-by-element addition and subtraction. The * operator performs scalar multiplication if one variable is a scalar, and it performs matrix multiplication if both arguments are matrices or one is a matrix and one is a vector. We also demonstrated how to define a matrix over the symbolic ring.

Other matrix methods

Matrix objects in Sage have many handy methods for calculating various scalars and matrices associated with a given matrix, such as its determinant, inverse matrix, and adjoint matrix.

Time for action – trying other matrix methods

Let's test out some other methods of the `Matrix` object:

```
A = matrix(QQ, [[2, 5, 4], [3, 1, 2], [5, 4, 6]])
print("Matrix A:")
show(A)
# Scalar operations
print("Determinant of A: {0}".format(A.det()))
print("Rank of A: {0}".format(A.rank()))
print("Euclidean norm: {0}".format(A.norm()))
print("Frobenius norm: {0}".format(A.norm('frob')))
# Matrix operations
print("Transpose of A:")
show(A.transpose())
print("Inverse of A:")
show(A.inverse())
print("Adjoint of A:")
show(A.adjoint())
print("Testing adj(A)/det(A) == inverse(A)")
A.adjoint()/A.det() == A.inverse()
```

The output should look like this:

Matrix A:

$$\begin{pmatrix} 2 & 5 & 4 \\ 3 & 1 & 2 \\ 5 & 4 & 6 \end{pmatrix}$$

Determinant of A: -16
Rank of A: 3
Euclidean norm: 11.346960
Frobenius norm: 11.661904
Transpose of A:

$$\begin{pmatrix} 2 & 3 & 5 \\ 5 & 1 & 4 \\ 4 & 2 & 6 \end{pmatrix}$$

Inverse of A:

$$\begin{pmatrix} \frac{1}{8} & \frac{7}{8} & -\frac{3}{8} \\ \frac{1}{2} & \frac{1}{2} & -\frac{1}{2} \\ -\frac{7}{16} & -\frac{17}{16} & \frac{13}{16} \end{pmatrix}$$

Adjoint of A:

$$\begin{pmatrix} -2 & -14 & 6 \\ -8 & -8 & 8 \\ 7 & 17 & -13 \end{pmatrix}$$

Testing adj(A)/det(A) == inverse(A)
True

What just happened?

We created an object that represents a 3 by 3 matrix of rational numbers, and used its methods to calculate the determinant and rank of A. We then calculated its inverse and its adjoint, and verified the relationship between them. We also used the `norm` method to compute two different norms of the matrix. When called with no arguments, `norm` returns the Euclidean norm. The available norms are:

Argument	Result
1	The largest column-sum norm
2	The Euclidean norm (default)
Infinity	The largest row-sum norm
'frob'	The Frobenius (sum of squares) norm

Eigenvalues and eigenvectors

Computing the eigenvalues and eigenvectors for a matrix is important for many areas of applied mathematics. Sage includes functions and methods that eliminate the tedious calculations that would be required to perform this important task by hand.

Time for action – computing eigenvalues and eigenvectors

Let's see how to compute the eigenvalues and eigenvectors for a 3x3 matrix. Evaluate the following code:

```
A = Matrix(QQ, [[2, -3, 1], [1, -2, 1], [1, -3, 2]])
print("Matrix A:")
show(A)
print("Eigenvalues:")
print(A.eigenvalues())
ev = A.eigenvectors_right()
for v in ev:
    print("Eigenvalue: {0}".format(v[0]))
    print("    Multiplicity: {0}".format(v[2]))
    print("    Eigenvectors:")
    for e in v[1]:
        print("    " + str(e))
print("Eigenmatrices:")
D, P = A.eigenmatrix_right()
print("D:")
show(D)
print("P:")
```

```
show(P)
print(A*P == P*D)
```

The output should look like this:

```
Matrix A:
```

$$\begin{pmatrix} 2 & -3 & 1 \\ 1 & -2 & 1 \\ 1 & -3 & 2 \end{pmatrix}$$

```
Eigenvalues:
[0, 1, 1]
Eigenvalue: 0
   Multiplicity: 1
   Eigenvectors:
   (1, 1, 1)
Eigenvalue: 1
   Multiplicity: 2
   Eigenvectors:
   (1, 0, -1)
   (0, 1, 3)
Eigenmatrices:
D:
```

$$\begin{pmatrix} 0 & 0 & 0 \\ 0 & 1 & 0 \\ 0 & 0 & 1 \end{pmatrix}$$

```
P:
```

$$\begin{pmatrix} 1 & 1 & 0 \\ 1 & 0 & 1 \\ 1 & -1 & 3 \end{pmatrix}$$

```
True
```

What just happened?

We defined a 3x3 matrix of rational numbers, and used the `eigenvalues` method to return a list of eigenvalues. We then used the `eigenvectors_right` method to return a list of tuples that contain data about the eigenvectors. We used a `for` loop to iterate through the list and print the information in a more readable format. Each element in the list is a tuple with three elements. The first is the eigenvalue, the second is the eigenvector, and the third is the multiplicity of the eigenvalue. Finally, we calculated and displayed the eigenmatrices D and P for matrix A, which satisfy the relation A*P=P*D.

Have a go hero – verifying the eigenvalues and eigenvectors

Let A be an m x n matrix with eigenvalues given by:

$$[\lambda_1, \lambda_2, \ldots, \lambda_n]$$

For each eigenvalue, there is an eigenvector x, which satisfies the relation:

$$A x_n = \lambda_n x_n$$

In the previous example, we found the eigenvalues and eigenvectors for matrix A. Use Sage to verify that each of those eigenvalues and eigenvectors satisfies the relation above.

Decomposing matrices

Another important task in applied mathematics is decomposing a matrix into a combination of special matrices. There are a variety of well-known decompositions (also known as factorizations) that are used to solve various practical problems in applied mathematics.

Time for action – computing the QR factorization

The QR factorization can be used to solve linear least squares problems. The QR factorization decomposes an m x n matrix A (with m≥n) into two matrices called Q and R, such that A=QR. Q is an m x n matrix with orthonormal columns and R is an n x n matrix that is upper triangular and invertible. In this example, we will see how easy it is to compute the QR factorization with Sage.

```
# This is an example where it's important to specify the correct ring
A = Matrix(RDF, [[1, -1, 4], [1, 4, -2], [1, 4, 2], [1, -1, 0]])
print("Matrix A:")
show(A)
```

```
Q, R = A.QR()
print("Matrix with orthonormal basis:")
show(Q)
print("Upper diagonal matrix:")
show(R)
print("Q*R recovers A:")
show(Q*R)
```

The output should look like this:

```
Matrix A:
```

$$\begin{pmatrix} 1.0 & -1.0 & 4.0 \\ 1.0 & 4.0 & -2.0 \\ 1.0 & 4.0 & 2.0 \\ 1.0 & -1.0 & 0.0 \end{pmatrix}$$

```
Matrix with orthonormal basis:
```

$$\begin{pmatrix} -0.5 & 0.5 & -0.5 & -0.5 \\ -0.5 & -0.5 & 0.5 & -0.5 \\ -0.5 & -0.5 & -0.5 & 0.5 \\ -0.5 & 0.5 & 0.5 & 0.5 \end{pmatrix}$$

```
Upper diagonal matrix:
```

$$\begin{pmatrix} -2.0 & -3.0 & -2.0 \\ 0.0 & -5.0 & 2.0 \\ 0.0 & 0.0 & -4.0 \\ 0.0 & -0.0 & -0.0 \end{pmatrix}$$

```
Q*R recovers A:
```

$$\begin{pmatrix} 1.0 & -1.0 & 4.0 \\ 1.0 & 4.0 & -2.0 \\ 1.0 & 4.0 & 2.0 \\ 1.0 & -1.0 & -6.66133814775 \times 10^{-16} \end{pmatrix}$$

What just happened?

We defined a 4 by 3 matrix called A over the ring called `RDF`, which is a shortcut for `RealDoubleField`. An `RDF` object is a double-precision approximation of a floating point number, while a `RealField` object can have an arbitrary number of bits of precision. This is another example where it is very important to choose the right ring. Matrix decompositions in Sage are only defined for matrices constructed on `RDF` and its counterpart `CDF`, or `ComplexDoubleField`. The `QR` method returns a tuple containing the matrices Q and R. We printed out the matrices and verified that A = Q*R.

Time for action – computing the singular value decomposition

The singular value decomposition, or SVD, has numerous applications in statistics, signal processing, and numerical analysis. An m x n matrix A is decomposed into three matrices: an m x m unitary matrix U, an m x n diagonal matrix sigma, and an n x n real unitary matrix V. These matrices satisfy the relation:

$$A = U \Sigma V^*$$

Here, **V*** denotes the transpose of the complex conjugate of V.

It's also easy to compute the SVD with Sage:

```
A = Matrix(RDF, [[1,1], [1,1], [0,0]])
print("Matrix A:")
show(A)

print "SVD:"
U, Sigma, V = A.SVD()
print("U:")
show(U)
print("Sigma:")
show(Sigma)
print("V:")
show(V)
print("U.Sigma.V* recovers A:")
show(U*Sigma*(V.conjugate().transpose()))
```

The result should look like this:

Matrix A:

$$\begin{pmatrix} 1.0 & 1.0 \\ 1.0 & 1.0 \\ 0.0 & 0.0 \end{pmatrix}$$

SVD:
U:

$$\begin{pmatrix} -0.707106781187 & -0.707106781187 & 0.0 \\ -0.707106781187 & 0.707106781187 & 0.0 \\ 0.0 & 0.0 & 1.0 \end{pmatrix}$$

Sigma:

$$\begin{pmatrix} 2.0 & 0.0 \\ 0.0 & 0.0 \\ 0.0 & 0.0 \end{pmatrix}$$

V:

$$\begin{pmatrix} -0.707106781187 & -0.707106781187 \\ -0.707106781187 & 0.707106781187 \end{pmatrix}$$

U.Sigma.V* recovers A:

$$\begin{pmatrix} 1.0 & 1.0 \\ 1.0 & 1.0 \\ 0.0 & 0.0 \end{pmatrix}$$

What just happened?

As in the previous example, we defined a 4 by 3 matrix called A over the field called `RDF`. The SVD method returns a tuple containing the matrices U, Sigma, and V. We displayed these matrices, and verified that they satisfy the mathematical relation shown in the introduction. Matrix objects in Sage have methods for computing other decompositions. The method `LU` computes the LU decomposition, and the method `cholesky_decomposition` computes the Cholesky decomposition.

The final line of this example shows that methods can be "chained" together. The methods are evaluated in order, from left to right. The reason this works is that the expression `v.conjugate()` returns a matrix object. We then call the method `transpose` of this matrix object. In many cases, chaining methods can make your code more concise and readable. Of course, it should be avoided if it makes the code less readable.

An introduction to NumPy

NumPy is a package that turns Python into a powerful numerical computing language. The core of NumPy is a powerful n-dimensional array class. The package also includes tools for numerical linear algebra, Fourier transforms, and many other commonly used numerical methods. To find out more about NumPy, check out `http://numpy.scipy.org/`.

The current release of Sage is 4.6.1, which includes NumPy version 1.5. Because NumPy is constantly evolving, the latest version of NumPy may differ slightly from the version included with the latest version of Sage. Be aware of this as you are looking at the documentation, especially if you are using a different version of NumPy in other Python code!

Time for action – creating NumPy arrays

The `array` class is the core of NumPy. Let's explore the various ways that we can create NumPy arrays:

```
import numpy

print("array:")
a = numpy.array([1,2,3,9,10,11])
print(a)

print("arange:")
b = numpy.arange(0.0, 10.0, 3.0/2)
print(b)

print("zeros:")
c = numpy.zeros(5,dtype=int)
print(c)

print("ones:")
d = numpy.ones((4,1), dtype=numpy.float64)
print(d)

print("ones, 2D array:")
e = numpy.ones((3,2))
print(e)

print("empty:")
f = numpy.empty((1,4), dtype=numpy.float32)
print(f)
```

The result should look like this:

```
array:
[ 1  2  3  9 10 11]
arange:
[ 0.   1.5  3.   4.5  6.   7.5  9. ]
zeros:
[0 0 0 0 0]
ones:
[[ 1.]
 [ 1.]
 [ 1.]
 [ 1.]]
ones, 2D array:
[[ 1.  1.]
 [ 1.  1.]
 [ 1.  1.]]
empty:
[[  0.00000000e+00   0.00000000e+00   2.31121656e-31   1.40129846e-45]]
```

What just happened?

In the first line of the script, we used the `import` statement to make NumPy functions and objects available to Sage. In order to keep NumPy types separate from Sage types with the same name, we access the NumPy types with the syntax `numpy.type`. In this example, we used several functions to create NumPy arrays. All of these functions accept the optional argument `dtype`, which specifies the type for the elements in the array (NumPy types are not the same as Sage types). We used the `print` function instead of the `show` function to display the arrays we created. Since NumPy objects return only plain text representations, there is no reason to use `show` to display NumPy objects.

Creating NumPy arrays

NumPy includes many convenient functions for creating arrays. The `array` function takes a Python list as an argument, and returns an array with the contents of the list, with each element converted to the specified type. `arange` is an extension of the `range` function that we learned about in Chapter 4. The basic syntax is as follows:

```
new_array = arange([start,] stop [,step] [,dtype])
```

If only one argument is provided, `start` is assumed to be zero and `step` is assumed to be one. If two arguments are given, the first is used as `start` and the second is assumed to be `stop`, and `step` is assumed to be one. `ones` and `zeros` return an array of the given shape and the specified type, with every element set to 1 or 0. The shape argument can be an integer or a tuple. An integer creates a "row" array, while a tuple of the form (n,1) creates a "column" array. Tuples of the form (m,n) or (m,n,p) create two-dimensional and three-dimensional arrays, respectively. `empty` is the fastest way to create an array of a specified shape. It allocates the appropriate amount of space for the elements, based on the specified type, but does not initialize the element values. Note that the values in an empty array will be different every time it is created.

NumPy types

Every NumPy array has a type, and all the elements in the array must have the same type. The following table will help you choose the appropriate type. When choosing a type, the main factors are the maximum value that needs to be stored, the amount of precision required, and the amount of memory required for the array. You must consider the amount of RAM needed to hold the array during calculations, and the amount of disk space required if you are going to save the array to a file. For the simple exercises in this chapter, you will be safe using the default 64-bit types:

`bool`	Boolean (True or False) stored as a byte
`int`	Default integer for the platform (normally either int32 or int64)
`int8`	Byte (-128 to 127)
`int16`	Integer (-32768 to 32767)
`int32`	Integer (-2147483648 to 2147483647)
`int64`	Integer (9223372036854775808 to 9223372036854775807)
`uint8`	Unsigned integer (0 to 255)
`uint16`	Unsigned integer (0 to 65535)
`uint32`	Unsigned integer (0 to 4294967295)
`uint64`	Unsigned integer (0 to 18446744073709551615)
`float`	Shorthand for `float64`
`float32`	Single precision float: sign bit, 8 bits exponent, 23 bits mantissa
`float64`	Double precision float: sign bit, 11 bits exponent, 52 bits mantissa
`complex`	Shorthand for `complex128`
`complex64`	Complex number, represented by two 32-bit floats (real and imaginary components)
`complex128`	Complex number, represented by two 64-bit floats (real and imaginary components)

Indexing and selection with NumPy arrays

All of the indexing and slicing tricks that we've learned so far also apply to NumPy arrays. NumPy adds a few indexing tricks that help with processing numeric data.

Time for action – working with NumPy arrays

Let's explore some ways to select elements and sub-arrays from NumPy arrays:

```
import numpy

a = numpy.arange(9.0)
print("Array a:")
print(a)

a = a.reshape((3,3))
print("Array a, reshaped:")
print(a)

print("Selecting an element: {0}".format(a[1,0]))
print("Selecting a row: {0}".format(a[1]))

print("Selecting a submatrix:")
print(a[1:3,1:3])

b = numpy.arange(9.0, 0.0, -1.0)
print("\nArray b: {0}".format(b))
indices, = numpy.where(b > 4.0)
print("Indices of elements of b > 4.0: {0}".format(indices))
print("b > 4.0: {0}".format(b[b > 4.0]))
```

The output should be as follows:

```
Array a:
[ 0.  1.  2.  3.  4.  5.  6.  7.  8.]
Array a, reshaped:
[[ 0.  1.  2.]
 [ 3.  4.  5.]
 [ 6.  7.  8.]]
Selecting an element: 3.0
Selecting a row: [ 3.  4.  5.]
Selecting a submatrix:
[[ 4.  5.]
 [ 7.  8.]]

Array b: [ 9.  8.  7.  6.  5.  4.  3.  2.  1.]
Indices of elements of b > 4.0: [0 1 2 3 4]
b > 4.0: [ 9.  8.  7.  6.  5.]
```

What just happened?

We used the `arange` function to create an array with nine floating-point elements. Since we only provided a single argument, NumPy assumes that the first element is zero and the increment is one. We then used the array's `reshape` method to return a two-dimensional array with three rows and three columns. `reshape` accepts a tuple that contains the dimensions of the new array. Note that `reshape` returns a new array instead of modifying the original array, so we have to use the syntax `a = a.reshape((3,3))` to overwrite the original array. Elements and subsets of this array were selected using the same slice notation that we used with Sage vectors and matrices.

We created a one-dimensional array to demonstrate how to select elements by value from NumPy arrays. In this case, we specified a negative step, so `arange` created an array with decreasing values. We used the `where` function to get a list of indices that met a specific condition. `where` returns a list of lists of indices, so we used tuple unpacking to obtain a single list. When `where` is used with multi-dimensional arrays, each list of indices corresponds to one dimension of the array. The final line of the example shows a shortcut for obtaining the elements of an array that meet a certain criterion.

Have a go hero – replacing lists with NumPy arrays

In Chapter 4, we used lists and loops to compute the analytical solution to a partial differential equation (see *Time for action – computing a solution to the diffusion equation*). Go back to that example and replace the lists with NumPy arrays.

- Replace the list called `x` with a NumPy array
- Use `arange` to replace the `for` loop that was used to define the x coordinates for the calculation
- Use `empty` to create an array to replace the list called `ideal_concentration`

NumPy matrices

NumPy also includes a matrix class, which is distinct from the two-dimensional array that we created in the previous example.

Time for action – creating matrices in NumPy

To illustrate some of the similarities and differences between the linear algebra features of Sage and NumPy, we'll repeat an earlier example in which we computed the singular value decomposition of a matrix:

```
import numpy as np
print "Two ways of creating a Numpy matrix:"
```

```
A = np.matrix('1 1; 1 1; 0 0')      # Matlab syntax
print(A)
A2 = np.matrix([[1,1], [1,1], [0,0]])
print(A2)

print("Singular value decomposition:")
U, s, Vstar = np.linalg.svd(A, full_matrices=False)
print("U:")
print(U)
print("s:")
print(s)
print("Transpose of conjugate of V:")
print(Vstar)

Sigma = np.diag(s)
print("Reconstructed matrix Sigma:")
print(Sigma)
print(np.dot(U, np.dot(Sigma, Vstar)))
```

The result should look like this:

```
Two ways of creating a Numpy matrix:
[[1 1]
 [1 1]
 [0 0]]
[[1 1]
 [1 1]
 [0 0]]
Singular value decomposition:
U:
[[-0.70710678 -0.70710678]
 [-0.70710678  0.70710678]
 [ 0.          0.        ]]
s:
[ 2.  0.]
Transpose of conjugate of V:
[[-0.70710678 -0.70710678]
 [-0.70710678  0.70710678]]
Reconstructed matrix Sigma:
[[ 2.  0.]
 [ 0.  0.]]
[[ 1.  1.]
 [ 1.  1.]
 [ 0.  0.]]
```

What just happened?

The example demonstrated two ways of creating a NumPy matrix object. To start with, we used the statement `import numpy as np` so that we can use `np` as a shortcut for `numpy`. This feature is handy for long package names that are used many times, but it can also lead to confusion when misused. We then tried two ways of creating NumPy matrix. The first way uses syntax that will be familiar to MATLAB users; the second uses standard Python notation.

We then computed the singular value decomposition using the `svd` function from NumPy. This function returns slightly different results than the `SVD` method of a Sage matrix object. `numpy.linalg.svd` returns the conjugate transpose of matrix V, instead of V. NumPy returns a vector instead of a full matrix for Sigma, so we had to construct matrix Sigma using the `diag` function. `diag` accepts an array (or other sequence type) as an argument, and returns a matrix with the elements of the array as the diagonal elements. For more about the `svd` function in NumPy, try the following:

```
np.linalg.svd?
```

Learning more about NumPy

This has been a very brief introduction to NumPy. We will use arrays in Chapter 6 when we learn about plotting, and again in Chapter 8 when we learn about numerical methods. Even then, we will barely begin to exploit the power of NumPy. Here are some resources to learn more:

- The official NumPy documentation page at `http://docs.scipy.org/doc/`
- The NumPy Tutorial at `http://www.scipy.org/Tentative_NumPy_Tutorial`
- Download the Guide to NumPy from `http://www.tramy.us/numpybook.pdf`

Summary

We have seen that Sage can reduce or eliminate the tedious computations that are required when doing linear algebra by hand. The capabilities of Sage are equivalent to those found in commercial mathematical software systems. Specifically, we covered:

- Creating vector spaces and vector objects, and performing basic operations like inner products and cross products
- Creating matrix objects, performing elementary row operations, and matrix algebra
- Using matrix methods to calculate scalars and matrices such as determinants, inverses, eigenvalues, and eigenvectors

- Using matrix methods to factorize and decompose matrices
- Creating and manipulating NumPy arrays and matrices for working with numerical data

In the next chapter, we will learn about the plotting and graphics capabilities of Sage.

6
Plotting with Sage

Graphs, plots, and charts are useful tools to understand the behaviour of functions and visualize data. Sage comes with some powerful plotting tools.

In this chapter we will:

- Learn how to plot functions of one variable
- Make various types of specialized 2D plots such as polar plots and scatter plots
- Use matplotlib to precisely format 2D plots and charts
- Make interactive 3D plots of functions of two variables

Let's start plotting!

Confusion alert: Sage plots and matplotlib

The 2D plotting capabilities of Sage are built upon a Python plotting package called matplotlib. The most widely used features of matplotlib are accessible through Sage functions. You can also import the matplotlib package into Sage, and use all of its features directly. This is very powerful, but it's also confusing, because there's more than one way to do the same thing. To further add to the confusion, matplotlib has two interfaces: the command-oriented Pyplot interface and an object-oriented interface. The examples in this chapter will attempt to clarify which interface is being used.

Plotting in two dimensions

Two-dimensional plots are probably the most important tool for visually presenting information in math, science, and engineering. Sage has a wide variety of tools for making many types of 2D plots.

Plotting symbolic expressions with Sage

We will start by exploring the plotting functions that are built in to Sage. They are generally less flexible than using matplotlib directly, but also tend to be easier to use.

Time for action – plotting symbolic expressions

Let's plot some simple functions. Enter the following code:

```
p1 = plot(sin, (-2*pi, 2*pi), thickness=2.0, rgbcolor=(0.5, 1, 0),
    legend_label='sin(x)')
p2 = plot(cos, (-2*pi, 2*pi), thickness=3.0, color='purple',
    alpha=0.5, legend_label='cos(x)')
plt = p1 + p2
plt.axes_labels(['x', 'f(x)'])
show(plt)
```

If you run the code from the interactive shell, the plot will open in a separate window. If you run it from the notebook interface, the plot will appear below the input cell. In either case, the result should look like this:

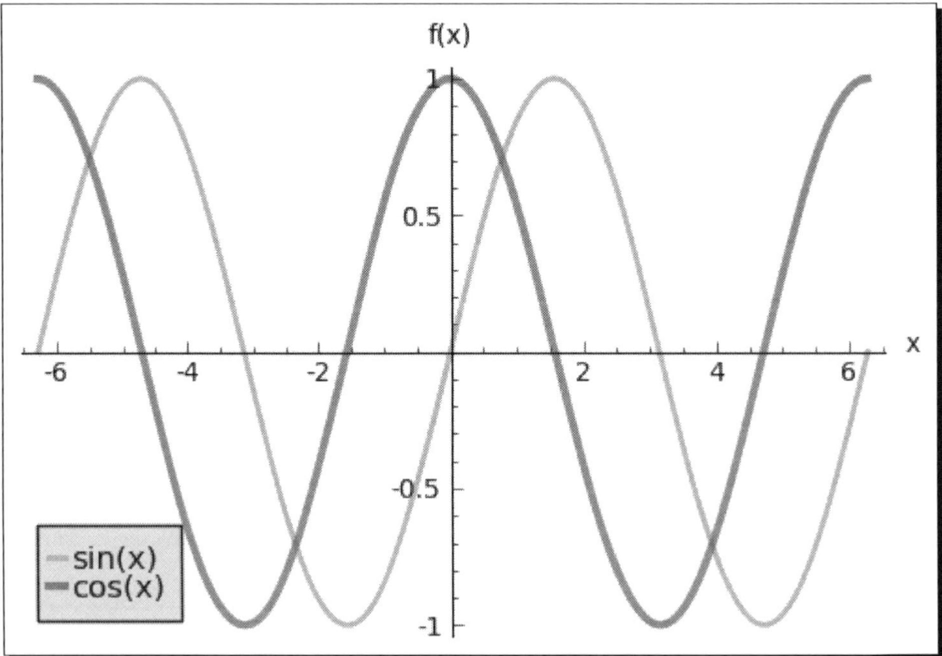

What just happened?

This example demonstrated the most basic type of plotting in Sage. The `plot` function requires the following arguments:

```
graphics_object = plot(callable symbolic expression, (independent_var,
ind_var_min, ind_var_max))
```

The first argument is a callable symbolic expression, and the second argument is a tuple consisting of the independent variable, the lower limit of the domain, and the upper limit. If there is no ambiguity, you do not need to specify the independent variable. Sage automatically selects the right number of points to make a nice curve in the specified domain. The `plot` function returns a graphics object. To combine two graphics objects in the same image, use the `+` operator: `plt = p1 + p2`. Graphics objects have additional methods for modifying the final image. In this case, we used the `axes_labels` method to label the x and y axes. Finally, the `show` function was used to finish the calculation and display the image.

The `plot` function accepts optional arguments that can be used to customize the appearance and format of the plot. To see a list of all the options and their default values, type:

```
sage: plot.options
{'fillalpha': 0.5, 'detect_poles': False, 'plot_points': 200,
'thickness': 1, 'alpha': 1, 'adaptive_tolerance': 0.01, 'fillcolor':
'automatic', 'adaptive_recursion': 5, 'exclude': None, 'legend_label':
None, 'rgbcolor': (0, 0, 1), 'fill': False}
```

Here is a summary of the options for customizing the appearance of a plot:

Keyword	Description
alpha	Transparency of the line (0=opaque, 1=transparent)
fill	True to fill area below the line
fillalpha	Transparency of the filled-in area (0=opaque, 1=transparent)
fillcolor	Color of the filled-in area
rgbcolor	Color of the line

Sage uses an algorithm to determine the best number of points to use for the plot, and how to distribute them on the x axis. The algorithm uses recursion to add more points to resolve regions where the function changes rapidly. Here are the options that control how the plot is generated:

Keyword	Description
adaptive_recursion	Max depth of recursion when resolving areas of the plot where the function changes rapidly
adaptive_tolerance	Tolerance for stopping recursion
detect_poles	Detect points where function value approaches infinity (see next example)
exclude	A list or tuple of points to exclude from the plot
plot_points	Number of points to use in the plot

Specifying colors in Sage

There are several ways to specify a color in Sage. For basic colors, you can use a string containing the name of the color, such as `red` or `blue`. You can also use a tuple of three floating-point values between 0 and 1.0. The first value is the amount of red, the second is the amount of green, and the third is the amount of blue. For example, the tuple (0.5, 0.0, 0.5) represents a medium purple color.

Some functions "blow up" to plus or minus infinity at a certain point. A simplistic plotting algorithm will have trouble plotting these points, but Sage adapts.

Time for action – plotting a function with a pole

Let's try to plot a simple function that takes on infinite values within the domain of the plot:

```
pole_plot = plot(1 / (x - 1), (0.8, 1.2), detect_poles='show',
    marker='.')
print("min y = {0}    max y = {1}".format(pole_plot.ymax(),
    pole_plot.ymin()))
pole_plot.ymax(100.0)
pole_plot.ymin(-100.0)

# Use TeX to make nicer labels
pole_plot.axes_labels([r'$x$', r'$1/(x-1)$'])

pole_plot.show()
```

The output from this code is as follows:

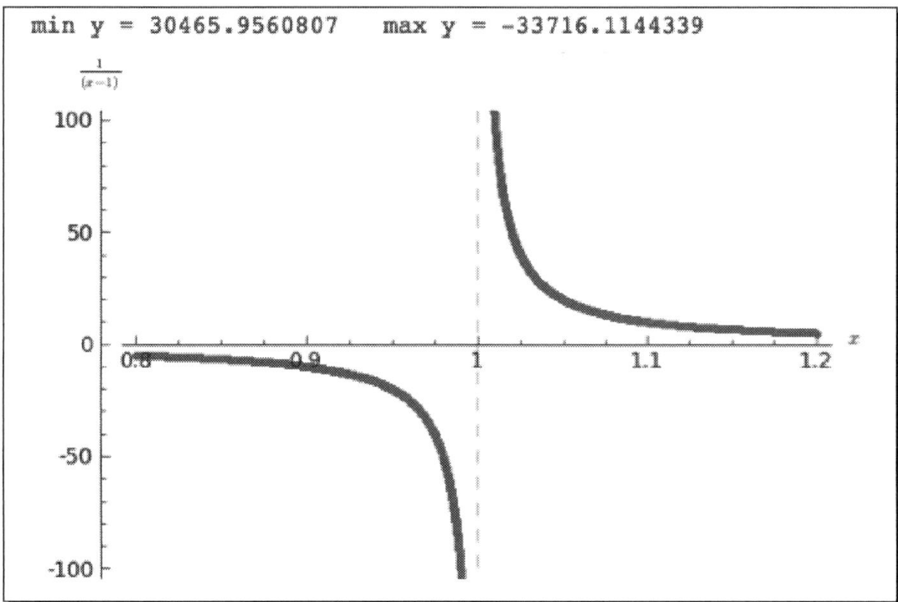

What just happened?

We did a few things differently compared to the previous example. We defined a callable symbolic expression right in the plot function. We also used the option `detect_poles='show'` to plot a dashed vertical line at the x value where the function returns infinite values. The option `marker='.'` tells Sage to use a small dot to mark the individual (x,y) values on the graph. In this case, the dots are so close together that they look like a fat line. We also used the methods `ymin` and `ymax` to get and set the minimum and maximum values of the vertical axis. When called without arguments, these methods return the current values. When given an argument, they set the minimum and maximum values of the vertical axis.

Finally, we labeled the axes with nicely typeset mathematical expressions. As in the previous example, we used the method `axes_labels` to set the labels on the x and y axes. However, we did two special things with the label strings:

```
r'$\frac{1}{(x-1)}$'
```

The letter **r** is placed in front of the string, which tells Python that this is a raw string. When processing a raw string, Python does not interpret backslash characters as commands (such as interpreting **\n** as a newline). Note that the first and last characters of the string are dollar signs, which tells Sage that the strings contain mark-up that needs to be processed before being displayed. The mark-up language is a subset of TeX, which is widely used for typesetting complicated mathematical expressions. Sage performs this processing with a built-in interpreter, so you don't need to have TeX installed to take advantage of typeset labels. It's a good idea to use raw strings to hold TeX markup because TeX uses a lot of backslashes. To learn about the typesetting language, see the matplotlib documentation at:

`http://matplotlib.sourceforge.net/users/mathtext.html`

In Chapter 10, we'll see how TeX and its relative LaTeX can help us typeset mathematical expressions.

Time for action – plotting a parametric function

Some functions are defined in terms of a parameter. Sage can easily plot parametric functions:

```
var('t')
pp = parametric_plot((cos(t), sin(t)), (t, 0, 2*pi),
    fill=True, fillcolor='blue')
pp.show(aspect_ratio=1, figsize=(3, 3), frame=True)
```

The output from this code is as follows:

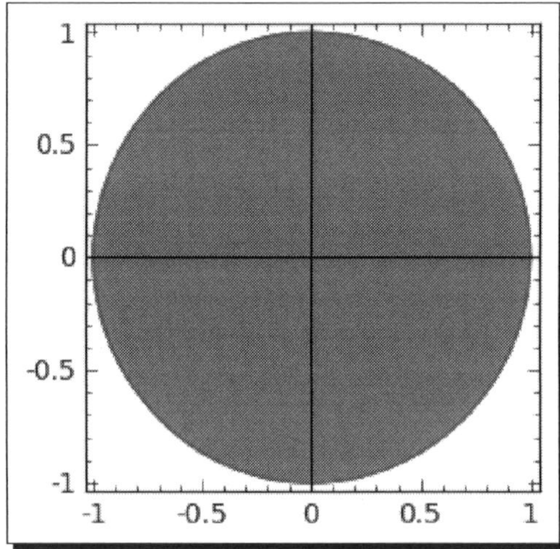

What just happened?

We used two parametric functions to plot a circle. This is a convenient place to demonstrate the `fill` option, which fills in the space between the function and the horizontal axis. The `fillcolor` option tells Sage which color to use for the fill, and the color can be specified in the usual ways. We also demonstrated some useful options for the `show` method (these options also work with the `show` function). The option `aspect_ratio=1` forces the x and y axes to use the same scale. In other words, one unit on the x axis takes up the same number of pixels on the screen as one unit on the y axis. Try changing the aspect ratio to 0.5 and 2.0, and see how the circle looks. The option `figsize=(x_size,y_size)` specifies the aspect ratio and relative size of the figure. The units for the figure size are relative, and don't correspond to an absolute unit like inches or centimetres. The option `frame=True` places a frame with tick marks around the outside of the plot.

Time for action – making a polar plot

Some functions are more easily described in terms of angle and radius. The angle is the independent variable, and the radius at that angle is the dependent variable. Polar plots are widely used in electrical engineering to describe the radiation pattern of an antenna. Some antennas are designed to transmit (or receive) electromagnetic radiation in a very narrow beam. The beam shape is known as the radiation pattern. One way to achieve a narrow beam is to use an array of simple dipole antennas, and carefully control the phase of the signal fed to each antenna. In the following example, we will consider seven short dipole antennas set in a straight line:

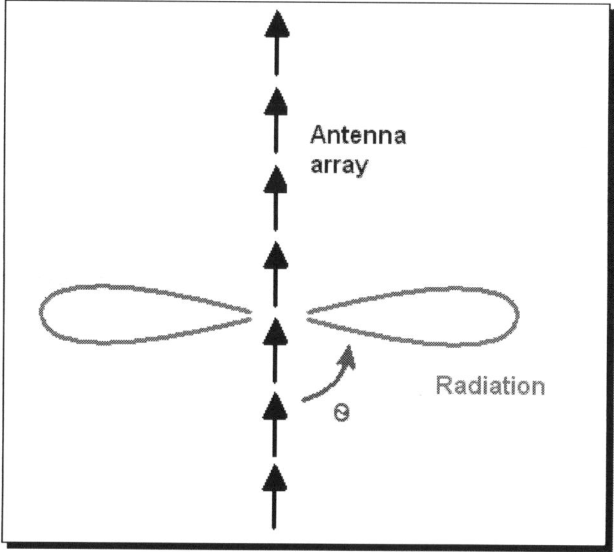

```
# A linear broadside array of short vertical dipoles
# located along the z axis with 1/2 wavelength spacing
var('r, theta')
N = 7
normalized_element_pattern = sin(theta)
array_factor = 1 / N * sin(N * pi / 2 * cos(theta)) \
/ sin(pi / 2 * cos(theta))
array_plot = polar_plot(abs(array_factor), (theta, 0, pi),
    color='red', legend_label='Array')
radiation_plot = polar_plot(abs(normalized_element_pattern
    * array_factor), (theta, 0, pi), color='blue',
    legend_label='Radiation')
combined_plot = array_plot + radiation_plot
combined_plot.xmin(-0.25)
combined_plot.xmax(0.25)
combined_plot.set_legend_options(loc=(0.5, 0.3))
show(combined_plot, figsize=(2, 5), aspect_ratio=1)
```

Execute the code. You should get a plot like this:

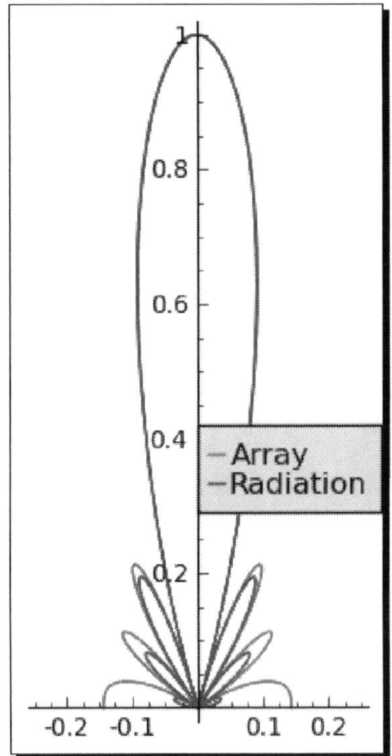

What just happened?

We plotted a polar function, and used several of the plotting features that we've already discussed. There are two subtle points worth mentioning. The function `array_factor` is a function of two variables, `N` and `theta`. In this example, `N` is more like a parameter, while `theta` is the independent variable we want to use for plotting. We use the syntax `(theta, 0, pi)` in the `plot` function to indicate that `theta` is the independent variable. The second new aspect of this example is that we used the methods `xmin` and `xmax` to set the limits of the x axis for the graphics object called `combined_plot`. We also used the `set_legend_options` of the graphics object to adjust the position of the legend to avoid covering up important details of the plot.

Time for action – plotting a vector field

Vector fields are used to represent force fields such as electromagnetic fields, and are used to visualize the solutions of differential equations. Sage has a special plotting function to visualize vector fields.

```
var('x, y')
a = plot_vector_field((x, y), (x, -3, 3), (y, -3, 3), color='blue')
b = plot_vector_field((y, -x), (x, -3, 3), (y, -3, 3), color='red')
show(a + b, aspect_ratio=1, figsize=(4, 4))
```

You should get the following image:

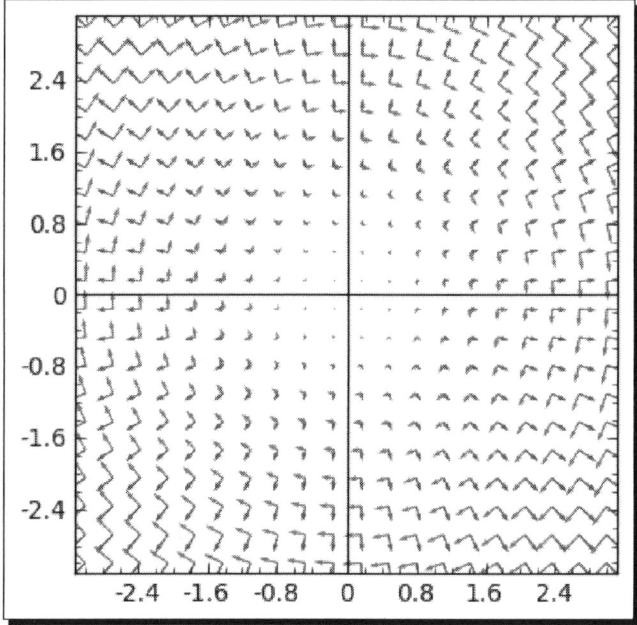

What just happened?

The `plot_vector_field` function uses the following syntax:

```
plot_vector_field((x_function,y_function), (x,x_min,x_max), (y,y_
min,y_max))
```

The keyword argument `color` specifies the color of the vectors.

Plotting data in Sage

So far, we've been making graphs of functions. We specify the function and the domain, and Sage automatically chooses the points to make a nice-looking curve. Sometimes, we need to plot discrete data points that represent experimental measurements or simulation results. The following functions are used for plotting defined sets of points.

Time for action – making a scatter plot

Scatter plots are used in science and engineering to look for correlation between two variables. A cloud of points that is roughly circular indicates that the two variables are independent, while a more elliptical arrangement indicates that there may be a relationship between them. In the following example, the x and y coordinates are contrived to make a nice plot. In real life, the x and y coordinates would typically be read in from data files. Enter the following code:

```
def noisy_line(m, b, x):
    return m * x + b + 0.5 * (random() - 0.5)

slope = 1.0
intercept = -0.5
x_coords = [random() for t in range(50)]
y_coords = [noisy_line(slope, intercept, x) for x in x_coords]
sp = scatter_plot(zip(x_coords, y_coords))
sp += line([(0.0, intercept), (1.0, slope+intercept)], color='red')
sp.show()
```

The result should look similar to this plot. Note that your results won't match exactly, since the point positions are determined randomly.

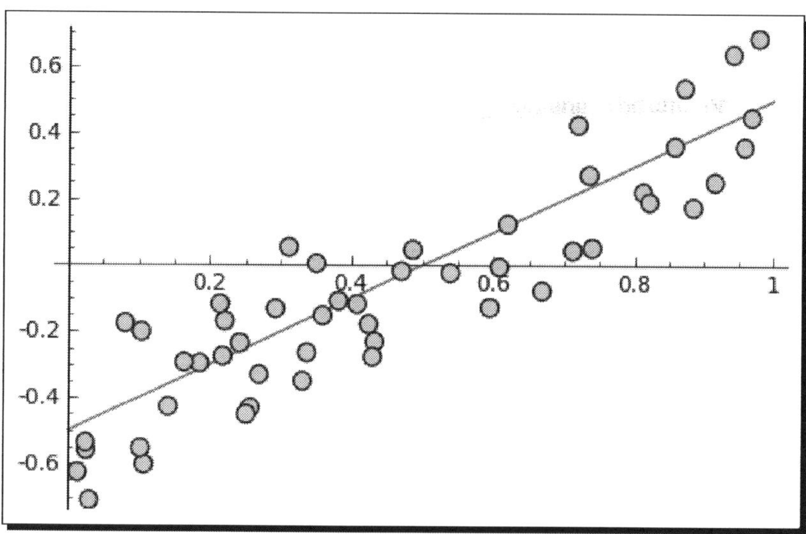

What just happened?

We created a list of randomized x coordinates using the built-in `random` function. This function returns a random number in the range $0 \leq x < 1$. We defined a function called `noisy_line` that we then used to create a list of randomized y coordinates with a linear relationship to the x coordinates. We now have a list of x coordinates and a list of y coordinates, but the `scatter_plot` function needs a list of `(x,y)` tuples. The `zip` function takes the two lists and combines them into a single list of tuples. The `scatter_plot` function returns a graphics object called sp. To add a line object to the plot, we use the following syntax:

```
sp += line([(x1, y1), (x2,y2)], color='red')
```

The `+=` operator is a way to increment a variable; `x+=1` is a shortcut for `x = x + 1`. Because the `+` operator also combines graphics objects, this syntax can be used to add a graphics object to an existing graphics object.

Time for action – plotting a list

Sometimes, you need to plot a list of discrete data points. The following example might be found in an introductory digital signal processing (DSP) course. We will use lists to represent digital signals. We sample the analogue function cosine(t) at two different sampling rates, and plot the resulting digital signals.

```
# Use list_plot to visualize digital signals
# Undersampling and oversampling a cosine signal

sample_times_1 = srange(0, 6*pi, 4*pi/5)
```

```
sample_times_2 = srange(0, 6*pi, pi/3)
data1 = [cos(t) for t in sample_times_1]
data2 = [cos(t) for t in sample_times_2]

plot1 = list_plot(zip(sample_times_1, data1), color='blue')
plot1.axes_range(0, 18, -1, 1)
plot1 += text("Undersampled", (9, 1.1), color='blue', fontsize=12)
plot2 = list_plot(zip(sample_times_2, data2), color='red')
plot2.axes_range(0, 18, -1, 1)
plot2 += text("Oversampled", (9, 1.1), color='red', fontsize=12)

g = graphics_array([plot1, plot2], 2, 1) # 2 rows, 1 column
g.show(gridlines=["minor", False])
```

The result is as follows:

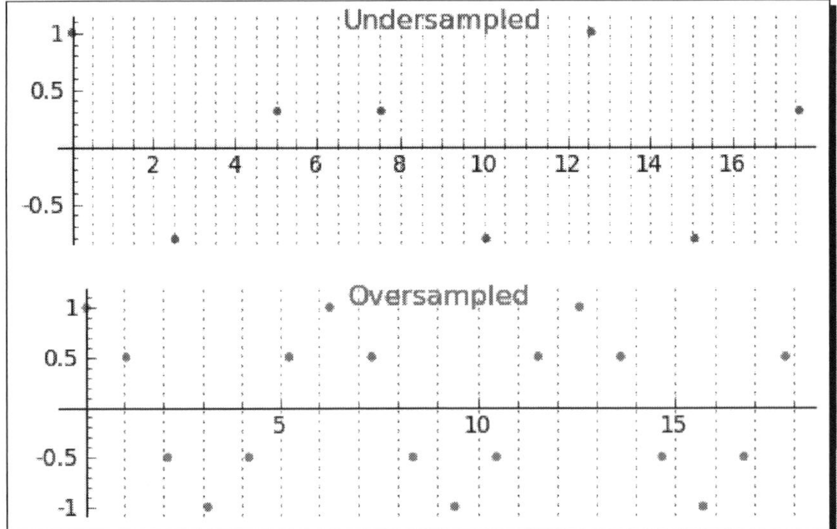

What just happened?

The function `list_plot` works a lot like `scatter_plot` from the previous example, so I won't explain it again. We used the method `axes_range(x_min, x_max, y_min, y_max)` to set the limits of the x and y axes all at once. Once again, we used the `+=` operator to add a graphics object to an existing object. This time, we added a text annotation instead of a line. The basic syntax for adding text at a given (x,y) position is `text('a string', (x,y))`. To see the options that text accepts, type the following:

```
sage: text.options
{'vertical_alignment': 'center', 'fontsize': 10, 'rgbcolor': (0, 0,
1),
'horizontal_alignment': 'center', 'axis_coords': False}
```

To display the two plots, we introduced a new function called `graphics_array`, which uses the basic syntax:

```
graphics_array([plot_1, plot_2, ..., plot_n], num_rows, num_columns)
```

This function returns another graphics object, and we used the `show` method to display the plots. We used the keyword argument `gridlines=["minor", False]` to tell Sage to display vertical lines at each of the minor ticks on the x axis. The first item in the list specifies vertical grid lines, and the second specifies horizontal grid lines. The following options can be used for either element:

"major"	Grid lines at major ticks
"minor"	Grid lines at major and minor ticks
False	No grid lines

Try playing with these options in the previous example.

Using graphics primitives

We've already seen that Sage has graphics primitives such as lines and text annotations. Sage has other types of graphics primitives that can be used for plotting.

Time for action – plotting with graphics primitives

A class of mathematical models called random sequential adsorption (RSA) models deals with the patterns that result when two-dimensional shapes are randomly deposited onto a plane. The following method can be used to visualize these kinds of models:

```
# Since the circles are random, your plot will not
# look exactly like the example!
circle_list = []
for i in range(15):
    x = -5 + 10 * random()
    y = -5 + 10 * random()
    circle_list.append(circle((x, y), 1, facecolor='red',
        edgecolor=(0, 0, 1), thickness=2, fill=True))
gr = sum(circle_list)
gr.axes(False)
gr.show(aspect_ratio=1, frame=True, gridlines=True, figsize=(4, 4))
```

You should get a plot that resembles the one below. Because the positions of the circles are randomly generated, your plot will not look exactly like this one.

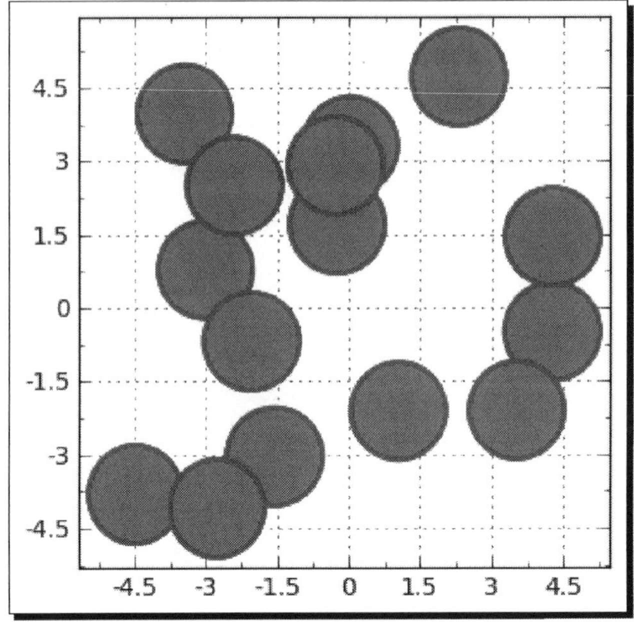

What just happened?

We created a list of graphics objects with a `for` loop and the `circle` function. The basic syntax for the circle function is as follows:

```
graphics_object = circle((center_x, center_y), radius)
```

In order to plot all the circles at once, we used the `sum` function to add up the list. We then prevented the axes from being drawn by calling the method `gr.axes(False)`. Finally, when calling the `show` method we used the keyword argument `frame=True` to draw a frame, with ticks and labels, around the outside of the plotting area. The argument `gridlines=True` is a shortcut to activate both horizontal and vertical grid lines. Sage has many other types of primitives, including elliptical arcs, arrows, disks, ellipses, points, and polygons, that are described in the Sage reference manual.

Using matplotlib

We can access matplotlib directly to do things that we can't do with Sage plotting functions. matplotlib has such a large number of options and features that it deserves a separate book. We will only touch on a few basic features. If you want to know more, the matplotlib website has excellent documentation:

`http://matplotlib.sourceforge.net/contents.html`

Time for action – plotting functions with matplotlib

To illustrate the similarities and differences between plotting with matplotlib and plotting with Sage, we will repeat the first example of this chapter using the Pyplot interface to matplotlib. Enter and evaluate the following code:

```
import numpy
import matplotlib.pyplot as plt

x = numpy.arange(-2 * numpy.pi, 2 * numpy.pi, 0.1)
func1 = numpy.sin(x)
func2 = numpy.cos(x)

plt.figure(figsize=(5.5, 3.7))    # size in inches
plt.plot(x, func1, linewidth=2.0, color=(0.5, 1,0),
label='$f(x)=sin(x)$')
plt.plot(x, func2, linewidth=3.0, color='purple', alpha=0.5,
label='$f(x)=cos(x)$')
plt.xlabel('$x$')
plt.ylabel('$f(x)$')
plt.title('Plotting with matplotlib')
plt.legend(loc='lower left')
plt.savefig('demo1.png')
plt.close()
```

The result should be as follows:

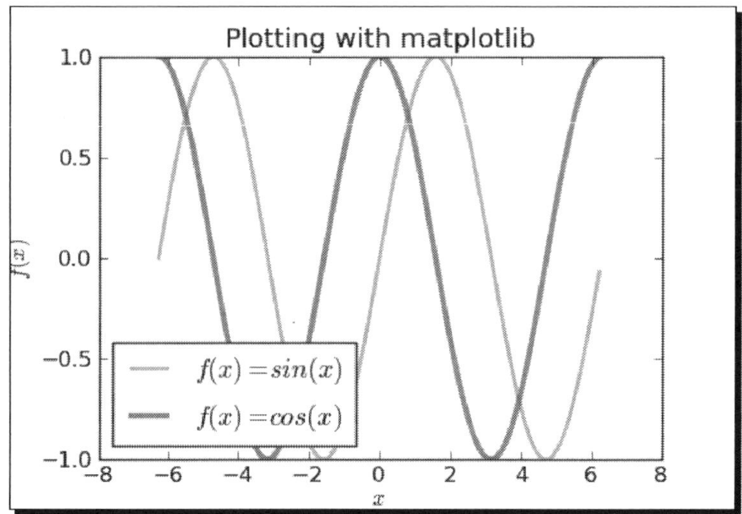

What just happened?

We gained access to matplotlib functions and types with the following line:

```
import matplotlib.pyplot as plt
```

We can now access these functions as `plt.function_name`. We also `import numpy` so that we can use its numerical arrays.

There is an important difference between the Sage `plot` function and the matplotlib `plot` function. matplotlib always plots lists or arrays of discrete points, rather than callable symbolic expressions. This block of code creates an array of x values:

```
x = numpy.arange(-2*numpy.pi, 2*numpy.pi, 0.1)
func1 = numpy.sin(x)
func2 = numpy.cos(x)
```

`func1` and `func2` are arrays of y values. Notice that we specify the NumPy version of `sin` and `cos`, since the Sage functions don't know what to do with NumPy arrays. The syntax for plotting with matplotlib is as follows:

```
plt.figure()
plt.plot(x_values, y_values)
```

The first line creates an empty figure. The optional argument `figsize=(x_size, y_size)` sets the figure size in inches. The second line plots the data points that are specified in the arrays or lists. By default, the points are connected with straight line segments. If you specify points that are too far apart, you will see the line segments instead of a smooth curve. The options for the `plt.plot` function are very similar to the options for the Sage `plot` function. The following code labels the x and y axes, and places a title above the figure:

```
plt.xlabel('$x$')
plt.ylabel('$f(x)$')
plt.title('Plotting with matplotlib')
plt.legend(loc='lower right')
```

The `legend` method places a legend on the figure. You can use TeX to format any text on the plot by wrapping the text in dollar signs. The following code actually displays the plot:

```
plt.savefig('demo1.png')
plt.close()
```

If you are running this example from the notebook interface, the graphic will automatically appear in the notebook. If you're running it in the interactive shell, you won't see any output. The `savefig` function will save an image file in your home directory. To specify a different path for saving files, pass a full or relative path in addition to the file name. For example:

```
sage: plt.savefig('Sage for Beginners/Chapter 6/Images/polar_plot.png')
```

matplotlib can save figures in a variety of image formats, such as png, pdf, ps (PostScript), eps (encapsulated PostScript), and svg (scalable vector graphics). It will automatically determine the correct format from the extension of the file name. You can also use the `format` keyword to specify the image format. PNG is a raster format, which is compatible with Microsoft Office and OpenOffice. For publications, it is best to use a vector format like PostScript, EPS, or PDF. The SVG format is used for displaying vector graphics on the Web.

Using matplotlib to "tweak" a Sage plot

Every Sage plot is actually an encapsulated matplotlib figure. We can get the underlying figure and modify it.

Time for action – getting the matplotlib figure object

Let's say you've made a plot with Sage, but you want to fix one or two formatting details, and Sage doesn't give you enough control. In this example, we'll use the object-oriented interface of matplotlib:

```
# Create a Sage plot, as shown in the first example
p1 = plot(sin, (-2*pi, 2*pi), thickness=2.0, rgbcolor=(0.5,1,0))
p2 = plot(cos, (-2*pi, 2*pi), thickness=3.0, color='purple',
alpha=0.5)
plt = p1 + p2

# Get the Matplotlib object
fig = plt.matplotlib()
from matplotlib.backends.backend_agg import FigureCanvasAgg
fig.set_canvas(FigureCanvasAgg(fig))    # this line is critical
ax = fig.gca()        # get current axes

# Add a legend and plot title
ax.legend(['sin(x)', 'cos(x)'])
ax.set_title('Modified with matplotlib')

# Add a y axis label in a custom location
ymin, ymax = ax.get_ylim()
ax.set_ylim(ymin, ymax*1.2)
ax.set_ylabel('$f(x)$', y=ymax*0.9)

# Fancy annotation of a point of interest
x_value = numerical_approx(-3*pi/4)
y_value = numerical_approx(cos(-3*pi/4))
ax.annotate('Point', xy=(x_value, y_value),
    xytext=(-6, -0.5), color='red',
    arrowprops=dict(arrowstyle="->", connectionstyle="angle3"))

# Show the matplotlib figure
fig.savefig('Sage_to_matplotlib.png')
```

The output should look like this:

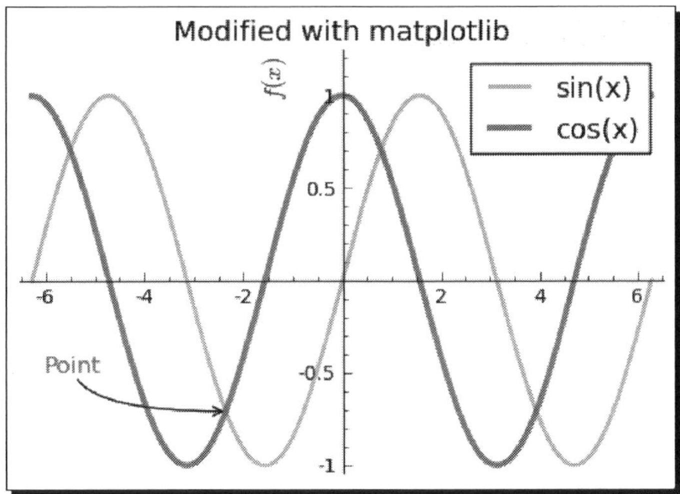

What just happened?

We modified a plot with matplotlib. First, we used Sage plotting commands to create a Sage graphics object. We then used the `matplotlib` method of the Sage graphics object to obtain the underlying matplotlib figure object. The rest of this example uses matplotlib functions, rather than Sage functions, to modify the figure. It is critical to use the following line of code:

```
fig.set_canvas(FigureCanvasAgg(fig))
```

The canvas is a "backend," which controls how matplotlib outputs the graphics it creates. Once we set the right canvas, we used the `gca` method of the figure object to get an object that represents the current axes. We then used methods of the axes object to modify the plot.

Time for action – improving polar plots

In a previous example, we made polar pots with the Sage function `polar_plot`. However, polar plots in matplotlib look nicer because they are plotted on special axes. Let's use matplotlib to make these plots again. This example uses the Pyplot interface to matplotlib:

```
import numpy
import matplotlib.pyplot as plt

# Repeat the antenna pattern example with the Pyplot interface
N = float(7)
theta = numpy.arange(0, numpy.pi, numpy.pi/100)
```

```
def normalized_element_pattern(theta):
    return abs(numpy.sin(theta))

def array_factor(theta, N):
    return abs(float(1 / N) * numpy.sin(float(N * pi / 2)
        * numpy.cos(theta))
        / numpy.sin(float(pi / 2) * numpy.cos(theta)))

plt.figure(figsize=(6, 4))
plt.subplot(121, polar=True)
plt.polar(theta, normalized_element_pattern(theta))
plt.title('Element factor')

plt.subplot(122, polar=True)
plt.polar(theta, array_factor(theta, N), color='red',
    label="Array factor")
plt.polar(theta, array_factor(theta, N) *
    normalized_element_pattern(theta),
    label="Pattern", color='blue')
plt.legend(loc='lower right', bbox_to_anchor = (1, 0))

plt.subplots_adjust(wspace=0.3)
plt.savefig('Polar_plot.png')
plt.close()
```

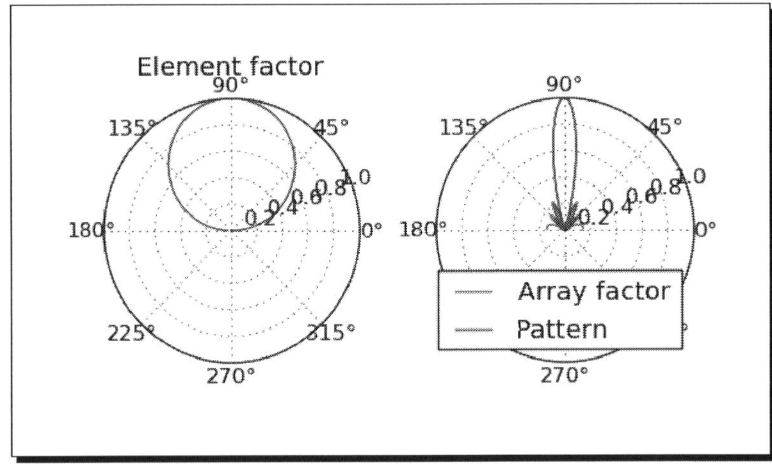

What just happened?

We made polar plots on nicely formatted polar axes. We introduced a new Pyplot function called `subplot`, which creates multiple axes on a single figure, arranged as a grid. Subplot accepts three integer arguments that specify the arrangement of axes and chooses one of the axes as the current axes object. The first integer specifies the number of columns in the grid, the second integer specifies the number of rows in the grid, and the third integer selects the current axes object. The first subplot, which is number one, is located in the upper-left corner of the figure. Subplot numbers increase from left to right across a row, and from top to bottom. It is possible, although not recommended, to omit the commas between arguments and pass a single three-digit integer value to `subplot`. This rather unusual syntax was chosen for compatibility with the `subplot` function in MATLAB. We used the `polar` keyword to choose polar axes for each of the subplots.

We also introduced a function called `subplots_adjust`, which we used to increase the amount of horizontal space between the plots. This command can be used to adjust the amount of space around and between subplots, using the following keyword arguments:

Keyword	Default	Meaning
left	0.125	Space to the left of the subplots
right	0.9	Space to the right of the subplots
bottom	0.1	Space below the subplots
top	0.9	Space above the subplots
wspace	0.2	Space between columns of subplots
hspace	0.2	Space between rows of subplots

Plotting data with matplotlib

Because matplotlib plots arrays of points, it is well suited to working with data. You can make many kinds of charts and publication-quality graphics with matplotlib.

Time for action – making a bar chart

Bar charts are often used to present experimental data in scientific papers. Let's make a chart with bars that represent the average value of some experimental data and add error bars to represent the standard deviation:

```
import numpy
import matplotlib.pyplot as plt

# Define experimental data
cluster1_data = numpy.array([9.7, 3.2])
```

```
cluster1_x = numpy.array([2,4])
cluster1_error = numpy.array([1.3, 0.52])

cluster2_data = numpy.array([6.8, 7.3])
cluster2_x = numpy.array([8,10])
cluster2_error = numpy.array([0.72, 0.97])

# Join data arrays for plotting
data = numpy.concatenate([cluster1_data, cluster2_data])
bar_centers = numpy.concatenate([cluster1_x, cluster2_x])
errors = numpy.concatenate([cluster1_error, cluster2_error])

# Plot
fig = plt.figure(figsize=(5,4))     # size in inches
plt.bar(bar_centers, data, yerr=errors,
    width=2.0, align='center', color='white', ecolor='black')
plt.ylabel('outcome')
plt.text(4, 4, '*', fontsize=14)

# Label ticks on x axis
axes = fig.gca()
axes.set_xticks(bar_centers)
axes.set_xticklabels(['trial 1', 'trial 2', 'trial 3', 'trial 4'])

plt.savefig('Bar_Chart.png')
plt.close()
```

The output should look like this:

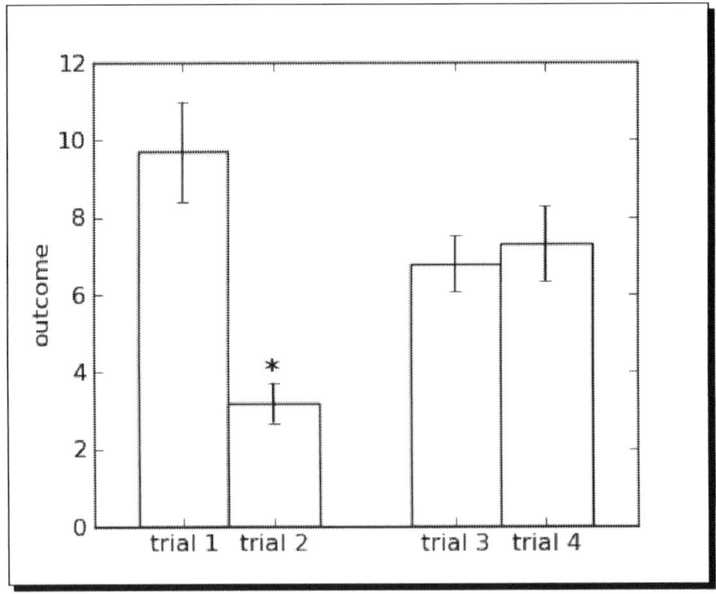

What just happened?

We created a publication-quality bar chart using the `bar` function from matplotlib. This function has two mandatory arguments. The first argument sets the horizontal location of each bar, and the second sets the height of each bar. Here is a summary of the optional arguments we used to customize the appearance of the plot:

Keyword	Description
yerr	Sets the size of the error bars on top of each bar.
width	Width of each bar.
align	Determines how the first argument is interpreted. If set to `'center'`, the array sets the location of the centre of each bar; otherwise, it sets the location of the left edge.
color	The color of the fill inside the bars.
ecolor	The color of the edge (outline) of the bars.

There are other optional arguments, which are described in the matplotlib documentation.

We used the `text` function to add text to the plot—in this case, an asterisk to indicate that one of the bars is statistically distinct from the others. The `text` function requires the x and y coordinates of the text, and a string containing the text to be displayed. The `fontsize` keyword allowed us to change the size of the text. In order to customize the tick labels on the x axis, we used the `gca` method of the figure object to get its axes object. We then passed an array of bar centres to the `set_xticks` method so that ticks will only be displayed at the centre of each bar. We used the `set_xticklabels` method to label the ticks with strings instead of numbers.

Time for action – making a pie chart

matplotlib can also make business graphics that are more commonly associated with spreadsheets. Let's try a pie chart:

```
import numpy
import matplotlib.pyplot as plt

data = [1.0, 10.0, 20.0, 30.0, 40.0]
explode = numpy.zeros(len(data))
explode[3] = 0.1

plt.figure(figsize=(4, 4))
plt.pie(data, explode=explode, labels=['a', 'b', 'c', 'd', 'e'])
plt.title('Revenue sources')

plt.savefig('Pie_chart.png')
plt.close()
```

The plot should look like this:

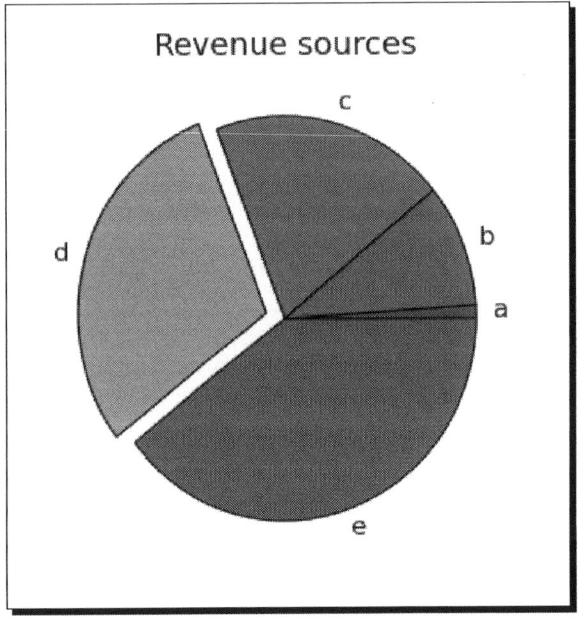

What just happened?

We made a pie chart. The `pie` function in matplotlib only requires one argument, which is a list of numbers that indicate the relative size of the slices. The `explode` option takes a list of numbers that show how far to offset each piece of the pie from the centre. In this case, we created an array of zeros and set the fourth element to 0.1, which offset the fourth slice of the pie. We used the keyword `explode` to pass this array to the `pie` function. We used the `labels` keyword to pass a list of strings to be used as labels for each slice.

Time for action – plotting a histogram

matplotlib has a built-in function for making histograms, which are used to visualize the distribution of values in a set of data. In this example, we will generate an array of random numbers that are drawn from a Gaussian distribution:

```
import numpy
import matplotlib.pyplot as plt
data = numpy.random.normal(0, 1, size=1000)
plt.figure(figsize=(4, 4))
plt.hist(data, normed=True, facecolor=(0.9, 0.9, 0.9))
plt.savefig('Histogram.png')
plt.close()
```

The result should be similar to the following plot. Because we are generating random data, your plot will not look exactly like this one:

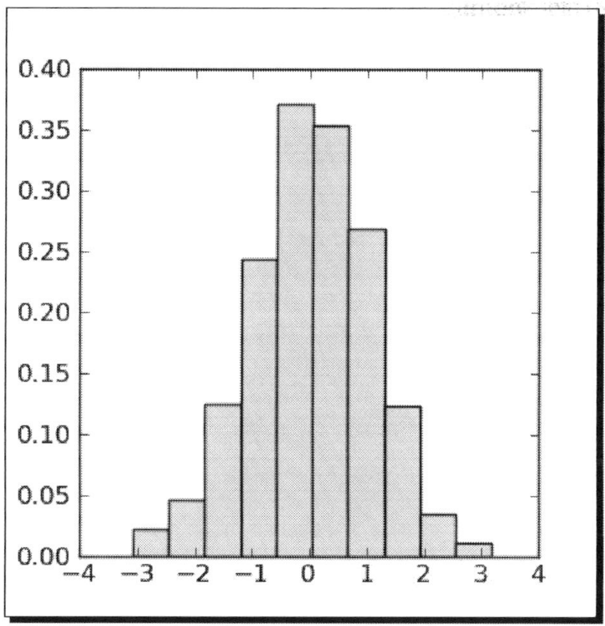

What just happened?

We used the `hist` function to visualize the distribution of values in an array of pseudo-random numbers. `hist` requires one argument, which is an array containing the data. In practice, the data would typically consist of experimental measurements, sensor data, or the results of a Monte Carlo simulation. We used the optional argument `normed=True` to indicate that the histogram should be normalized, which means that its integral is one. The `facecolor` keyword was used to specify the fill color of the bars as a tuple of R, G, B values.

Plotting in three dimensions

Sage can make 3D plots for visualizing functions of two variables, as well as parametric plots that create three-dimensional surfaces. It also has a variety of tools for making two-dimensional representations of three-dimensional surfaces.

Time for action – make an interactive 3D plot

Let's make an interactive 3D plot.

```
var('x, y')
p3d = plot3d(y^2 + 1 - x^3 - x, (x, -pi, pi), (y, -pi, pi))
p3d.show()
```

If you run this example in the notebook interface, a Java applet called Jmol will run in the cell below the code. If you run it from the interactive shell, Jmol will launch as a stand-alone application. Clicking and dragging on the figure with the left mouse button will rotate the plot in 3D space. Clicking and dragging with the centre button, or moving the scroll wheel, zooms in and out. Right-clicking brings up a menu that allows you to set various options for Jmol. Since Jmol is also used to visualize the 3D structures of molecules, some of the options are not relevant for plotting functions. Here is a screenshot of the function, plotted with Jmol:

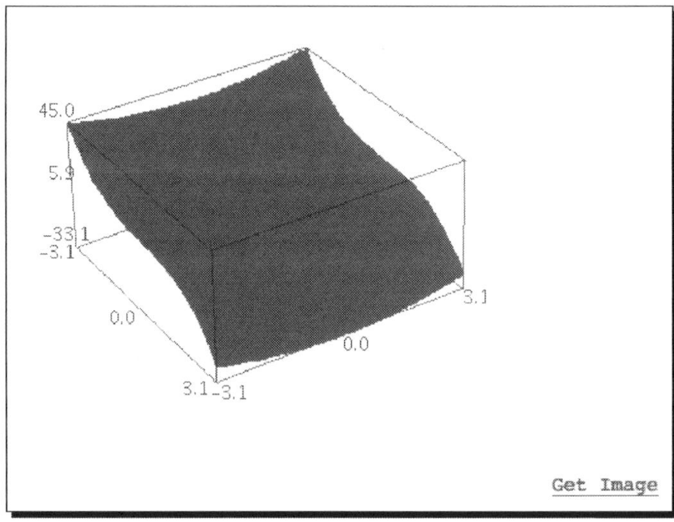

What just happened?

We made a cool 3D plot that allowed us to explore a function of two variables. When running Jmol as an applet in a worksheet, you can click on the "Get Image" link below the plot to save an image of the plot in its current state. However, the image quality is not particularly high because it is saved in JPEG format. When Jmol is called from the command line, it runs as a stand-alone application, and more options are available. You can save files in JPEG, GIF, PPM, PNG, or PDF format. Note that the PDF format is a bitmap embedded in a PDF file, rather than a true vector representation of the surface. The syntax for using plot3d is very simple:

```
plot3d(f(x,y), (x, x_min, x_max), (y, y_min, y_max))
```

There are a few optional arguments to the `show` method that you can use to alter the appearance of the plot. Setting `mesh=True` plots a mesh on the surface, and setting `dots=True` plots a small sphere at each point. You can also use the `transformation` keyword argument to apply a transformation to the data—see the `plot3d` documentation for more information.

Higher quality output

We can improve the quality of saved images using ray tracing, which is an algorithm for generating images that is based on optical principles. Sage comes with ray tracing software called Tachyon, which can be used to view 3D plots. To activate Tachyon, use the `show` method with the `viewer` keyword as shown below:

```
p3d.show(viewer='tachyon', frame=False, axes=True)
```

Depending on the speed of your computer, the ray tracing may require a few seconds to a few minutes.

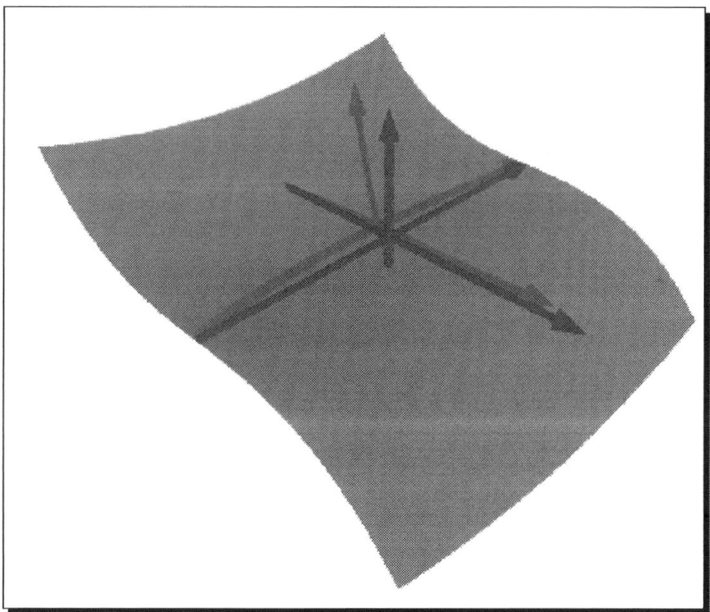

The `frame` keyword selects whether or not to draw a box around the outer limits of the plot, while the `axes` keyword determines whether or not the axes are drawn.

Parametric 3D plotting

Sage can also plot functions of two variables that are defined in terms of a parameter. You can make very complex surfaces in this way.

Time for action – parametric plots in 3D

We will plot two interlocking rings to demonstrate how complex surfaces are easily plotted using three functions of two parameters:

```
var('u, v')
f1 = (4 + (3 + cos(v)) * sin(u), 4 + (3 + cos(v)) * cos(u),
    4 + sin(v))
f2 = (8 + (3 + cos(v)) * cos(u), 3 + sin(v), 4 + (3 + cos(v))
    * sin(u))
p1 = parametric_plot3d(f1, (u, 0, 2 * pi), (v, 0, 2 * pi),
    texture="red")
p2 = parametric_plot3d(f2, (u, 0, 2 * pi), (v, 0, 2 * pi),
    texture="blue")
combination = p1 + p2
combination.show()
```

The result should look like this:

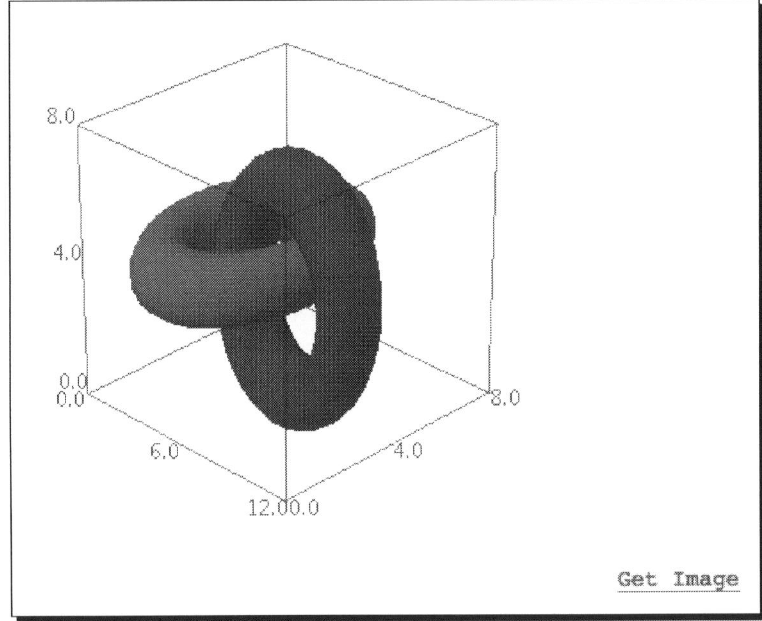

What just happened?

We made a very complex 3D shape using the `parametric_plot3d` function. The optional arguments for this function are the same as the options for the `plot3d` function.

Contour plots

Sage can also make contour plots, which are 2-D representations of 3-D surfaces. While 3D plots are eye-catching, a 2D plot can be a more practical way to convey information about the function or data set.

Time for action – making some contour plots

The following code will demonstrate four different ways to make a 2D plot of a 3D surface with Sage:

```
var('x, y')
text_coords = (2, -3.5)

cp = contour_plot(y^2 + 1 - x^3 - x, (x, -3, 3), (y, -3, 3),
    contours=8, linewidths=srange(0.5, 4.0, 0.5), fill=False,
    labels=True, label_colors='black', cmap='gray', colorbar=False)
cp += text("Contour", text_coords)

ip = implicit_plot(y^2 + 1 - x^3 - x, (x, -3, 3), (y, -3, 3))
ip += text("Implicit", text_coords)

rp = region_plot(y^2 + 1 - x^3 - x < 0, (x, -3, 3), (y, -3, 3),
    incol=(0.8, 0.8, 0.8))    # color is an (R,G,B) tuple
rp += text("Region", text_coords)

dp = density_plot(y^2 + 1 - x^3 - x, (x, -3, 3), (y, -3, 3))
dp += text("Density", text_coords)

show(graphics_array([cp, ip, rp, dp], 2, 2), aspect_ratio=1,
    figsize=(6, 6))
```

The output should be as follows:

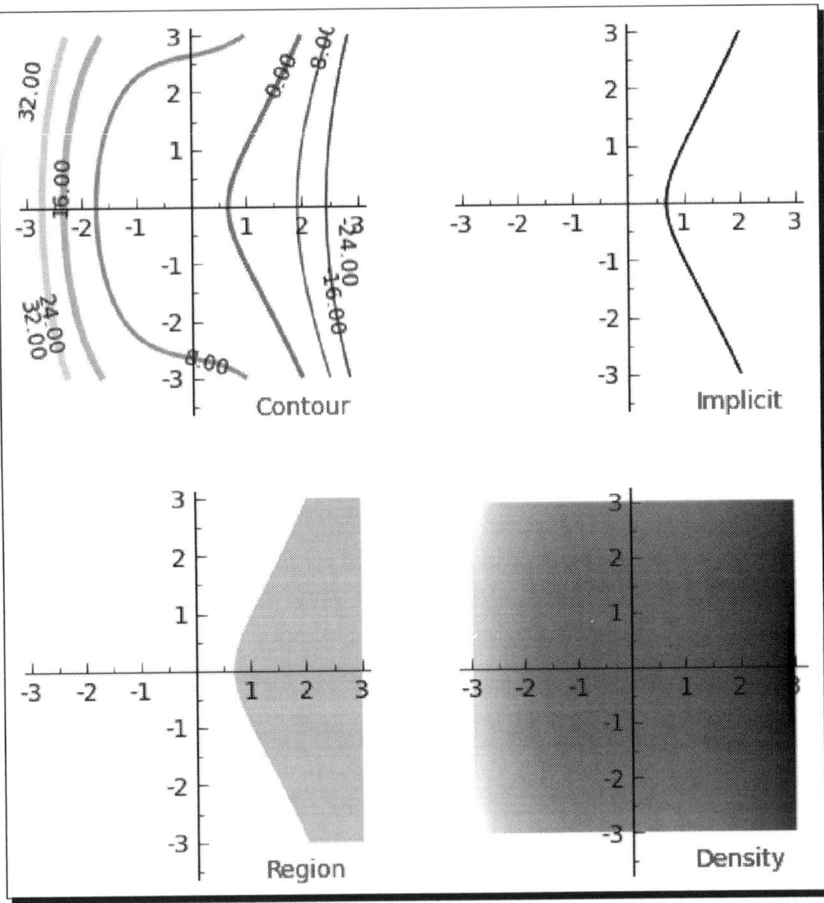

What just happened?

The plots we made demonstrate four different ways of visualizing the function we plotted in the previous example. All four functions follow the same syntax as `plot3d`:

```
contour_plot(f(x,y), (x, x_min, x_max), (y, y_min, y_max))
```

`contour_plot` plots level curves on the surface. In other words, z is constant on each curve. `implicit_plot` does the same thing, but only plots the curve where z=0. `region_plot` determines the curve for which z=0, and then fills in the region where z<0. Finally, `density_plot` converts the z value of the function to a color value and plots a color map of the z values over the x-y plane. We used the contour plot to demonstrate some of the keyword arguments that can be used to control the appearance of the plot. Here is a summary of the options we used:

Keyword	Description
contours	The number of contours to draw
linewidths	A list of line widths, corresponding to the number of contours
fill	True to fill in between the contours
labels	True to label each contour
label_colors	Color to use for labels
cmap	Color map to use for contour lines
colorbar	True to display the a scale bar showing the color map

Summary

We have seen that Sage has powerful graphics capabilities. Specifically, we learned about:

- Plotting functions of one variable, in rectangular and polar coordinates
- Setting options that control the appearance of plots
- Visualizing data with `list_plot` and `scatter_plot`
- Using graphics primitives to customize
- Using matplotlib to gain more control over the formatting of plots
- Making various types of charts for presenting data
- Making three-dimensional plots and contour plots

In the next chapter, we will learn how to use the powerful symbolic capabilities of Sage to solve difficult problems in mathematics, engineering, and science.

7
Making Symbolic Mathematics Easy

Every engineer, scientist, and mathematician has taken classes that introduced calculus, and many have learned more advanced mathematics such as differential equations. Unfortunately, the majority of a student's time is often spent performing algebra rather than understanding advanced concepts. Sage has powerful tools that automate the tedious process of moving symbols around in algebraic expressions. Further, Sage is capable of differentiating and integrating complicated functions, and performing Laplace transforms that would otherwise need to be looked up in a reference book. In fact, Sage can perform integrals and Laplace transforms that can't realistically be performed by hand. Students and professionals will find it worth their time to learn how to utilize Sage to perform tedious mathematics so that they can focus on understanding important concepts and performing creative problem-solving.

Although this chapter will focus on undergraduate-level mathematics, Sage is also useful for mathematical research, as evidenced by the list of publications that reference Sage (`http://sagemath.org/library-publications.html`). The lead developer of Sage is a number theorist, and Sage is ahead of its commercial competitors in the area of number theory.

In this chapter, we will learn how to:

- Create symbolic functions and expressions, and learn to manipulate them
- Solve equations and systems of equations exactly, and find symbolic roots
- Automate calculus operations like limits, derivatives, and integrals
- Create infinite series and summations to approximate functions
- Perform Laplace transforms
- Find exact solutions to ordinary differential equations

So let's get on with it...

Using the notebook interface

All of the examples in this chapter were written using the notebook interface. I highly recommend using the notebook for performing symbolic calculations. The `show` function (or method) generates nicely formatted output that is much easier to read than the text representation that you get on the command line.

Calling Maxima directly

Sage uses Maxima, an open-source computer algebra system, to handle many symbolic calculations. You can interact directly with Maxima from a Sage worksheet or the interactive shell by using the `maxima` object. For a complete tutorial with many examples, see `http://www.sagemath.org/doc/reference/sage/interfaces/maxima.html`.

Defining symbolic expressions

Before we can start doing integrals, derivatives, and transforms, we have to define the variables and functions that we are going to be working with. Functions and relations in Sage are called symbolic expressions.

Time for action – defining callable symbolic expressions

In Chapter 3, we learned how to define a mathematical function as a callable symbolic expression. Since we'll be working with callable symbolic expressions extensively in this chapter, let's learn a little more about how to use them. Enter the following code into an input cell in a worksheet, and evaluate the cell:

```
var('a, b, c, x')
f(x) = a * x^2 + b * x + c    # A callable symbolic expression
print("f(x):")
f.show()
print("Variables in f: {0}  Arguments in f: {1}".format(
    f.variables(), f.arguments()))
print("Type of f: {0}".format(type(f)))

g(x) = f.derivative(x)
print("g(x):")
g.show()
print("Variables in g: {0}  Arguments in g: {1}".format(
    g.variables(), g.arguments()))

g_plot = plot(g(a=1, b=-1), (-1, 1))
g_plot.axes_labels(['x', 'g(x)'])
show(g_plot, figsize=(3,3), aspect_ratio=1.0)
```

The output is shown below:

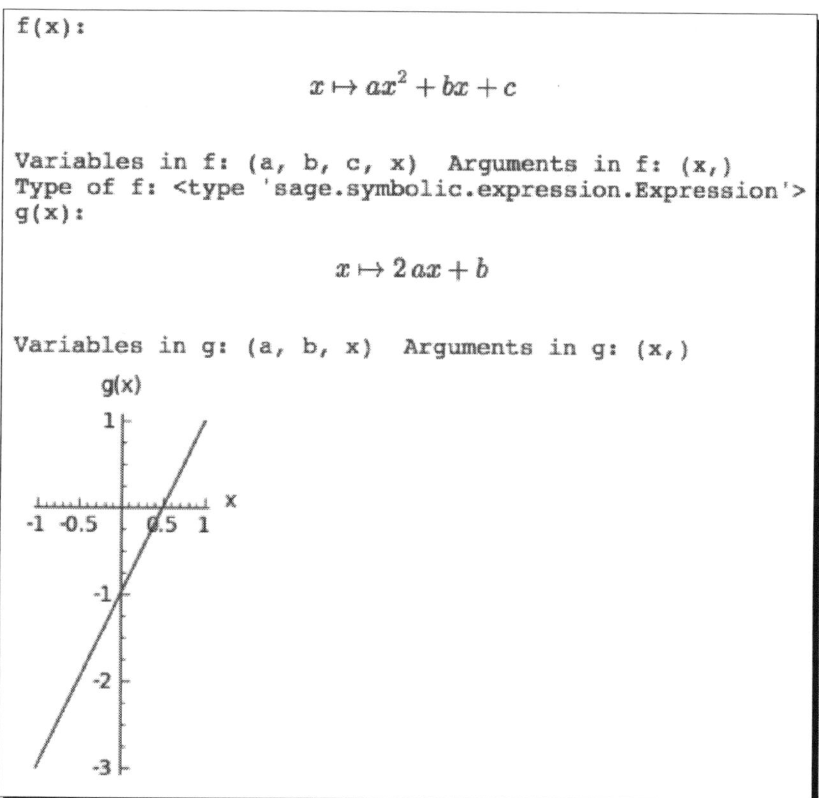

f(x):
$x \mapsto ax^2 + bx + c$
Variables in f: (a, b, c, x) Arguments in f: (x,)
Type of f: <type 'sage.symbolic.expression.Expression'>
g(x):
$x \mapsto 2\,ax + b$
Variables in g: (a, b, x) Arguments in g: (x,)
g(x)
1
-1
-2
-3
x
-1
-0.5
0.5
1

What just happened?

We started with a `var` statement to tell Sage that `x`, `a`, `b`, and `c` are symbolic variables, which also erases any previous values that we may have assigned to these variables. Technically, we could have omitted `x` from this list, since Sage automatically assumes that any variable called `x` is a symbolic variable. We then defined a callable symbolic expression `f(x)`. We used the `variables` method to list all of the variables that are present in `f`. We also used the method `arguments` to determine which variables are arguments. In this case, `x` is the only argument because we defined `f` to be a function of `x`. In Sage, an argument is an independent variable, while the other variables are more like parameters that are expected to take on fixed values.

We used the `derivative` method to compute the derivative of `f` with respect to `x`, and assign the result to another callable symbolic expression called `g`. Again, the methods `variables` and `arguments` were used to see which variables and arguments are present in `g`. Notice that the variable `c` is not present in `g`. Finally, we plotted function `g` to demonstrate how to plot a callable symbolic expression with one argument and multiple variables. In order to make a plot, Sage needs to have numerical values for the parameters `a` and `b`. In the `plot` function call, we used keyword syntax to set values for these variables, and we set limits for the domain of `x` in the usual way.

Relational expressions

A symbolic expression doesn't have to define a mathematical function. We can also express equality and inequality with symbolic expressions.

Time for action – defining relational expressions

Let's express some simple inequalities as relational expressions to see how they work:

```
exp1 = SR(-5) < SR(-3)     # use the symbolic ring
print("Expression {0} is {1}".format(exp1, bool(exp1)))

exp2 = exp1^2
print("Expression {0} is {1}".format(exp2, bool(exp2)))

forget()
exp3 = x^2 + 2 >= -3 * x^2
print("Expression {0} is {1}".format(exp3, bool(exp3)))

p1 = plot(exp3.lhs(), (x, -5, 5), legend_label='lhs')
# also lhs() or left_hand_side()

p2 = plot(exp3.rhs(), (x, -5, 5), color='red', legend_label='rhs')
# also rhs() or right_hand_side()

show(p1 + p2)
```

The output is shown in the following screenshot:

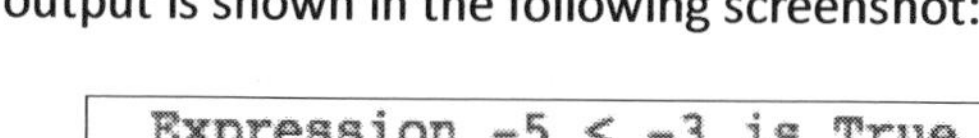

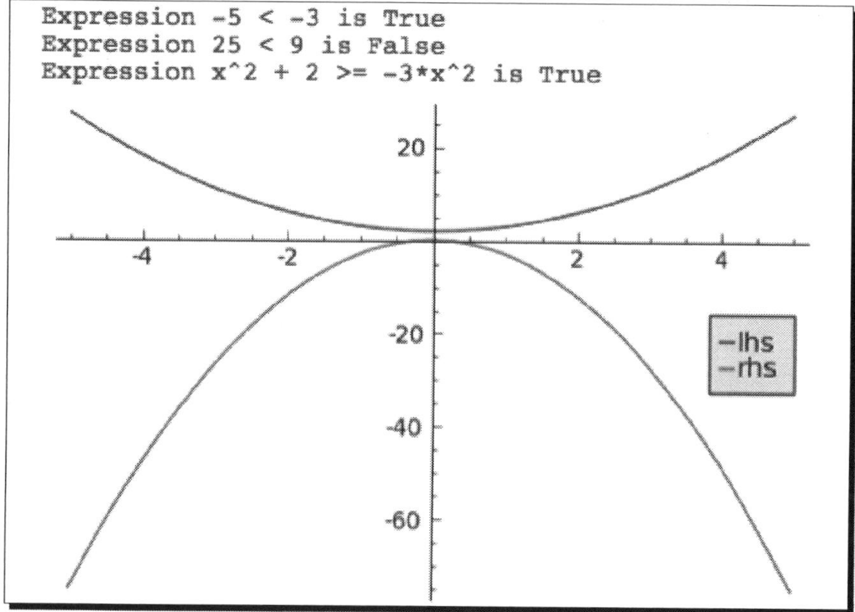

What just happened?

We defined a simple relational expression that expresses an inequality between two integers. We used the `SR` function to create symbolic objects, rather than integer objects, that represent the values -5 and -3. This is important because we need to give Sage a symbolic expression to work with. To evaluate the truth of the inequality, we used the `bool` function. Next, we used the syntax `exp1^2` to square both sides of the inequality, and used `bool` to evaluate the new inequality. This would not have worked if we had defined the inequality using integers.

We then created a relational symbolic expression involving the symbolic variable `x`. Since the expression involves at least one symbolic variable, Sage treats the entire expression as a symbolic expression. That's why we didn't need to use `SR` to create symbolic variables instead of numerical variables. We called the `forget` function before evaluating the expression, which clears any assumptions about any variables that may have been set (we'll cover assumptions in the next example). To help understand why this expression evaluates to `True`, we plotted each side of the expression on the same axes. The method `left` (and its synonyms `lhs` and `left_hand_side`) return the left-hand side of an expression, while the method `right` (and its synonyms `rhs` and `right_hand_side`) return the right-hand side. The plot shows that the right-hand side is less than the left-hand side for all values of `x`, so the expression evaluates to `True`. If the inequality is false for only one point in the domain, then it evaluates to `False`.

Time for action – relational expressions with assumptions

Let's try a more complicated expression that states an inequality between two functions. We'll use plots to illustrate what's happening:

```
forget()

expr = -20 * x - 30 <= 4 * x^3 - 7 * x
print("Expression {0} is {1}".format(expr, bool(expr)))

p1 = plot(expr.left(), (x, -5, 5), legend_label='lhs')
p2 = plot(expr.right(),(x, -5, 5), color='red', legend_label='rhs')

assume(x > 0)
print("Now assume x > 0")
print("Expression {0} is {1}".format(expr, bool(expr)))
show(p1 + p2)
```

The output is shown in the following screenshot:

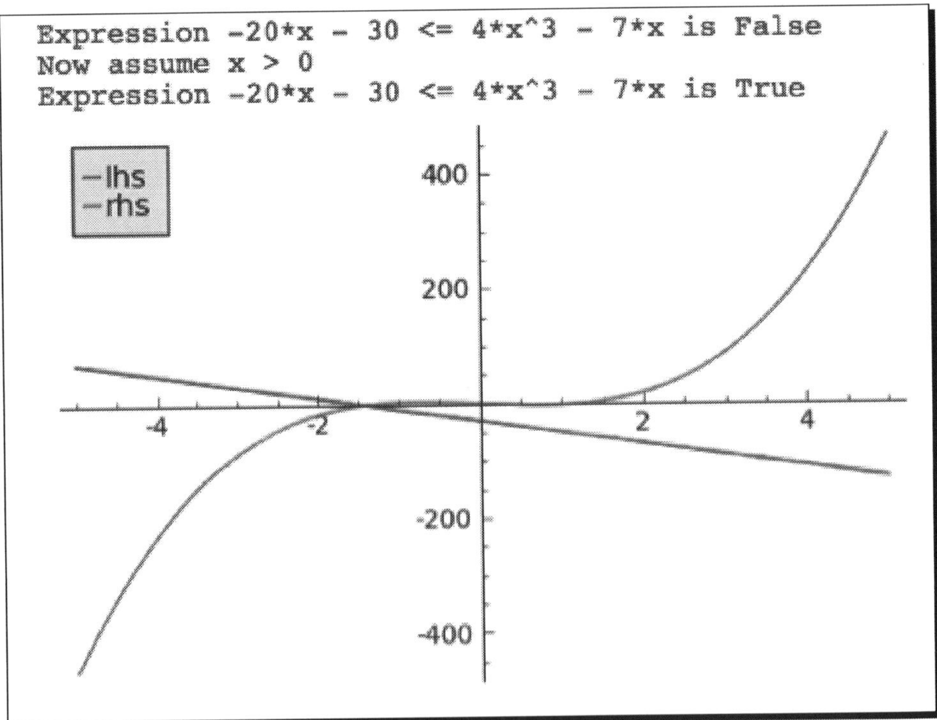

What just happened?

We started the example with a call to the `forget` function, to clear any assumptions that we may have made in other cells. The first expression evaluated to `False`, because the expression on the left-hand side is greater than the expression on the right-hand side over part of the domain. However, when we used the `assume` statement to assert that x>0, the expression evaluated to `True`. Looking at the plot, we can see why this is true.

Manipulating expressions

We've already seen how to square both sides of a relational expression. There are many ways to manipulate relational expressions with Sage.

Time for action – manipulating expressions

Enter the following code into an input cell in a worksheet, and evaluate the cell:

```
var('x, y')
expr = (y - 7) / (x^2 + 1) == x^3 - 5
print("Expression:")
expr.show()

print("Two ways of multiplying both sides:")
show(expr.multiply_both_sides(x^2 + 1))
show(expr * (x^2 + 1))
# also divide_both_sides

expr = expr * (x^2 + 1)

print("Two ways of adding to both sides:")
show(expr.add_to_both_sides(7))
show(expr+7)
# also subtract_from_both_sides
```

The results are shown in the following screenshot:

Expression:

$$\frac{y-7}{x^2+1} = x^3 - 5$$

Two ways of multiplying both sides:

$$y - 7 = (x^2+1)(x^3-5)$$

$$y - 7 = (x^2+1)(x^3-5)$$

Two ways of adding to both sides:

$$y = (x^2+1)(x^3-5) + 7$$

$$y = (x^2+1)(x^3-5) + 7$$

What just happened?

This example showed how to perform one of the most basic algebraic re-arrangements: performing the same operation on both sides of a relation. We can do this by using methods of the symbolic expression object (`add_to_both_sides`, `subtract_from_both_sides`, `multiply_both_sides`, `divide_both_sides`). We can also use the arithmetic operators `+`, `-`, `*`, and `/` to perform the same operation on both sides of a relation. Note that these operations return a new symbolic expression, instead of modifying the existing expression. To modify the expression, we use the syntax `expr = expr * (x^2 + 1)`. We can also use the shortcuts `+=`, `-=`, `*=`, and `/=`, just like ordinary arithmetic.

Manipulating rational functions

Sage has special operations that are useful for working with rational functions. A rational function is any function that can be written as the ratio of two polynomial functions. Rational functions often occur when using the Laplace transform to solve ordinary differential equations.

Time for action – working with rational functions

Let's say you have used the Laplace transform to solve an ordinary differential equation. You have a rational function in the `s` domain, and you need to transform it back to the original problem domain. Here are some tools you can use to manipulate the symbolic expression to make it easier to perform the inverse Laplace transform:

```
var('s')
F(s) = (s + 1) / (s^2 * (s + 2)^3)
show(F)

print("Numerator: ")
show(F.numerator())
print("Denominator: ")
show(F.denominator())

print("Expanded:")
show(F.expand_rational())

print("Partial fraction expansion:")
pf(s) = F.partial_fraction()
show(pf)
```

The results are shown in the following screenshot:

$$s \mapsto \frac{s+1}{(s+2)^3 s^2}$$

Numerator:

$$s \mapsto s+1$$

Denominator:

$$s \mapsto (s+2)^3 s^2$$

Expanded:

$$s \mapsto \frac{1}{(s+2)^3 s} + \frac{1}{(s+2)^3 s^2}$$

Partial fraction expansion:

$$s \mapsto \frac{1}{16\,(s+2)} - \frac{1}{4\,(s+2)^3} - \frac{1}{16\,s} + \frac{1}{8\,s^2}$$

What just happened?

We defined a rational function, and demonstrated the utility methods `numerator` and `denominator` to obtain different parts of the expression. The method `expand_rational` separates the expression into a sum of terms by multiplying out products of sums and exponentials, splitting the numerator into terms, and distributing multiplication over addition. The method `partial_fraction` returns the partial fraction expansion of the expression. This is an extremely tedious calculation to perform by hand, and it is often the most time-consuming step in solving a differential equation with the Laplace transform.

Substitutions

When working with symbolic expressions, it is often necessary to substitute one variable or function for another. Substitution is often a critical step when deriving an equation or simplifying an expression.

Time for action – substituting symbols in expressions

Let's see how to perform symbolic substitutions with Sage.

```
var('x, y')
f(x) = 1 / x + 3 * x^2 + cos(x)
f.show()
print("Substitute for x with a keyword:")
show(f.subs(x=(7 * x)))
print("Substitute for x with a relational expression:")
show(f.substitute(x == 7 * x))

print("Substitute sine for cosine:")
show(f.substitute_function(cos, sin))
print("Substitute using a dictionary:")
show(f.substitute({1 / x: y^3, cos(x):sin(x)}))
```

The results are shown in the following screenshot:

$$x \mapsto 3x^2 + \frac{1}{x} + \cos(x)$$

```
Substitute for x with a keyword:
```

$$x \mapsto 147x^2 + \frac{1}{7x} + \cos(7x)$$

```
Substitute for x with a relational expression:
```

$$x \mapsto 147x^2 + \frac{1}{7x} + \cos(7x)$$

```
Substitute sine for cosine:
```

$$3x^2 + \frac{1}{x} + \sin(x)$$

```
Substitute using a dictionary:
```

$$x \mapsto 3x^2 + y^3 + \sin(x)$$

What just happened?

We used several methods to substitute both variables and functions in a callable symbolic expression. The methods called `subs` and `substitute` are identical. If you only need to replace a single symbol, a keyword argument can be used to specify which variable is to be replaced, and what expression should take its place. Multiple keywords can be used to make multiple substitutions at the same time. A relational expression can be used to replace a single symbol, or a sub-expression. We then used the method `substitute_function` to replace one function (sine) with another (cosine). Finally, we demonstrated that a dictionary can be passed to the `substitute` (or `subs`) method to specify the substitution. Each key:value pair in the dictionary describes one substitution. The key is the expression to be replaced, and the value is the replacement. Using a dictionary is very flexible, because you can replace a variable, a sub-expression (such as 1/x), or a function. When you use a dictionary to replace a function, note that you have to describe the functions as `cos(x)` and `sin(x)`, rather than `cos` and `sin`.

Another way to perform substitutions is with the `substitute_expression` method (and its synonym `subs_expr`). These methods use the `subst` command in Maxima, which performs a formal pattern substitution. The results may not be mathematically meaningful, so it is best to avoid these two methods if possible.

Expanding and factoring polynomials

Expanding a polynomial is the process of converting the polynomial from a product of sums to a sum of products. Factoring is the opposite process, in which a sum of products is converted into a product of factors.

Time for action – expanding and factoring polynomials

A number of methods are especially useful when working with polynomials. Let's see how they work:

```
var('x')
exp1 = (x + 3)^3 == (x - 1)^2
show(exp1)

print("Expanded expression:")
exp2 = exp1.expand()
show(exp2)

print("Expand left-hand side only:")
show(exp1.expand('left'))
lhs = exp1.expand('left').lhs()

print("Factor LHS:")
show(lhs.factor())

print("Information about the expanded LHS:")
print("  Highest degree of x on LHS: {0}".format(lhs.degree(x)))
print("  Coefficients: {0}".format(lhs.coeffs(x)))
print("  Coefficient of x^2: {0}".format(lhs.coeff(x,2)))
print("  Trailing coefficient of LHS: {0}".format
    (lhs.trailing_coefficient(x)))
```

The output is shown in the following screenshot:

$$(x+3)^3 = (x-1)^2$$

```
Expanded expression:
```

$$x^3 + 9x^2 + 27x + 27 = x^2 - 2x + 1$$

```
Expand left-hand side only:
```

$$x^3 + 9x^2 + 27x + 27 = (x-1)^2$$

```
Factor LHS:
```

$$(x+3)^3$$

```
Information about the expanded LHS:
  Highest degree of x on LHS: 3
  Coefficients: [[27, 0], [27, 1], [9, 2], [1, 3]]
  Coefficient of x^2: 9
  Trailing coefficient of LHS: 27
```

What just happened?

We defined a relational symbolic expression that equates two polynomials. We used the `expand` method (with no arguments) to multiply out the polynomials on each side of the equality. We also used the `expand` method with the optional argument `'left'` to expand only the left-hand side (you can also use `'right'`). We then used the `factor` method to factor the expanded left-hand side of the expression, and recovered its original form. These two methods are complementary, and can be used to move back and forth between different representations of a polynomial.

We also demonstrated some methods that return information about polynomials. The method `degree` returns the largest exponent of the given symbol in the polynomial. The method `coeffs` (or `coefficients`) returns a list that contains the coefficients of each term in the polynomial. Each item in the list is another list. The first item is the coefficient, and the second item is the degree of the term with that coefficient. The `coeff` (or `coefficient`) method allows us to get the coefficient for a specific term. Its first argument specifies a symbol, and its second argument specifies the power of that symbol. You may need to expand or factor the polynomial before calling this method. Finally, the method `trailing_coefficient` (or `trailing_coeff`) was used to obtain the coefficient for the smallest power of `x` in the left-hand side.

> The `factor` function in Sage is used to factor both polynomials and integers. This behaviour is different from Mathematica, where `Factor[]` is used to factor polynomials and `FactorInteger[]` is used to factorize integers.

Manipulating trigonometric expressions

Expressions involving trigonometric functions can be difficult to manipulate because of the numerous trigonometric identities that can be used (`http://en.wikipedia.org/wiki/List_of_trigonometric_identities`). Fortunately, Sage can automate this process.

Time for action – manipulating trigonometric expressions

Sage has several methods that are used primarily when an expression involves trigonometric functions. Let's try them out.

```
var('x, y')
f(x, y) = sin(x) * cos(x)^3 + sin(y)^2
print("f(x, y)")
f.show()
g(x, y) = f.reduce_trig()     # also trig_reduce
print("After trig_reduce:")
g.show()
print("After expanding:")
show(g.expand_trig())        # also trig_expand
print("Simplify to get original expression:")
show(g.expand_trig().trig_simplify())    # also simplify_trig
```

The output is shown in the following screenshot:

```
f(x,y)
```

$$(x,y) \mapsto \sin(x)\cos(x)^3 + \sin(y)^2$$

```
After trig_reduce:
```

$$(x,y) \mapsto \frac{1}{4}\sin(2x) + \frac{1}{8}\sin(4x) - \frac{1}{2}\cos(2y) + \frac{1}{2}$$

```
After expanding:
```

$$(x,y) \mapsto -\frac{1}{2}\sin(x)^3\cos(x) + \frac{1}{2}\sin(x)\cos(x)^3 + \frac{1}{2}\sin(x)\cos(x) + \frac{1}{2}\sin(y)^2 - \frac{1}{2}\cos(y)^2 + \frac{1}{2}$$

```
Simplify to get original expression:
```

$$(x,y) \mapsto \sin(x)\cos(x)^3 + \sin(y)^2$$

What just happened?

We demonstrated some useful methods that are specifically designed to manipulate expressions that involve trigonometric functions. `expand_trig` and `reduce_trig` (or `trig_expand` and `trig_reduce`) are complementary methods that have a similar function to those used in the previous example. We also introduced the method called `trig_simplify` (or `simplify_trig`), which attempts to represent an expression in the most compact way.

Logarithms, rational functions, and radicals

There are special rules for manipulating logarithms and radicals, so Sage has special methods for expanding and simplifying expressions involving these operations. There is also a separate method for simplifying rational expressions.

Time for action – simplifying expressions

In the following example, we will see how Sage can be used to simplify expressions that involve exponentials, logarithms, rational functions, and square roots:

```
var('x')

# Logs
f(x) = log(x^2 * sin(x) / sqrt(1 + x))
print("Original function:")
f.show()
print("This form is easier to work with:")
show(f.expand_log())
print("Simplify expanded form:")
show(f.expand_log().simplify_log())

# Rational functions
f(x) = (x + 1) / (x^2 + x)

print("Original function:")
f.show()
print("Simplified:")
show(f.simplify_rational())

# Radicals
f(x) = sqrt(x^2+x)/sqrt(x)
print("Original function:")
f.show()
print("Simplified:")
show(f.simplify_radical())
```

The output is shown in the following screenshot:

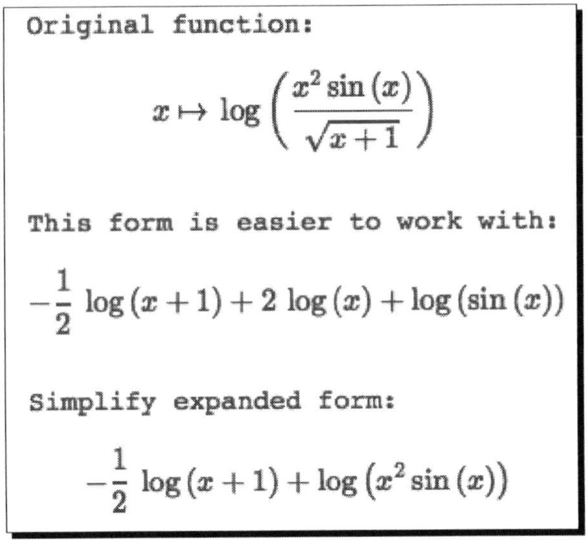

Original function:

$$x \mapsto \log\left(\frac{x^2 \sin(x)}{\sqrt{x+1}}\right)$$

This form is easier to work with:

$$-\frac{1}{2} \log(x+1) + 2 \log(x) + \log(\sin(x))$$

Simplify expanded form:

$$-\frac{1}{2} \log(x+1) + \log\left(x^2 \sin(x)\right)$$

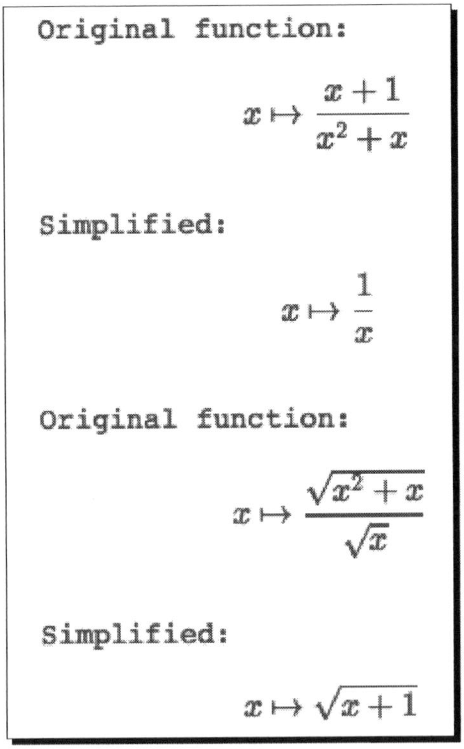

Original function:

$$x \mapsto \frac{x+1}{x^2+x}$$

Simplified:

$$x \mapsto \frac{1}{x}$$

Original function:

$$x \mapsto \frac{\sqrt{x^2+x}}{\sqrt{x}}$$

Simplified:

$$x \mapsto \sqrt{x+1}$$

What just happened?

We demonstrated some special methods for expanding and simplifying expressions involving logs, rational functions, and radicals. The following table summarizes the methods available in Sage for simplifying and expanding expressions:

Method(s)	Description
`expand_log` `log_expand`	Expands logarithms of powers, logarithms of products, and logarithms of quotients
`simplify_log` `log_simplify`	Attempt to simplify an expression involving logarithms
`simplify_rational` `rational_simplify`	Attempt to simplify an expression involving rational expressions
`radical_simplify` `simplify_radical` `exp_simplify` `simplify_exp`	Attempt to simplify an expression involving radicals
`simplify_factorial` `factorial_simplify`	Simplify an expression by combining factorials and expanding binomials into factorials
`simplify_full` `full_simplify`	Applies the following operations, in order: `simplify_factorial`, `simplify_trig`, `simplify_rational`, `simplify_radical`, `simplify_log`, and again `simplify_rational`

It can be tricky to get an expression in the form that you want. You may have to experiment with various combinations of expanding, simplifying, and factoring an expression. Part of the problem is that it is difficult to quantify the "simplest" form of an expression. Most of the commands in Sage that factor, expand, or simplify expressions accept optional arguments that control how they work. Look at the documentation for each method for more information.

Logarithms in Sage

The `log` function in Sage assumes the base of the logarithm is `e`. If you want to use a different base (such as 10), use the optional argument with keyword `base` to specify the base. For example: `log(x, base=10)`

Solving equations and finding roots

Solving equations is a fundamental task in mathematics. A related task is finding the values of the independent variables for which a function is equal to zero, which is known as finding its roots.

Time for action – solving equations

Enter the following code into an input cell in a worksheet, and evaluate the cell:

```
var('x, y')
# Solve a single equation
f(x) = x^3 - 1
solution1 = solve(f == 0, x)
for solution in solution1:
    print(solution)
# Solve a system of equations
solutions = solve([x^2 + y^2 == 1, y^2 == x^3 + x + 1], x, y,
    solution_dict=True)
print("\nSolution to system:")
for solution in solutions:
    print("x = {0}   y = {1}".format(solution[x], solution[y]))

# Solve an inequality
print("\nSolution to inequality:")
solve(-20 * x - 30 <= 4 * x^3 - 7 * x, x)
# Plotted in previous example
```

The output is shown in the following screenshot:

```
x == 1/2*I*sqrt(3) - 1/2
x == -1/2*I*sqrt(3) - 1/2
x == 1

Solution to system:
x = -1/2*I*sqrt(3) - 1/2   y = -1/2*sqrt(-I*sqrt(3) + 3)*sqrt(2)
x = -1/2*I*sqrt(3) - 1/2   y = 1/2*sqrt(-I*sqrt(3) + 3)*sqrt(2)
x = 1/2*I*sqrt(3) - 1/2   y = -1/2*sqrt(I*sqrt(3) + 3)*sqrt(2)
x = 1/2*I*sqrt(3) - 1/2   y = 1/2*sqrt(I*sqrt(3) + 3)*sqrt(2)
x = 0   y = -1
x = 0   y = 1

Solution to inequality:
[[x >= -1.42233228276]]
```

What just happened?

We used the `solve` function to solve an equation, a system of equations, and an inequality. The first argument to `solve` is an equation or a list of equations. The next argument (or arguments) is the variable or variables to solve for. By default, the solutions are returned as a list of symbolic expressions. The optional keyword argument `solution_dict=True` causes the solutions to be returned as a list of dictionaries. Each dictionary has a key for each variable that was solved for, and the value for a key is the solution for that variable. Solving an inequality uses the same syntax. In this case, Sage was unable to find a symbolic solution to the inequality.

Finding roots

Finding the roots of an equation (also known as the zeros of the equation) is closely related to solving an equation. Callable symbolic expressions in Sage have a special method that finds their roots.

Time for action – finding roots

Enter the following code into an input cell in a worksheet, and evaluate the cell:

```
# A problem we already know the answer to
var('a, b, c, x')
f(x) = a * x^2 + b * x + c
root_list = f.roots(x)
for root in root_list:
    print("Root with multiplicity {0}:".format(root[1]))
    show(root[0])

# Something more complicated
g(x) = expand((x^2 - 1)^3 * (x^2 + 1) * (x - 2));
g.show()
root_list = g.roots(x)
for root in root_list:
    print("Root: {0}  multiplicity: {1}".format(root[0], root[1]))
p1 = plot(g, (-2, 2))
p1.ymin(-10)
p1.show()
```

The output is shown in the following screenshot:

```
Root with multiplicity 1:
```

$$\frac{-b+\sqrt{-4ac+b^2}}{2a}$$

```
Root with multiplicity 1:
```

$$\frac{-b-\sqrt{-4ac+b^2}}{2a}$$

$$x \mapsto x^9 - 2x^8 - 2x^7 + 4x^6 + 2x^3 - 4x^2 - x + 2$$

```
Root: -I  multiplicity:1
Root: I  multiplicity:1
Root: 2  multiplicity:1
Root: 1  multiplicity:3
Root: -1  multiplicity:3
```

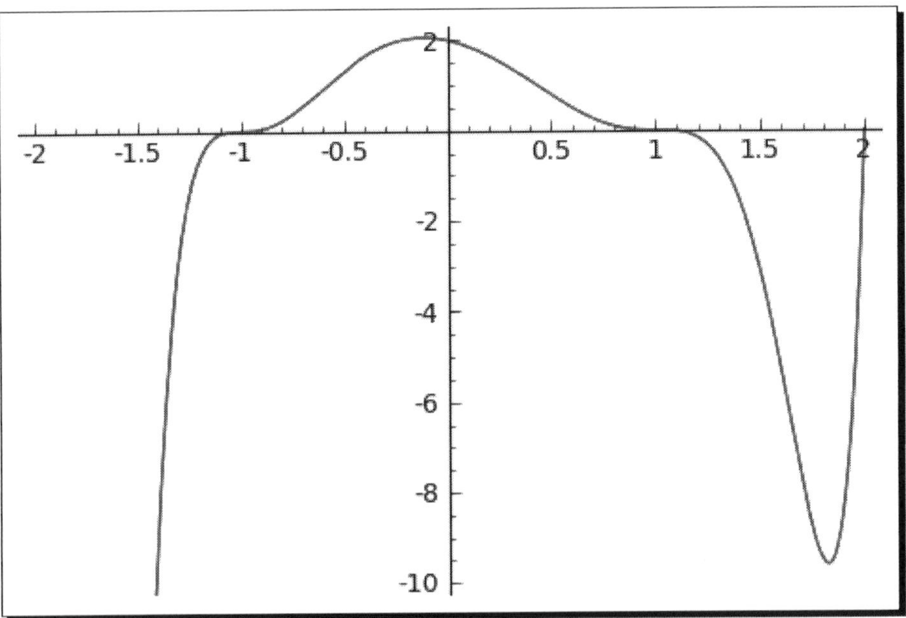

What just happened?

We started off by finding the roots for the general second-order polynomial with the `roots` method. The result is a list of tuples that represent the roots. The first item in each tuple is the multiplicity, and the second item is the root. We passed the variable `x` to `roots`. If this argument is not provided, `roots` formulates the solution in terms of the default variable. We then looked at a higher-order polynomial, which has three real roots and two complex roots. The analytical results are confirmed by a plot of the function that shows the real roots of the function. The `roots` method accepts several optional arguments that control its behaviour:

Keyword	Default	Description
explicit_solutions	True	If False, also include implicit roots
multiplicities	True	If False, return a list of roots without multiplicities
ring	None	If a ring is specified, the expression is converted to a polynomial over the ring, and the roots are found over the ring

Differential and integral calculus

Many branches of advanced mathematics are built upon a foundation of basic calculus. The following examples will demonstrate how to use Sage to compute limits, derivatives, and integrals of symbolic functions.

Time for action – calculating limits

The concept of the limit is often used to define the integral and the derivative. Run the following code to see how to compute limits with Sage:

```
var('x')

# Something easy
f(x) = 1 / x
print("Limit of 1/x as x->0+: {0}".format(limit(f, x=0,
    dir='plus')))
print("Limit of 1/x as x->0-: {0}".format(limit(f, x=0
    dir='minus')))
p1 = plot(f, (x, -1, 1), detect_poles='show')
p1.axes_range(-1, 1, -10, 10)
p1.show()

# Something more complex
g(x)=(2 * x + 8) / (x^2 + x - 12)
g.show()
print("Limit of g(x) as x->-4: {0}".format(limit(g, x=-4)))
```

```
h(x) = (x^2 - 4) / (x - 2)
h.show()
print("Limit of h(x) ax x->2: {0}".format(lim(h, x=2)))
```

The results are shown in the following screenshot:

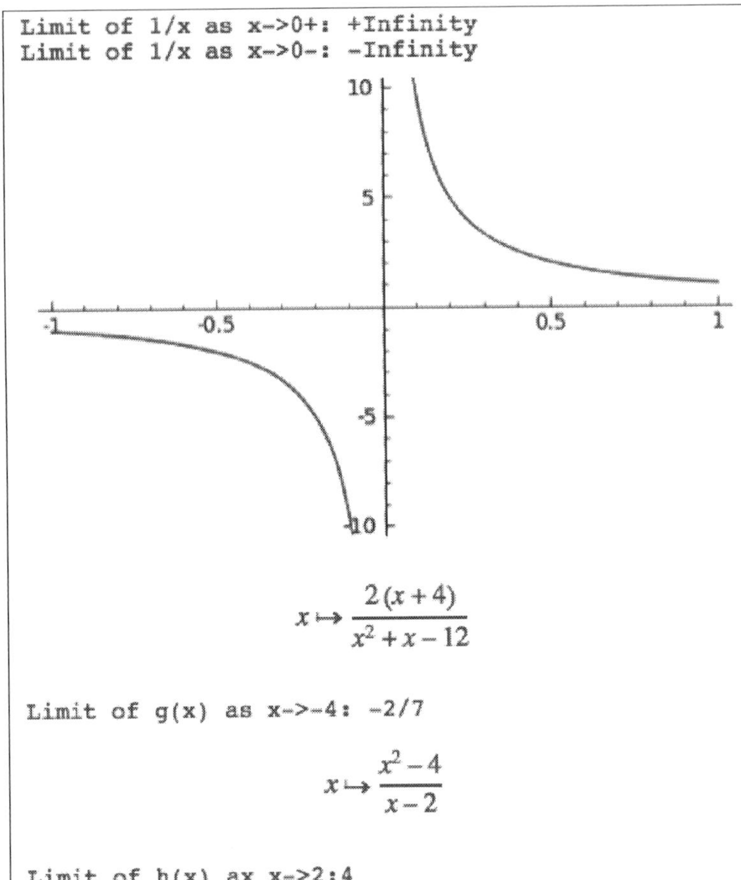
Limit of 1/x as x->0+: +Infinity
Limit of 1/x as x->0-: -Infinity
10
5
-5
-10
-1
-0.5
0.5
1
x ↦ 2(x + 4) / (x^2 + x − 12)
Limit of g(x) as x->-4: -2/7
x ↦ (x^2 − 4) / (x − 2)
Limit of h(x) ax x->2:4

What just happened?

We started out by defining a simple function with a discontinuity at zero. We used the function `limit` (or `lim`) to compute the limit as x approaches zero. The first argument to `limit` is a function, and the second argument is the value at which to compute the limit. If the `dir` keyword argument is present, a one-sided limit is computed from either above or below the specified value. The values `'+'`, `'plus'`, or `'right'` compute the limit from above, while `'-'`, `'minus'`, or `'left'` compute the limit from below. If `dir` is omitted, a two-sided limit is computed. `limit` also accepts the keyword argument `taylor`, which is `False` by default. If `taylor=True`, then a Taylor series is used to approximate the function when computing the limit. The second function we defined looks more complicated, although the limit calculation is straightforward. The third case demonstrated that Sage is able to handle indeterminate forms, where the function evaluates to 0/0 at the given point.

Derivatives

The derivative describes how a function responds to an infinitesimal change in one of its independent variables. Derivatives are used to compute rates of change.

Time for action – calculating derivatives

Run the following code to see how to compute derivatives with Sage:

```
var('x, y')
f(x, y) = 3 * x^4 * y^3 + 9 * y * x^2 - 4 * x + 8 * y
print("f(x,y):")
f.show()
dfdx(x, y) = diff(f, x)
print("df/dx:")
dfdx.show()
dfdy(x, y) = diff(f, y)
print("df/dy:")
dfdy.show()
print("Second derivative:")
d2fdx2(x, y) = derivative(f, x, 2)     # Synonym for diff
d2fdx2.show()
# Trigonometric functions
g(x) = sqrt(x^3 + csc(x))
print("g(x):")
g.show()
dgdx(x) = g.diff(x)
print("dg/dx:")
dgdx.show()
```

```
# Implicit differentiation
# The next line tells Sage that y is a function of x
y(x) = function('y', x)
expr = 5 * y^2 + sin(y) == x^2
print("Expression:")
expr.show()

# take the derivative and solve for dy/dx
dydx = solve(diff(expr), diff(y))
print("dy/dx:")
dydx[0].show()
```

The results are shown in the following screenshot:

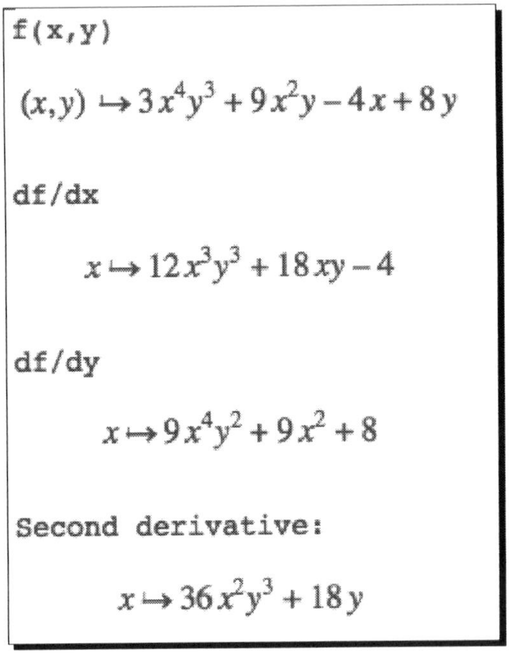

f(x,y)

$$(x,y) \mapsto 3x^4y^3 + 9x^2y - 4x + 8y$$

df/dx

$$x \mapsto 12x^3y^3 + 18xy - 4$$

df/dy

$$x \mapsto 9x^4y^2 + 9x^2 + 8$$

Second derivative:

$$x \mapsto 36x^2y^3 + 18y$$

```
g(x)
```

$$x \mapsto \sqrt{x^3 + \csc(x)}$$

```
dg/dx
```

$$x \mapsto \frac{3\,x^2 - \csc(x)\cot(x)}{2\,\sqrt{x^3 + \csc(x)}}$$

```
Expression
```

$$x \mapsto 5\,y(x)^2 + \sin(y(x)) = x^2$$

```
dy/dx
```

$$D[0](y)(x) = \frac{2\,x}{\cos(y(x)) + 10\,y(x)}$$

What just happened?

Sage is able to compute derivatives for many types of functions. You can use a function called `diff` (or `differentiate` or `derivative`), or an equivalent method with the same names. In the example, we used both the function form and the method form. When calling `diff` as a function, the first argument is a function which is differentiated against the variable specified in the second argument. If a third argument is present, it is the degree of the derivative (the default is one, for the first derivative). We started by defining a long polynomial function of two variables, `x` and `y`. We then differentiated with respect to each variable. We also computed the second derivative. We didn't have to change anything to compute the derivative of a trigonometric function. In the final part of the example, we demonstrated how to do implicit differentiation. The function `y(x)` was defined implicitly by a relational symbolic expression. We used the syntax `y(x) = function('y', x)` to create a new symbolic function called `y` that is a function of `x`. The first argument of `function` is a string that contains the name of the new function. The next argument is the argument of the symbolic function (it can have multiple arguments). We then used the `diff` function to compute the derivative of the entire expression, and then used the `solve` function to isolate the derivative.

Integrals

Sage is able to integrate many symbolic functions that would need to be looked up in a table of integrals, or computed using laborious methods like integration by parts. Sage can easily compute symbolic integrals that cannot be found in any book.

Time for action – calculating integrals

Run the following example to see how to compute integrals with Sage:

```
var('x')
print("Elementary integrals:")
f = x^2
print(f.integrate(x))
print(integral(e^x,x))
print(integral(1/x,x))
print(integral(sinh(x), x))
print(integral(1/sqrt(1+x^2),x))
print("\nIntegration by parts:")
print(integral(e^x*cos(x), x))
print(integral(sqrt(x^2-25)/x, x))
print("\nDefinite integral:")
print(integral(1/(1+x^2), x, -1, 1))
print("\nImproper integral:")
print(integral(1/(1+x^2), x, -infinity, infinity))
print("\nDivergent integral:")
print(integral(1/(1-x), x, 1,2))     # Diverges
```

The results are shown in the following screenshot:

```
Elementary integrals:
1/3*x^3
e^x
log(x)
cosh(x)
arcsinh(x)

Integration by parts:
1/2*(sin(x) + cos(x))*e^x
sqrt(x^2 - 25) + 5*arcsin(5/abs(x))

Definite integral:
1/2*pi

Improper integral:
pi

Divergent integral:
Traceback (click to the left of this block for traceback)
...
ValueError: Integral is divergent.
```

What just happened?

The function integrate (or integral) is used to compute integrals, and the methods called integrate and integral do exactly the same thing. We started out by showing that Sage knows about lots of the elementary integrals. We then showed that Sage easily handles functions that need to be integrated by parts, which can be very tedious to do by hand. If integrate is called as a function, the first argument is the function to be integrated, and the second argument is the variable of integration. If there are no additional arguments, the integral is assumed to be indefinite. If two additional arguments are present, they are used as the limits of integration. We showed that Sage can compute definite integrals and improper integrals (one or more limits at infinity.) In the final case, we showed what happens when an integral diverges: Sage simply prints an appropriate error message and exits. integrate also accepts the optional keyword argument algorithm to choose the integration algorithm, which can be set to 'maxima' (the default), 'sympy', or 'mathematica_free' (which uses http://integrals.wolfram.com/).

Series and summations

An infinite series is a summation of a sequence with an infinite number of terms. Truncated series are useful for approximating functions. In this section, we'll look at the capabilities that Sage has for computing infinite sequences and computing their sums.

Time for action – computing sums of series

Enter the following code into an input cell in a worksheet, and evaluate the cell:

```
var('x, n, k')

f(x) = sin(x) / x^2
f.show()

print("Power series expansion around x=1:")
s(x) = f.series(x==1, 3)
s.show()

print("Sum of alternating harmonic series:")
h(k) = (-1)^(k + 1) * 1 / k
print h.sum(k, 1, infinity)

print("Sum of binomial series:")
h(k) = binomial(n, k)
print h.sum(k, 1, infinity)

print("Sum of harmonic series:")
h(k) = 1 / k
print h.sum(k, 1, infinity)     # Diverges
```

The results are shown in the following screenshot:

$$x \mapsto \frac{\sin(x)}{x^2}$$

```
Power series expansion around x=1:
```

$$x \mapsto (\sin(1)) + (-2\sin(1) + \cos(1))(x-1) + (\frac{5}{2}\sin(1) - 2\cos(1))(x-1)^2 + O\left((x-1)^3\right)$$

```
Alternating harmonic series:
k |--> log(2)
Binomial series:
k |--> 2^n - 1
Harmonic series:
Traceback (click to the left of this block for traceback)
...
ValueError: Sum is divergent.
```

What just happened?

We started by defining a function and using the `series` method to compute a power series around the point x=1. The first argument to `series` is the point at which to create the series, and the second argument is the order of the computed series. Notice that Sages uses "big O" notation to denote the order of the series.

We then created several infinite series and computed their sums. Sage can compute the sum of any convergent series using the `sum` method. The first argument to `sum` is the summation variable, the second argument is the lower endpoint, and the third argument is the upper endpoint of the series. We used this method to compute the sum of the alternating harmonic series and the binomial series. However, we ran into trouble when we tried to compute the sum of the harmonic series, which is divergent. Fortunately, Sage handled this problem gracefully.

Taylor series

A Taylor series is a series expansion of a function around a point. If the point is zero, the series is known as a Maclaurin series. Taylor series are often used to approximate functions.

Time for action – finding Taylor series

Run the following code to see how to compute a one-dimensional Taylor series with Sage.

```
var('x,k')
colors=['red', 'black', 'green', 'magenta']

x1 = pi/2
```

```
xmin = x1 - pi;     xmax = x1 + pi
f(x) = sin(x)
p1 = plot(f, (xmin, xmax), color='blue')
Taylor_series_3(x) = f.taylor(x, x1, 3)
p1 += plot(Taylor_series_3, (xmin, xmax), legend_label='3',
    color='red')
Taylor_series_5(x) = f.taylor(x, x1, 5)
p1 += plot(Taylor_series_5, (xmin, xmax), legend_label='5',
    color='green')
Taylor_series_7(x) = f.taylor(x, x1, 7)
p1 += plot(Taylor_series_7, (xmin, xmax), legend_label='7',
    color='black')
Taylor_series_7.show()
show(p1)
```

The results are shown in the following screenshot:

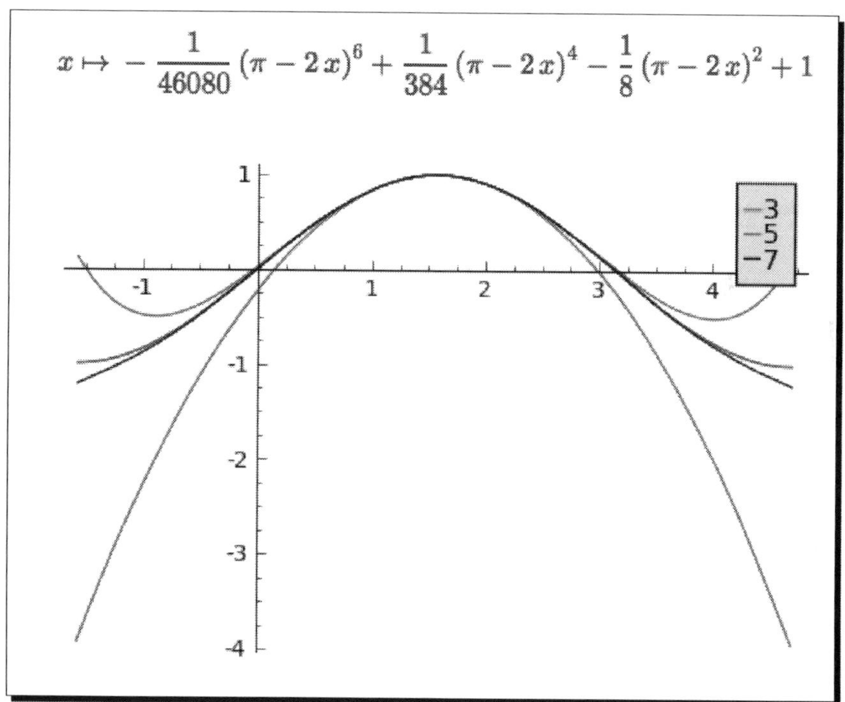

What just happened?

The Taylor series expansion approximates the behaviour of a function in the vicinity of a point. With an infinite number of terms, the series should match the function exactly in a small region near the point. However, the Taylor series provides a good approximation with only a finite number of terms. We used Sage to create a plot that illustrates how the Taylor series approaches the function sin(x) near the point pi/2 as the number of terms in the series increases.

We used the `taylor` method to create the Taylor series. The first argument is the independent variable, the second argument is the point, and the third argument is the order of the series. In this case, we constructed Taylor series of order 3, 5, and 7 and plotted them on the same axes with the sine function, in the vicinity of the point pi/2. We also displayed the seventh-order Taylor series.

Have a go hero – Taylor series

Compute the Taylor series for the `exp` function about the point x=1. Use a plot to see how well the Taylor series approximates the function as you increase the order of the Taylor series.

Laplace transforms

The Laplace transform is defined as the integral:

$$F(s) = \int_0^{\infty} e^{-st} f(t)\, dt$$

This is for functions that are defined for t ≥ 0. The Laplace transform is widely used for solving ordinary differential equations. It has applications in the theory of electrical circuits, control systems, and communication systems. If you need to learn or review the basics of Laplace transforms, you may want to consult *Shaum's Outline of Laplace Transforms* by Murray Spiegel (McGraw-Hill, 1965).

Time for action – computing Laplace transforms

Evaluate the following code to see how to compute Laplace transforms with Sage:

```
var('t, a, k, s')
print("Elementary transform:")
f(t) = sin(k * t)
F(s) = f.laplace(t, s)
```

```
F.show()

print("Inverse transform:")
G(s) = 1 / ((s - 1) * (s + 2) * (s + 4))
G.show()
g(t) = G.inverse_laplace(s, t)
g.show()
```

The results are shown in the following screenshot:

Elementary transform:

$$s \mapsto \frac{k}{k^2 + s^2}$$

Inverse transform:

$$s \mapsto \frac{1}{(s-1)(s+2)(s+4)}$$

$$t \mapsto \frac{1}{10} e^{(-4\,t)} - \frac{1}{6} e^{(-2\,t)} + \frac{1}{15} e^{t}$$

What just happened?

We used Sage to compute the Laplace transform and the inverse Laplace transform. Normally, finding the Laplace transform would have required looking up the elementary forms in a table. Computing the inverse transform requires performing a partial fraction expansion and then finding the resulting terms in a table. The process is much faster with Sage, and Sage can compute transforms that cannot practically be computed by hand. We used the `laplace` method to compute the forward transform, and `inverse_laplace` to compute the reverse transform. Each of these methods computes the transform with respect to a variable (the first argument) using a transform parameter (the second argument.) It's easier to think of the first argument as the variable you are transforming *from*, and the second as the variable you are transforming *to*.

Solving ordinary differential equations

Ordinary differential equations (ODEs) are widely used in applied mathematics, engineering, and the sciences. Sage enables you to find exact solutions to many ODEs.

Time for action – solving an ordinary differential equation

The following code demonstrates how to solve ordinary differential equations with Sage:

```
var('x, x1, x2, t')

# Finding a general solution
print("General solution:")
y = function('y', x)
ode = 4*diff(y, x, 2) + 36 * y == csc(3 * x)
y(x) = desolve(ode, y)
y.show()

# Solving an initial-value problem
print("Solving an initial-value problem:")
y = function('y', x)
ode = diff(y, x, 2) - 4 * diff(y, x) + 13 * y == 0
y(x) = desolve(ode, y, [0, -1, 2], ivar=x)
y.show()

# Solving a system of first-order equations
print("Solving a system of first-order ODEs:")
x1 = function('x1', t)
x2 = function('x2', t)
ode1 = 2 * diff(x1, t) + diff(x2, t) - x2 == t
ode2 = diff(x1, t) + diff(x2, t) == t^2
y1, y2 = desolve_system([ode1, ode2], [x1, x2],
    ics=[0, 0, 0])
y1.show()
y2.show()
```

The results are shown in the following screenshot:

General solution:

$$x \mapsto k_1 \sin(3x) + k_2 \cos(3x) - \frac{1}{12} x \cos(3x) + \frac{1}{36} \log(\sin(3x)) \sin(3x)$$

Solving an initial-value problem:

$$x \mapsto \frac{1}{3}(4 \sin(3x) - 3 \cos(3x)) e^{(2x)}$$

Solving a system of first-order ODEs:

$$x_1(t) = \frac{1}{3} t^3 - 2t^2 + 5t + 5e^{(-t)} - 5$$

$$x_2(t) = 2t^2 - 5t - 5e^{(-t)} + 5$$

What just happened?

The first step towards solving a differential equation with Sage is to create a symbolic function that represents the solution. In this example, we used `function` to create a symbolic function called `y` that is a function of `x`. We then created a relational symbolic expression called `ode` that implicitly defines `y(x)`. Once the problem is set up, it is simple to call the `desolve` function to obtain the solution. `desolve` requires two arguments: the relational expression that defines the differential equation, and the dependent variable. It returns an expression for the general solution of the ODE. If the function has more than one independent variable, then the independent variable must be specified using the `ivar` keyword.

In the next part of the example, we used `desolve` to solve an initial-value problem with a second-order ODE. The initial values of the independent variable, the dependent variable, and the first derivative of the dependent variable are used to form a list (in this order), which was passed as an argument to `desolve`. Sage solves the initial-value problem and returns the solution as a symbolic expression. In the third part of the example, we used `desolve_system` to solve a system of two first-order ODEs. `desolve_system` can solve systems of many first-order differential equations. Since a higher-order ODE can be written as a system of first-order ODEs, this does not limit the usefulness of `desolve_system`. We defined two symbolic functions, `x1` and `x2`, which are functions of `t`. The first argument of `desolve_system` is a list of differential equations, and the second argument is a list of dependent variables to solve for. We used the optional argument with keyword `ics` to set initial conditions for the independent variable (`t`), `x1`, and `x2`, respectively. The result is a pair of symbolic expressions for `x1` and `x2`. In the next chapter, we'll see how Sage can help us solve differential equations numerically.

Summary

We covered a lot of material in this chapter. Sage makes it fast and easy to do tedious symbolic tasks like computing integrals and Laplace transforms for complicated functions. In fact, the hardest part is making sure that you have defined your functions and expressions correctly.

Specifically, we covered:

- Working with symbolic expressions
- Manipulating symbolic expressions to put them in the form you want
- Performing basic calculus operations like computing limits, derivatives, and integrals
- Finding series representations, and computing their sums
- Computing Laplace transforms
- Finding exact solutions to ordinary differential equations

Sage has powerful symbolic capabilities. However, many real-world problems simply don't have analytical solutions. In other cases, Sage might not be able to find an analytical solution, even when it exists—software is never perfect! Some symbolic operations may consume so much memory or CPU time that they become impractical. Integrals, systems of equations, and differential equations often require numerical methods of solution. Sage also has powerful numerical capabilities, which we'll explore in the next chapter.

8
Solving Problems Numerically

The previous chapter described how to use Sage to solve many difficult problems in symbolic mathematics. While this capability is very useful, many real-world problems do not lend themselves to symbolic computation. Some differential equations don't have closed-form solutions, and not every integral can be computed in terms of elementary functions. In other cases, a function value may have to be computed from a look-up table that was derived from experimental results, which precludes symbolic computation. In this chapter, we will demonstrate some of the tools in Sage that allow us to solve problems numerically.

We will learn how to:

- Find the roots of an equation
- Compute integrals and derivatives numerically
- Find minima and maxima of functions
- Compute discrete Fourier transforms, and apply window functions
- Numerically solve an ordinary differential equation (ODE), and systems of ODEs
- Use optimization techniques to fit curves and find minima
- Explore the probability tools in Sage

Let's get started!

Sage and NumPy

One potential source of confusion in this chapter is that Sage incorporates functions from NumPy, Maxima, the GNU Scientific Library (GSL), and other sources. Whenever possible, we will use functions in Sage. However, sometimes we need to go to NumPy to perform a particular calculation. To minimize the possibility of confusion, do *not* use the syntax `from numpy import *`. This imports every name from NumPy into Sage, overriding some pre-defined Sage functions and objects. Use the syntax shown in the examples, which keeps NumPy functions separate from Sage functions.

Solving equations and finding roots numerically

We've already looked at solving systems of linear equations in Chapter 5, when we learned about linear algebra. We created matrices using integers or symbols, but you can just as easily create vectors and matrices with real numbers or floating-point numbers. Chapter 5 also covered some numerical operations on matrices, such as computing the QR factorization and singular value decomposition. Now, we will learn how to find roots of equations numerically in Sage.

Time for action – finding roots of a polynomial

Let's start by finding the roots of a polynomial.

```
g(x) = expand((x^2 - 1)^3 * (x^2 + 1) * (x - 2));
g.show()

print("Root at x = {0}".format(g.find_root(-2,2)))
print("Root at x = {0}".format(g.find_root(-2,0)))
print("Root at x = {0}".format(g.find_root(0.5,1.5)))

plt = plot(g, (x, -1.2, 2.01))
show(plt, figsize=(4, 3))
```

The output is shown in the following screenshot:

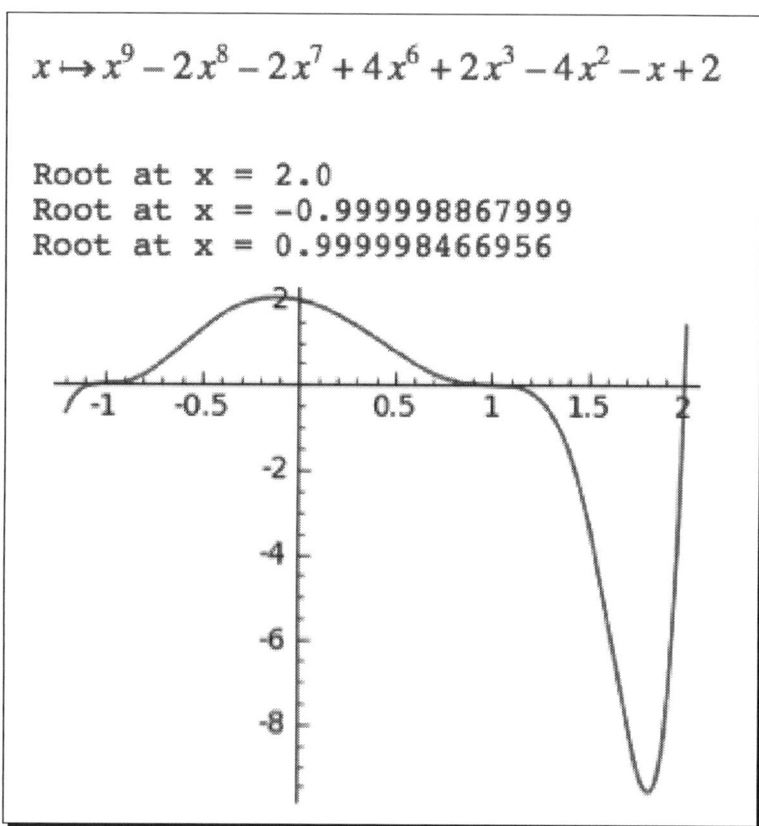

What just happened?

We defined a fairly complicated polynomial equation with a number of real and imaginary roots. We can see that the function will have real roots at 1, -1, and 2 simply by looking at the factored form of the function, which can be confirmed by looking at the plot. When trying out a new numerical method, it's always a good idea to start with a problem that you know the answer to, so that you can evaluate the accuracy and reliability of the method. The `find_root` function is a relatively simple way to find a single root within a given domain, specified by the given end points. In the first call, we gave `find_root` a wide span that contained three roots, and it happened to find the root at x=2. In the next two calls, we used a narrower span that only included a single root in each span. Finding roots numerically is relatively simple, but you have to understand the equation you are working with to find the correct root.

Finding minima and maxima of functions

Sometimes, we are interested in the minima or maxima of a function, rather than the zero crossings. For example, an engineer might define a function that estimates the cost of a product. Finding the minimum of this function will help the engineer design a product with the lowest cost. Conversely, one might want to maximize a function that represents the performance of a system. The problem of finding minima and maxima is a form of numerical optimization, which we'll cover later in the chapter.

Time for action – minimizing a function of one variable

We'll define another function of one variable and let Sage find the minimum:

```
var('x')
f = lambda x: 3 * x^3 - 7 * x^2 + 2
minval, x_min = find_minimum_on_interval(f, 0, 3)
print("Min on interval [0,3]: f({0}) = {1}".format(x_min, minval))
maxval, x_max = find_maximum_on_interval(f, -1, 1)
print("Max on interval [-1,1]: f({0}) = {1}".format(x_max, maxval))
f_plot = plot(f, (x, -1, 2.5))
min_point = point((x_min, minval), color='red', size=50)
max_point = point((x_max, maxval), color='black', size=50)
show(f_plot + min_point + max_point, figsize=(4, 4))
```

The results are shown in the following screenshot:

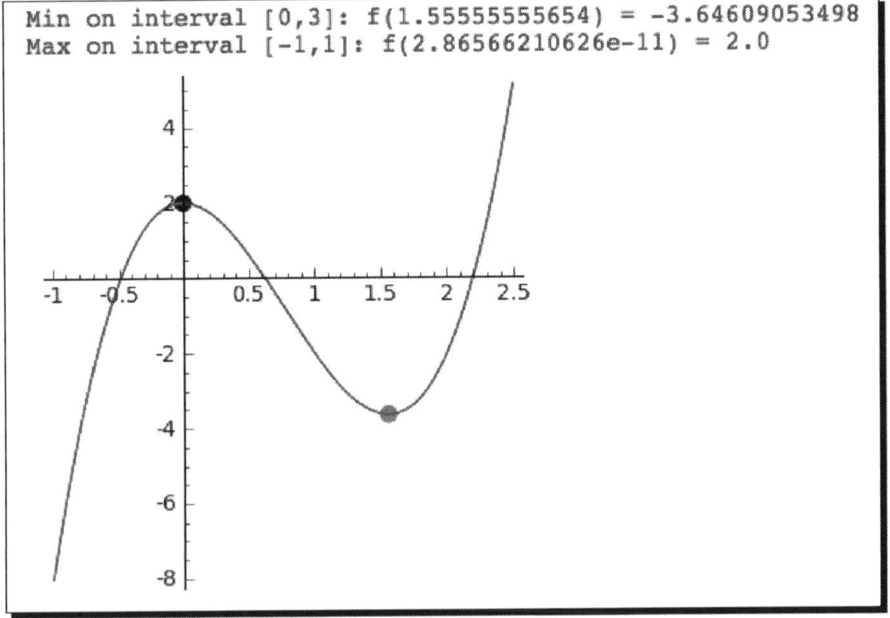

What just happened?

We defined a function that represents a cubic polynomial using the `lambda` construct. Recall from Chapter 4 that `lambda` is a shorthand way of defining a Python function. We used a Python function, rather than a callable symbolic expression, because numerical methods are designed to work with functions that return real numbers. The functions `find_minimum_on_interval` and `find_maximum_on_interval` work in a similar way to `find_root`. Each function accepts the endpoints of an interval and finds the minimum or maximum of the function on that interval, and returns a tuple that contains the (x,y) coordinates of the minimum or maximum. These functions also accept the keyword argument `tol` to specify the tolerance determines when the algorithm has converged on a maximum or minimum (the default is 1.48e-8). The keyword argument `maxfun` sets a limit on the maximum number of function evaluations (default 500) that will be used to find the point of interest. Finally, we used the `point` graphics function to illustrate the points that we found.

Functions of more than one variable

Finding minima of a function of multiple variables is a more challenging problem because each independent variable adds a new dimension to the search space. Sage uses a more sophisticated function for minimizing functions of two or more variables.

Time for action – minimizing a function of several variables

Now, we'll minimize a function of two variables, and use a contour plot to illustrate the results:

```
var('x, y')
f = 100 * (y - x^2)^2 + (1 - x)^2 + 100 * (2 - y^2)^2 + (1 - y)^2
min = minimize(f, [0,0], disp=0)

plt = contour_plot(f, (x, -0.3, 2), (y, -0.3, 2), fill=False,
    cmap='hsv', labels=True)

pt = point(min, color='red', size=50)
show(plt+pt, aspect_ratio=1, figsize=(4, 4))
```

The plot is shown below:

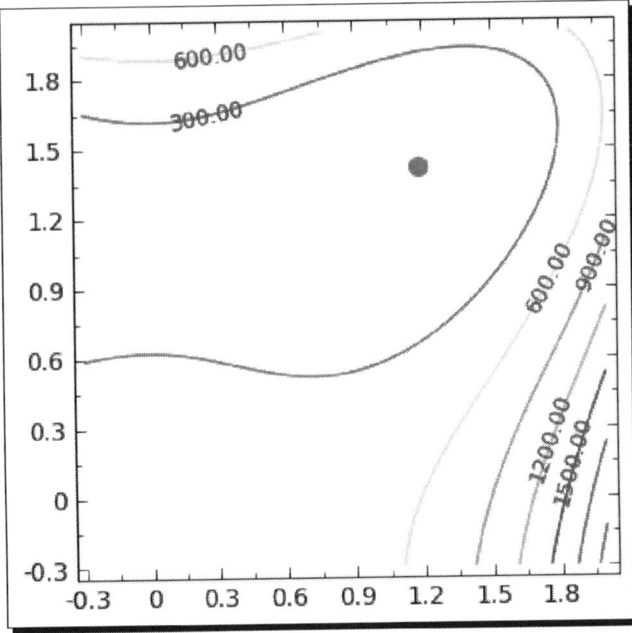

What just happened?

We started out by defining a callable symbolic expression that represents a polynomial function of two variables. We then used `minimize` to find a minimum of the function near the point (0,0). `minimize` works a little differently from the functions in the previous examples. Rather than specifying limits on the domain of the problem, you need to pass an initial guess to `minimize` so that it knows where to start searching for a minimum. Like the functions `find_root` and `find_minimum_on_interval`, `minimize` will only find a minimum in the vicinity of its starting point (if it exists), which is known as a local minimum. We used the keyword argument `disp=0` to prevent the function from displaying text that summarizes its solution process.

We will pause here to clarify the concept of local and global minima. A local minimum is the lowest value that a function takes on over a portion of its domain. A function can have many local minima. A function's global minimum is the lowest value of the function over its entire domain. There is no general algorithm that can find the global minimum of an arbitrary function. Therefore, `minimize` (and all the other minimum-finding functions in Sage) are only guaranteed to find a local minimum (assuming one exists), which may happen to also be the global minimum.

Minimizing a function of several variables is significantly more complicated than minimizing a function of one variable. `minimize` is actually an interface to several minimization algorithms. If the function to be minimized is symbolic, the default algorithm is the Broyden-Fletcher-Goldfarb-Shannon (bfgs) algorithm. If the function is a Python function, the simplex algorithm is the default. The following table summarizes the options that can be passed to `minimize`:

Keyword	Description
disp	0 disables text output (default is 1)
algorithm	A string value that specifies algorithm: `'default'` chooses default (see text) `'simplex'` chooses the simplex method `'powell'` chooses Powell's conjugate gradient descent method `'bfgs'` chooses Broyden-Fletcher-Goldfarb-Shannon (bfgs) `'cg'` chooses conjugate-gradient (requires gradient) `'ncg'` chooses Newton-conjugate-gradient (requires gradient and Hessian)
gradient	Function that computes the gradient
hessian	Function that computes the Hessian

If the function to be minimized is symbolic, you do not have to provide the Hessian or the gradient because Sage will compute them symbolically. If the function to be minimized is a Python function and you choose an algorithm that requires the Hessian or the gradient, you will have to provide functions that compute the Hessian and/or the gradient. The Sage reference manual has an example that demonstrates how to minimize a Python function with an algorithm that requires a gradient: `http://www.sagemath.org/doc/reference/sage/numerical/optimize.html`

Numerical approximation of derivatives

In the previous chapter, we learned how to use Sage to compute derivatives of symbolic functions. Now, we will learn how to approximate derivatives numerically.

Time for action – approximating derivatives with differences

Let's start by defining a function of one variable. We'll use NumPy to estimate the derivative numerically, and we'll plot the estimate with matplotlib.

```
import numpy as np
import matplotlib.pyplot as plt

import matplotlib as mpl
mpl.rc('font', size=10)       # set default font size
```

```
dx = 0.01
x = np.arange(0, 2, dx)
f = power(x, 3)
dfdx = 3*power(x, 2)

plt.figure(figsize=(4, 4))
plt.plot(x, f, label='f(x)')
plt.plot(x, dfdx, color='red', label='Analytical df/dx')

df = np.diff(f)
plt.plot(x[:-1], df/dx, color='black', label='Numerical df/dx')

plt.xlabel('x')
plt.ylabel('f(x)')
plt.legend(loc='best')
plt.savefig('diff.png')
plt.close()
```

The output is shown in the following screenshot:

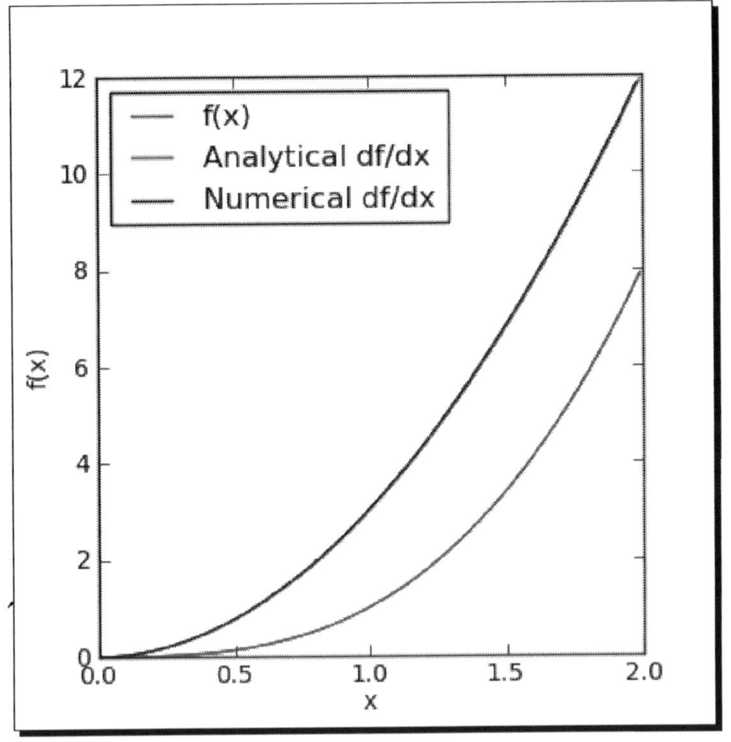

What just happened?

We defined a simple polynomial, $f(x)=x^3$. Its derivative can easily be calculated in closed form: $f'(x)=3x^2$. We defined a NumPy array of x values and computed the value of the function at each point. We then used the `diff` function from NumPy to compute the forward finite difference at each point in the domain. The forward finite difference is defined as:

$$\Delta f_P \equiv f_{P+1} - f_P$$

`diff` accepts three arguments. The first is a NumPy array containing values of the function. The optional keyword argument `n` specifies which order difference to take (the default is one, which approximates the first derivative). The optional keyword argument `axis` specifies which axis of the array to use (if the array has more than one dimension). This keyword allows `diff` to be used to approximate a partial derivative of a function of several variables. To estimate the derivative, the finite difference at each point is divided by the distance between points, which we have defined as `dx`. We then plotted the numerical estimate of the derivative along with the analytical derivative and verified that they match.

In this example, we evaluated a new numerical method by solving a problem with a known answer. If used incorrectly, a numerical technique may give an invalid result without any warning. It's important to replicate a known result to make sure you are using the method correctly.

Computing gradients

For functions of multiple variables, we can use partial derivatives to compute the derivative with respect to one of the independent variables. The gradient gives the direction of steepest descent at any given point in the domain.

Time for action – computing gradients

Enter the following code into a cell in a Sage worksheet, and evaluate it:

```
import numpy as np
import matplotlib.pyplot as plt
def func(x,y):
    return exp(-1 / 3 * x^3 + x - y^2)

dx = 0.2; dy = 0.2
grid = np.ogrid[-2 : 2 + dx : dx, -2 : 2 + dx : dx]
xlen = max(grid[0].shape)
ylen = max(grid[1].shape)
f = np.empty([xlen, ylen])
```

```
for i in range(xlen):
    for j in range(ylen):
        f[i, j] = func(grid[0][i], grid[1][0,j])

plt.figure(figsize=(5, 5))
c = plt.contour(grid[0].flatten(), grid[1].flatten(), f)
plt.clabel(c)          # label contours
plt.axis('scaled')     # aspect ratio=1.0

# Compute and plot gradient of function
grad = np.gradient(f, dx, dy)
plt.quiver(grid[0].flatten(), grid[1].flatten(), grad[0], grad[1])

plt.savefig('contour.png')
plt.close()
```

A contour plot of the function is shown below, with overlaid vectors representing the gradient:

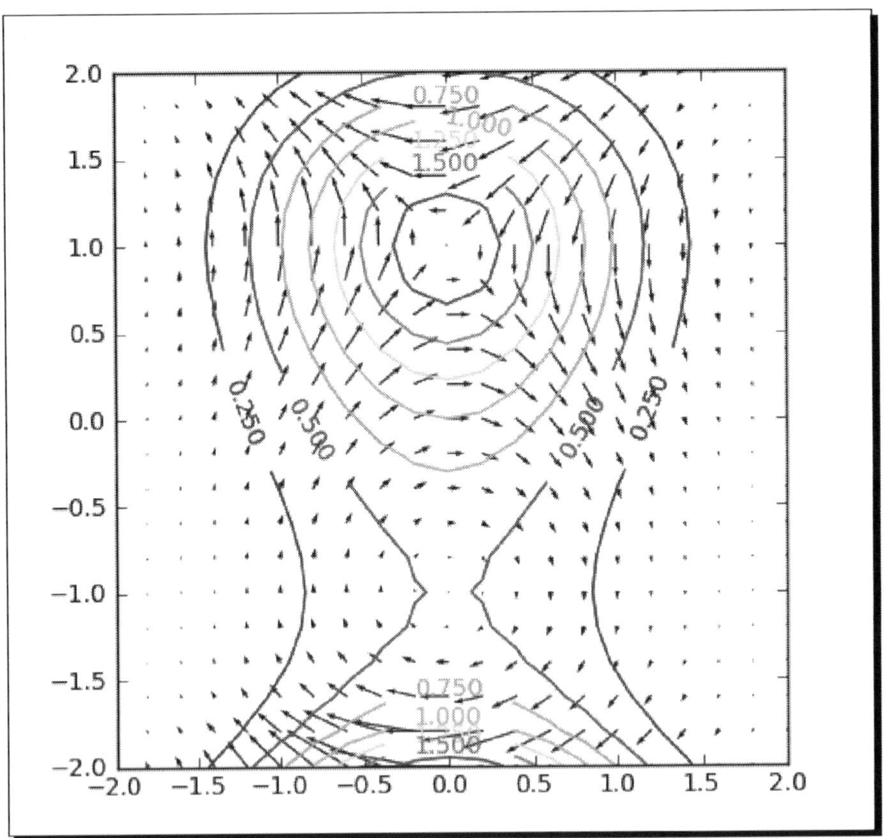

What just happened?

Computing the gradient is actually the easiest aspect of this example. Since we are using NumPy, we first need to define a two-dimensional grid of points. We use the `ogrid` function from NumPy, which does exactly that. We then used two nested `for` loops to compute the value of the function at each point in the grid. We used the `contour` function from Pyplot to display the level contours of the function, and used the `gradient` function to compute the gradient at each point of the grid. `gradient` is very similar to `diff`, except that it expects an N-dimensional array as its first argument. The next N arguments specify the grid spacing for each dimension of the array. Finally, we used the `quiver` plotting function from Pyplot to display a vector that represents the gradient at each point of the grid. We can see that the gradient is normal to the contour lines at each point.

Numerical integration

Numerical integration (known in older literature as "quadrature") is another fundamental operation in numerical mathematics.

Time for action – numerical integration

Let's start by using Sage functions to numerically integrate a symbolic function of one variable:

```
var('x')
f(x) = e^x * cos(x)
f.show()

a = 0
b = 8
p = plot(f, (x, a, b))
p.show(figsize=(4, 3))

print("Integral of f(x) from {0} to {1}:".format(a,b))
print("  Analytical definite integral: {0}"
    .format(f.integral(x, a, b).n()))

integral_value, tolerance, num_evals, error_code = \
    f.nintegral(x, a, b)

print("  Using nintegral: {0}".format(integral_value))
# also nintegrate

integral_value, tolerance = numerical_integral(f, a, b)
print("  Using numerical_integral: {0}".format(integral_value))
```

A plot of the function, along with the integration results, is shown below:

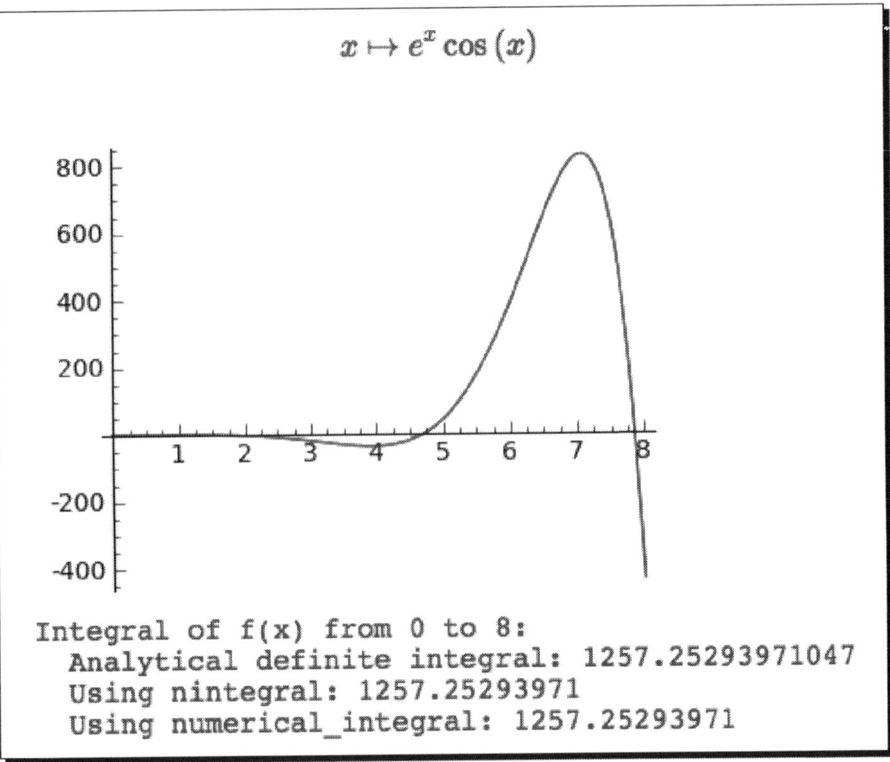

What just happened?

We defined a symbolic function f(x) and defined an interval on which to compute the definite integral. As a point of reference, we used the symbolic integration method `integral` with limits to compute the definite integral symbolically. We used the method `n` (which is a shortcut for numerical_approx) to convert the symbolic result into a decimal number for comparison to the results of numerical integration.

Sage has two types of numerical integration. We used the numerical integration method `nintegral` (also called `nintegrate`) to perform the integration numerically. These methods call Maxima to perform the computation, and return a tuple with four elements:

- Approximation to the integral (float)
- Estimated absolute error of the approximation (float)
- The number of integrand evaluations (integer)
- An error code (integer)

We repeated the calculation with `numerical_integral`, which uses the GNU Scientific Library. This function returns a tuple that contains the integral value and an estimate of the error. `numerical_integral` can be used to integrate functions that are defined as callable symbolic expressions or as Python functions. Both methods of numerical integration use algorithms that automatically adapt to the function that is being integrated. We can see that all three types of integration obtain equivalent results.

Numerical integration with NumPy

Sometimes, we may need to integrate a function that cannot be defined by a Python function or a symbolic expression. This situation may occur if the function values come from experimental measurements or simulation results. For example, if we have an array of flux values over time, we can integrate the flux over time to obtain the total amount of substance. If the values of a function are stored in an array, we can use NumPy to perform the integration.

Time for action – numerical integration with NumPy

We'll repeat the calculation from the previous example with NumPy. Execute the following code and see what happens:

```
import numpy as np
def func(x):
    return np.exp(x) * np.cos(x)

a=0; b=8
dx = 0.1

for i in range(4):
    x = np.arange(a, b + dx, dx)
    f = func(x)

    print("dx = {0}  integral = {1}".format(dx, np.trapz(f,x)))
    dx = dx / 10
```

The output is shown in the following screenshot:

```
dx=0.100000000000000  integral=1254.43366792
dx=0.0100000000000000  integral=1257.22474007
dx=0.00100000000000000  integral=1257.25265771
dx=0.000100000000000000  integral=1257.25293689
```

What just happened?

We defined a Python function that represents the mathematical function used in the previous example. We then used a `for` loop to numerically integrate the function with `trapz`, using different spacing of the independent variable `x`. The first argument to `trapz` is a NumPy array that contains the values of the function to be integrated. The `x` values can be specified as either an array of values (which do not have to be uniformly spaced) or a single scalar value `dx` that defines the spacing between points. If the array containing the function values has more than one dimension, the `axis` keyword can be used to specify the axis of integration.

Remember that all NumPy functions operate on arrays of discrete points. The `trapz` function is a very simple integrator that uses the trapezoidal rule to integrate a sequence of points. Unlike the integration functions in Sage, `trapz` cannot adapt to the function being integrated. To demonstrate this, we performed the integral with four different step sizes. You can see that the precision of the integral increases as the step size decreases.

Discrete Fourier transforms

The Fourier transform is used in optics, acoustics, radio engineering, and many other fields. It is most often used to transform a time-domain signal into the frequency domain so that its frequency components can be analysed. Because most applications involve signals that are sampled at discrete times, the discrete Fourier transform (DFT) is an important part of numerical computing.

Time for action – computing discrete Fourier transforms

Since the discrete Fourier transform operates on an array of samples from a signal, we'll use the signal-processing tools in NumPy:

```
import numpy as np
import matplotlib.pyplot as plt

dt = 0.01
t = np.arange(-10, 10, dt)
f = np.sinc(t)

plt.figure(figsize=(6, 3))
plt.plot(t, f)
plt.savefig('f.png')
plt.close()

fourier_transform = np.fft.fft(f)
spectrum = np.absolute(fourier_transform)
phase = np.angle(fourier_transform)
```

```
freq = np.fft.fftfreq(t.shape[-1], d=dt)

spectrum = np.fft.fftshift(spectrum)
phase = np.fft.fftshift(phase)
freq = np.fft.fftshift(freq)

plt.figure(figsize=(6,3))
plt.plot(freq, spectrum)
plt.title('Magnitude')
plt.axis([-1.5, 1.5, spectrum.min(),spectrum.max()])
plt.savefig('spectrum.png')

plt.figure(figsize=(6,3))
plt.plot(freq, phase)
plt.title('Phase')
plt.axis([-1.5,1.5, phase.min(),phase.max()])
plt.savefig('phase.png')

plt.close()
```

The following plots show the function, its magnitude spectrum, and its phase spectrum:

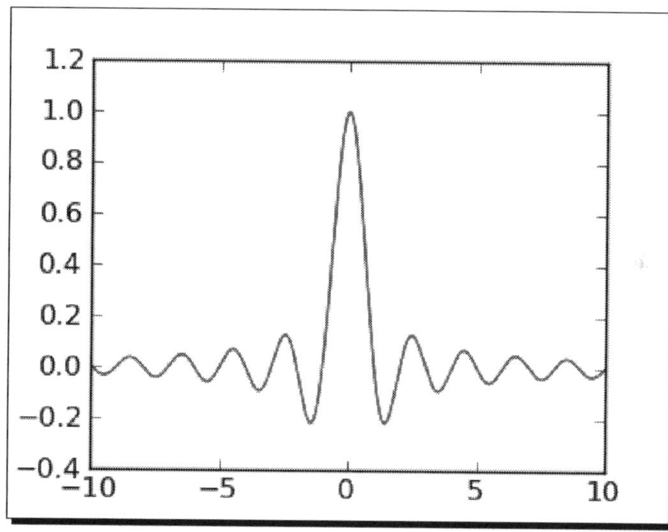

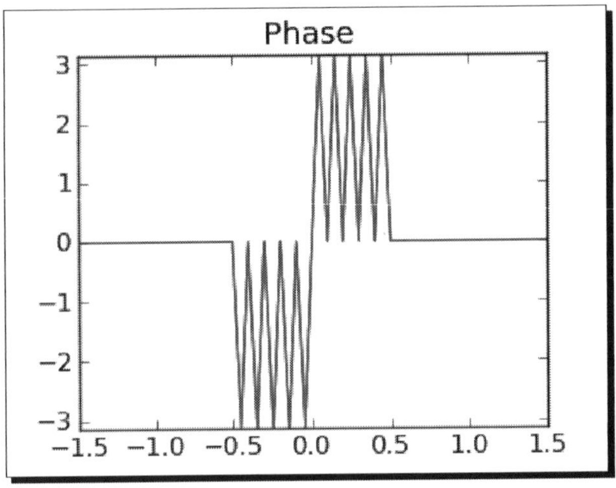

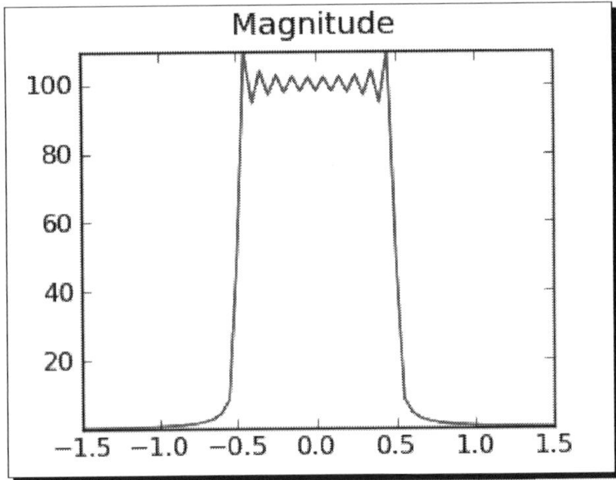

What just happened?

We first generated a time-domain signal to work with. The `arange` function was used to create a series of sample times, and the `sinc` function was used to compute the sinc function at those times. The first plot shows the time-domain function that we are going to analyse. We then used the `fft` function to compute the Fourier transform, which returns a NumPy array of complex values. It is customary to plot the frequency spectrum as magnitude and phase, so we used the `absolute` function to get the magnitude and the `angle` function to get the phase. The `fftfreq` function accepts an array of sample times and the time step, and uses them to compute the frequency values for plotting the frequency spectrum. The `fftshift` function was used to shift the magnitude and phase arrays and the frequency array so that the zero-frequency point was in the centre of the array. This is helpful for making plots.

Window functions

The `sinc` function that we used in the previous example is actually an approximation to the true sinc function, which extends from negative infinity to positive infinity. Because we used finite data to compute the Fourier transform, we introduced a distortion into the frequency spectrum. One way of reducing this distortion is by applying a window function to the signal before performing the transform. All the common window functions are built into NumPy.

Time for action – plotting window functions

Let's plot the window functions available in NumPy:

```
import numpy as np
import matplotlib.pyplot as plt
plt.figure(figsize=(6,4))
plt.plot(np.bartlett(51), label="Bartlett")
plt.plot(np.blackman(51), label="Blackman")
plt.plot(np.hamming(51), label="Hamming")
plt.plot(np.hanning(51), label="Hanning")
plt.plot(np.kaiser(51,3), label="Kaiser")
plt.legend(loc='best')
plt.savefig('window_functions.png')
plt.close()
```

The output is shown below:

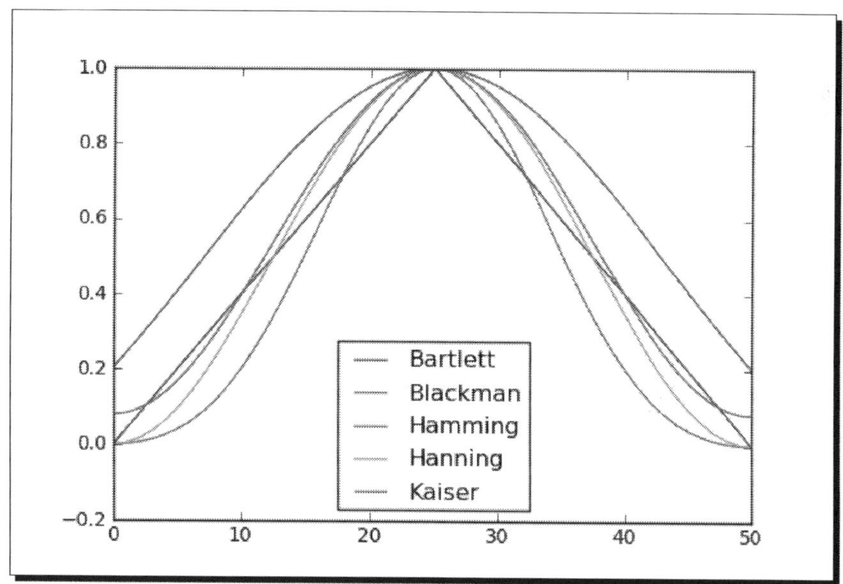

What just happened?

Calling the function `hamming`(51) returns an array containing 51 samples of the Hamming window function. The sample at the centre of the array corresponds to the centre of the window, where it reaches the value of 1. The other window functions work the same way, except that the Kaiser window also requires a shape parameter.

Have a go hero – using window functions

Apply some of the window functions to the sinc function in the example and compute the DFT to see how the window functions affect the frequency spectrum.

HINT: Generate an array of samples of the window function that has the same number of samples as the array containing the sinc function, and multiply the two arrays before performing the DFT.

Solving ordinary differential equations

In the previous chapter, we looked at some tools for finding exact solutions to ordinary differential equations (ODEs). Sometimes, finding an exact solution is impossible or impractical. Sage also has a powerful set of tools for solving ordinary differential equations numerically.

Time for action – solving a first-order ODE

Let's start by solving a single, first-order, ordinary differential equation. We'll compare the exact solution to the numerical solution:

```
var('x, y')
y = function('y', x)
ode = diff(y, x) + 1 / x * y == x * y^2
sol = desolve(ode, y, ics=[10, 1])
sol.show()
exact_plot = plot(sol, (x, 0.1, 10), color='red', marker='.')

rk4_plot = desolve_rk4(ode, y, ics=[10, 1], output='slope_field',
    end_points=[0, 10])
show(exact_plot + rk4_plot, figsize=(4, 3))
```

The symbolic solution is shown in the following screenshot, and its graph is plotted on the same axes as the numerical solution and the slope field:

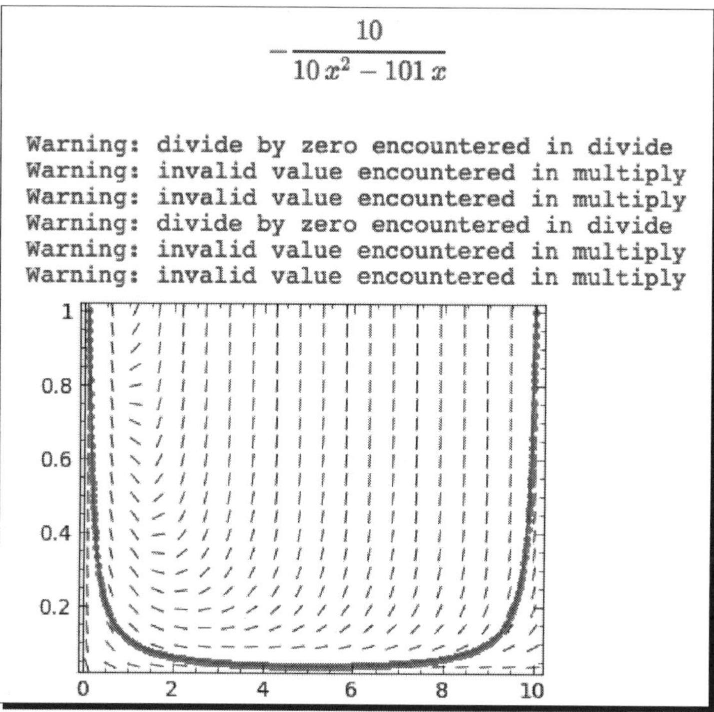

What just happened?

As we explained in the previous chapter, we defined a symbolic ordinary differential equation and found the solution using `desolve`. The warning messages occur during the calculation of the slope field, and can be safely ignored. We then used the `desolve_rk4` function to compute the solution numerically. As its name implies, the functions use the 4th order Runge-Kutta method to integrate a single first-order ordinary differential equation numerically (the function `rk` from Maxima's dynamics package is used to perform the integration). `desolve_rk4` accepts the following keyword arguments:

Keyword	Default	Description
`ics`	`None`	List of initial conditions for each variable.
`ivar`	`None`	Independent variable. Only required if there is more than one choice for the independent variable.
`end_points`	`None`	The end points of the interval of integration. If `end_points` is a or [a], integrate between `min(ics[0],a)` and `max(ics[0],a)`. If `end_points` is `None`, then `end_points=ics[0]+10`. If `end_points` is `[a,b]` integrate between `min(ics[0],a)` and `max(ics[0],b)`.

Keyword	Default	Description
`step`	0.1	Step size for the independent variable.
`output`	`'list'`	`'list'` returns a list of lists of [x,y] values. `'plot'` returns a plot of the solution as a graphics object. `'slope_field'` returns a plot of the solution and the slope field as a graphics object.

Solving a system of ODEs

Sage also has tools to solve systems of ordinary differential equations numerically. We can use this capability to solve any higher-order ODE, since any higher-order ODE can be broken down into a system of first-order differential equations. For the next two examples, we will look at the van der Pol oscillator:

$$\frac{d^2x}{dt^2} - \mu\left(1 - x^2\right)\frac{dx}{dt} + x = 0$$

It can be written in terms of two first-order ODEs:

$$\frac{dx}{dt} = y$$

$$\frac{dy}{dt} = \mu\, y\left(1 - x^2\right) - x$$

Time for action – solving a higher-order ODE

Let's see if Sage can find a symbolic solution:

```
var('t')
x = function('x', t)
y = function('y', t)
u = 1.0

de1 = diff(x,t) - y == 0
de2 = diff(y,t) + x - u * y * (1 - x^2) == 0

Van_der_Pol = [de1, de2]
desolve_system(Van_der_Pol, [x, y], ics=[0, 2, 0])
```

If you run this code, Sage will return an error. It is unable to find a symbolic solution. Now, let's try to solve it numerically:

```
var('t, x, y')
u = 1.0

Van_der_Pol = [y, -x + u * y * (1 - x^2)]
sol = desolve_system_rk4(Van_der_Pol, [x, y], ivar=t,
    ics=[0, 2, 0], end_points=[0, 20])
t = [i for i, j, k in sol]
x_sol = [j for i, j, k in sol]
y_sol = [k for i, j, k in sol]

# Plot results
import matplotlib.pyplot as plt
plt.figure(figsize=(4, 3))
plt.plot(t, x_sol)
plt.xlabel('t')
plt.ylabel('y(t)')
plt.subplots_adjust(bottom=0.15)
plt.savefig('Van_der_Pol_rk4.png')
plt.close()

# Limit cycle in the phase plane
plt.figure(figsize=(4, 4))
plt.plot(x_sol, y_sol)
plt.axis('scaled')
plt.xlabel('x')
plt.ylabel('y')
plt.savefig('Van_der_Pol_rk4_phase.png')
plt.close()
```

The results should look like this:

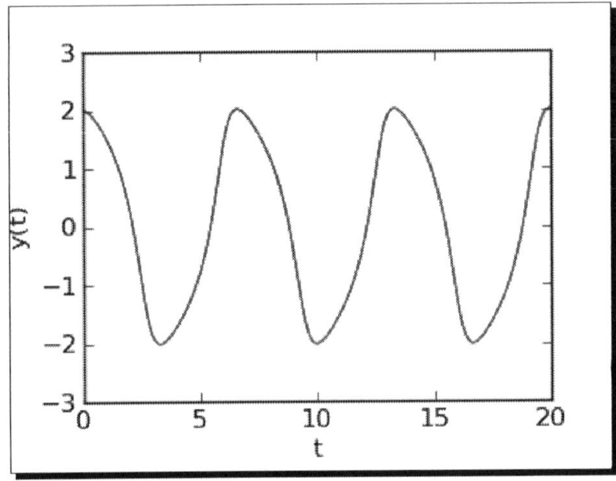

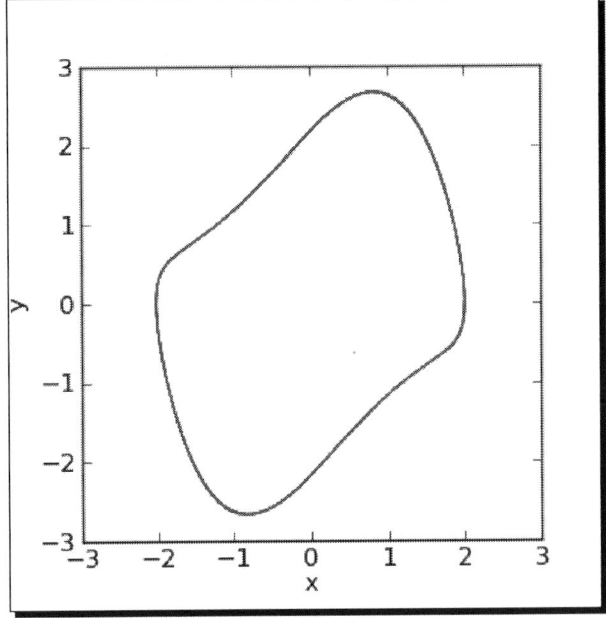

What just happened?

We used the function `desolve_system_rk4` to solve the system. This function operates just like `desolve_rk4`, except that it accepts a list of differential equations as its first argument (both of these functions utilize the `rk` function from Maxima to compute the solution.). An initial condition must also be provided for each variable—three, in this case. We had to use the `ivar` keyword to specify that `t` is the independent variable. The function returns the solution as a list of lists:

```
[[0, 2, 0],
[0.1, 1.99093050354, -0.172638259608],
[0.2, 1.96694849768, -0.300697407982],
...
[0.4, 1.88817476497, -0.47282676678]]
```

We used list comprehensions to separate the solutions for x, y, and t into three different lists. Since we are working with lists of points, we used matplotlib for plotting. The first plot is the time-varying solution to the van der Pol differential equation. Note that we used the matplotlib function `subplots_adjust` to ensure that the label for the `t` axis is visible. For certain combinations of figure size, font size, and plot size you will occasionally have to use `subplots_adjust` to make a figure look right. In the second plot, we plotted x vs. y to create a phase-plane plot. This is known as the limit cycle. Try varying the value of u in the range of 0 to 5 to see how it impacts the solution.

Solving the system using the GNU Scientific Library

Sage is a collection of tools. You often have a choice of several methods for accomplishing the same task. While this can be confusing, one algorithm may be able to solve a problem that another one couldn't. For solving ODEs, Sage also allows you to access the ODE solver from the GNU Scientific Library (GSL). This solver gives you access to more solution algorithms.

Time for action – alternative method of solving a system of ODEs

We'll solve the same problem again, using the numerical ODE solver from the GSL.

```
def f_1(t, y, params):
    return [y[1], -y[0] - params[0] * y[1] * (y[0]**2 - 1.0)]
def j_1(t, y, params):
    return [ [0.0, 1.0], [-2.0 * params[0] * y[0] * y[1] - 1.0,
    -params[0] * (y[0] * y[0] - 1.0)] ]
T = ode_solver()
T.algorithm = "rk8pd"
T.function = f_1
T.jacobian = j_1
T.ode_solve(y_0=[2, 0], t_span=[0, 20], params=[1.0],
```

```
    num_points=1000)
interpolator = T.interpolate_solution()
plot(interpolator, (0, 20), axes_labels=('t','y'), figsize=(4,3))
```

The output is shown in the following screenshot:

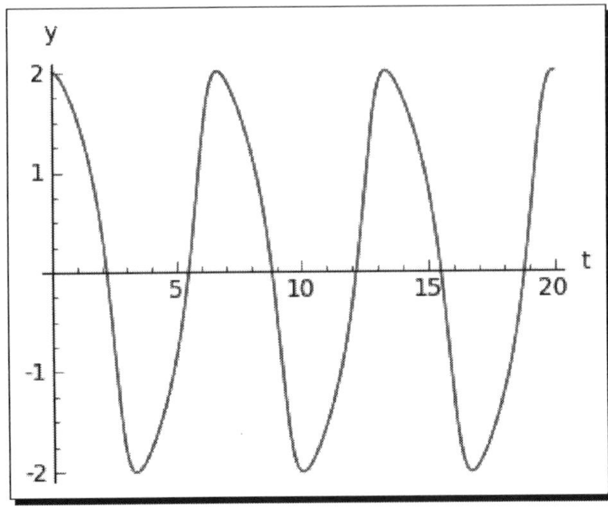

What just happened?

This solver has a very different interface from the one in the previous example. The ordinary differential equations are defined by a Python function called f_1. The first argument to this function is the independent variable, the second is a list of dependent variables, and the third is a list of parameters. y[0] represents the variable y, and y[1] represents x. In this case, the parameter list has only one element, which is the value of u. We used similar syntax to define the Jacobian function, j_1. The Jacobian is only required for certain integration algorithms; see the `ode_solver` documentation for more details.

The code `T = ode_solver()` creates a solver object. We used the attribute `algorithm` to choose the `rk8pd` (Runge-Kutta Prince-Dormand 8,9) algorithm, and used the attributes `function` and `jacobian` to pass in the functions we just defined. We called the method `ode_solve` to solve the system, which accepts the following arguments:

Keyword	Description
`y_0`	List of initial conditions. Note that y[0] is y and y[1] is x, which is backwards compared to the previous example!
`t_span`	Domain of solution, specified as a list: [start, stop].
`params`	List of parameter values (in this case, u=1).
`num_points`	Number of points for the solution.

Finally, we used the method `interpolate_solution` to obtain a spline object that contains the solution. We used the `plot` function to plot the solution. The `ode_solver` object is very powerful, and it is described in detail in the Sage documentation.

Numerical optimization

We briefly touched on numerical optimization in the section on finding minimum values of functions. In general, optimization is a process of choosing the best element from a set of possible elements. The criteria for choosing the "best" element are quantified in the form of an objective function that is to be minimized or maximized. The elements may be discrete elements, or they may take on a continuous range of values. In general, optimization is a very difficult problem that can be approached in many different ways. We will focus on the case in which we seek to minimize a scalar-valued objective function by choosing the values of variables from a continuous set. The values of the variables may be limited by constraints. Optimization is of great importance in science and engineering, where it is used for fitting functions to data sets and finding optimal combinations of design parameters.

Time for action – linear programming

First, we'll solve a linear programming problem with Sage. Although it is limited to solving problems in which the objective function and the constraints are linear functions of the variables, linear programming is widely taught in applied mathematics courses and has many practical applications. Let's see how Sage can help us visualize what's going on in an example problem from the Sage documentation. The problem to be solved is as follows:

Minimize $-4x_1-5x_2$ subject to the following linear inequality constraints:

$2x_1+x_2\leq 3$

$x_1+2x_2\leq 3$

$x_1\geq 0$

$x_2\geq 0$

```
var('x, y')
c=vector(RDF,[-4, -5])
G=matrix(RDF,[[2, 1], [1, 2], [-1, 0], [0, -1]])
h=vector(RDF,[3, 3, 0, 0])
sol=linear_program(c, G, h)
print("Minimum: {0}".format(sol['x']))
print("Slack variables: {0}" .format(sol['s']))
c1_plot = implicit_plot(2 * x + y == 3, (x,0,2), (y,0,2))
c2_plot = implicit_plot(x + 2 * y == 3, (x,0,2), (y,0,2))
c3_plot = implicit_plot(x == 0, (x,0,2), (y,0,2))
```

```
c4_plot = implicit_plot(y == 0, (x,0,2), (y,0,2))
min_plot = point(sol['x'], color='red', size=50)
rp = region_plot([2 * x + y <= 3, x + 2 * y <= 3, x >= 0,  y >= 0],
    (x,0,2), (y,0,2))

g = graphics_array([c1_plot+c2_plot+c3_plot+c4_plot+min_plot,
    rp], 1, 2)
g.show(aspect_ratio=1)
```

The output is shown below:

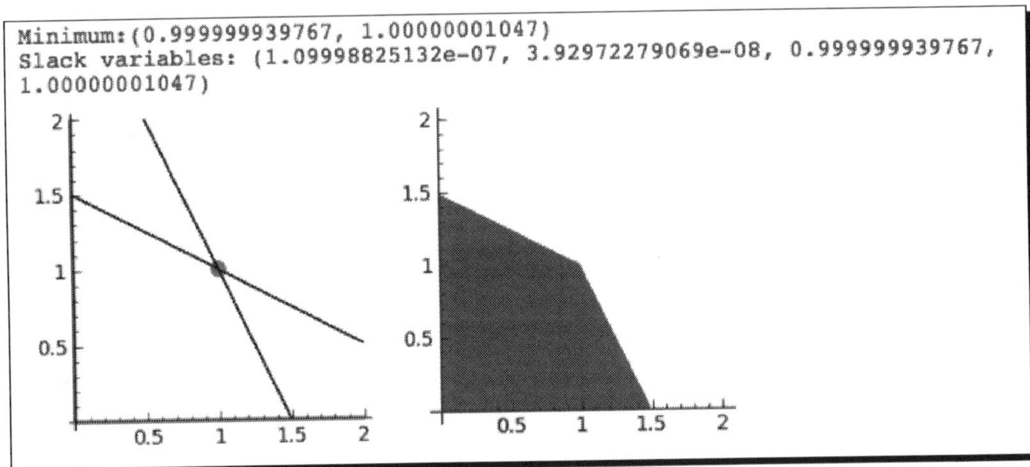

What just happened?

A linear program consists of a linear function to be minimized or maximized, and a set of linear constraints. In this case, there are only two variables, which makes it easier to visualize what's going on. We specified the function as a vector of coefficients called `c`. We created a matrix `G` that represents the left-hand side of the constraints. Each row in the matrix is a vector of coefficients for that constraint. Note that `linear_program` expects all constraints to specified as lhs < rhs, so we have to enter the third and fourth constraints with negative coefficients. The right-hand sides of the constraints were used to form another vector called `h`. The two vectors and the matrix were passed as arguments to `linear_program`, which returns the solution as a dictionary. The dictionary contains information about the solution, the minimized parameters, the slack variables, and the solution to the dual program (for more about slack variables and the dual program, see `http://en.wikipedia.org/wiki/Linear_programming` or an optimization textbook). `linear_program` accepts an optional argument with the keyword `solver`, which determines which solver is used. If the value is `None` (the default), the solver from the Python package CVXOPT is used. If `solver='glpk'`, the solver from the GNU Linear Programming Kit (GLPK) is used.

The plotting features of Sage can help us visualize the problem and the solution. We formulated the constraints as equalities, and utilized the `implicit_plot` function to plot the resulting lines in the x-y plane. We used the `point` function to add a dot to indicate the location of the minimum. We also used `region_plot` to plot the region defined by the inequalities. Going further, we could use a contour plot to show how the objective function varies over the domain.

Fitting a function to a noisy data set

Fitting a function to data is one of the most common applications of numerical optimization for engineers and scientists. This is often referred to as "least squares fitting," because an optimal fit is achieved when the sum of squared errors is minimized.

Time for action – least squares fitting

The following is adapted from an example in the Sage documentation:

```
var('a, b, c, x')
set_random_seed(0.0)
data = [(i, 1.2 * sin(0.5 * i - 0.2) + 0.1 *
    normalvariate(0, 1)) for i in xsrange(0, 4 * pi, 0.2)]
data_plot = list_plot(data)

model(x) = a * sin(b * x - c)

fitted_params = find_fit(data, model, solution_dict=True)
print("a = {0}".format(fitted_params[a]))
print("b = {0}".format(fitted_params[b]))
print("c = {0}".format(fitted_params[c]))

g(x) = model.subs(a=fitted_params[a], b=fitted_params[b], c=fitted_
params[c])
fitted_plot = plot(g(x), (x, 0, 4 * pi), color='red')
show(data_plot + fitted_plot, figsize=(4, 3))
```

The noisy data, and the fitted function, are shown below:

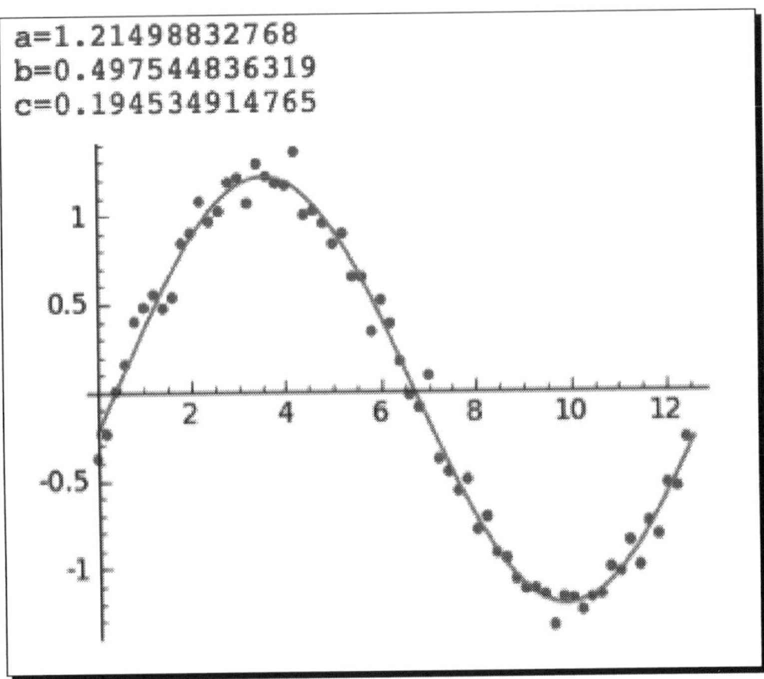

What just happened?

After declaring some symbolic variables, we called the `set_random_seed` function to fix the seed for the pseudo-random number generator. A pseudo-random number generator will always generate the same sequence of numbers for a given seed value. Setting the seed ensures that the plot you create will be identical to the one in the example. We used a fairly complex list comprehension to construct the pseudo-random data set. We also defined a callable symbolic expression called `model` that has one variable and three variable parameters. We then used `find_fit` to vary the parameters until an optimal fit was achieved. `find_fit` has only two required arguments: a list containing the data and the model to be fitted. The keyword argument `solution_dict=True` tells the function to return the fitted values as a dictionary, rather than a list of relations. Having the parameter values in a dictionary allows us to substitute the values back into the model, using the `subs` method. Finally, we plotted the fitted function. `find_fit` accepts several additional optional arguments:

Keyword	Default	Description
`initial_guess`	1 for each parameter	List containing an initial guess for each parameter.

Keyword	Default	Description
parameters	None	List of parameters (only required if the model is a Python function).
variables	None	List of variables (only required if the model is a Python function).

Constrained optimization

Constrained optimization is useful when there are constraints on the parameter values. These may be simple constraints, such as a parameter that must be greater than zero. The constraints can also be more complicated functions that involve several parameters.

Time for action – a constrained optimization problem

The following example is adapted from a textbook on operations research:

```
#Ronald L. Rardin. "Optimization in Operations Research."
# Prentice-Hall, Upper Saddle River, NJ, 1998.  Example 14.3, p. 792

# Global constants
d1 = 2.5
d2 = 40
t1 = 0.6
t2 = 1.0
p0 = 200

initial_guess = [20, 500]

def x3(x):
    return 36.25 * (d2 - x[0]) * (t2 - t1) / t1 * log(x[1] / p0)
def x4(x):
    return 348300 * (d2 - x[0]) * (t2 - t1)/ x[1]


def f(x):
    return 61.8 + 5.72 * x[0] + 0.0175 * x3(x)^0.85 + \
        0.0094 * x4(x)^0.75 + 0.006 * t1 * x3(x)


c_1 = lambda p: p[0]
c_2 = lambda p: p[1]
c_3 = lambda p: t2 * p[0] - d1 * t1 - d2 * (t2 - t1)
c_4 = lambda p: p[1] - p0

(x1, x2) = minimize_constrained(f, [c_1,c_2,c_3,c_4], initial_guess)

print('x1 = {0}'.format(x1))
print('x2 = {0}'.format(x2))
print('x3 = {0}'.format(x3([x1,x2])))
```

```
print('x4 = {0}'.format(x4([x1,x2])))
print('x5 = {0}'.format(f([x1,x2])))
```

The fitted values are:

```
x1 = 17.5
x2 = 473.692826399
x3 = 468.843924104708
x4 = 6617.57963242
x5 = 173.746171538638
```

What just happened?

First, we defined some constants that are used in the models. These are fixed values that are not optimized. This problem has four parameters, but only the first two are independent. Parameters x3 and x4 are functions of x1 and x2, so we defined Python functions to calculate their values. We also defined the objective function `f`, which is the function that we want to minimize. The objective function has one argument, which is a list that contains the two parameters to be fitted. We then defined four constraint functions using the `lambda` construct (we could also have used normal function definitions). We called `minimize_constrained` to perform the actual optimization. It requires three arguments: the objective function, a list of constraints, and a list of initial guesses for each parameter. The optional parameter `gradient` is a function that is required if the constraints are given as a list of intervals. The keyword parameter `algorithm` can be used to specify the algorithm. Currently, the only alternative is `'l-bfgs-b'`.

Probability

We will end this chapter with a brief introduction to probability in Sage. Many applications, such as Monte Carlo simulations, require a series of pseudorandom numbers that are drawn from a specified distribution. Sage has many built-in probability distributions that can be used to generate pseudorandom numbers, as well as obtaining analytical distributions.

Time for action – accessing probability distribution functions

In the following code, we will see how to access probability distributions in Sage, obtain random variates from a specified distribution, and plot their distribution:

```
import matplotlib.pyplot as plt

variance = 0.75

# GNU Scientific Library
gaussian = RealDistribution('gaussian', variance)
```

```
gaussian.set_seed(0.0)
random_values = [gaussian.get_random_element() for i in range(1000)]
gaussian_plot = gaussian.plot((-5, 5))
# Get the Matplotlib object for the Gaussian plot
fig = gaussian_plot.matplotlib()
from matplotlib.backends.backend_agg import FigureCanvasAgg
fig.set_canvas(FigureCanvasAgg(fig))    # this line is critical
ax = fig.gca()
# Add a histogram
ax.hist(np.array(random_values), normed=True, facecolor='white')
ax.axis([-3, 3, 0, 0.6])
fig.savefig('hist.png')
```

The result should look like this:

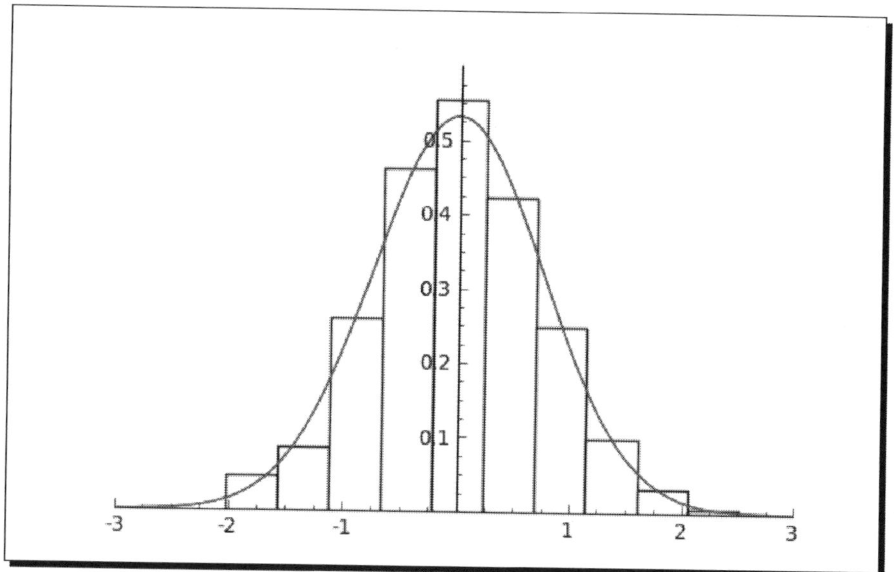

What just happened?

We first called `RealDistribution`, which returns a Sage probability distribution object. Sage uses the random number generators from the GNU Scientific Library. In this case, we specified a Gaussian distribution with a variance of 0.75. We then called the `set_seed` method to ensure that the histogram generated in this example would match the plot you obtain when you run the code. To get a single real number drawn from this distribution, call the `get_random_element` method. To plot a histogram from a bunch of random numbers, we used a list comprehension to call this method repeatedly. If you are not concerned about the formatting of the plot, you can use the `generate_histogram_plot` method of the `RealDistribution` object to plot a histogram showing the distribution of random values from the specified distribution.

In this example, we wanted to make a plot that shows a normalized histogram superimposed on a plot of the normal distribution. Unfortunately, Sage does not yet have a function for plotting histograms. We called the `plot` method of the `RealDistribution` object to plot the analytical Gaussian distribution. We then obtained a matplotlib figure from the Sage graphics object, following the procedure described in Chapter 6. We obtained the current axes using the `gca` function and added a histogram plot, using the matplotlib function `hist` as described in Chapter 6.

NumPy also features high-quality random number generators, which can be found in the `numpy.random` module. You can generate an entire NumPy array of random variates with a single function call, which avoids the need to use a list comprehension. If you need to generate a very large number of random variates, using NumPy can speed up your code significantly because it avoids the relatively slow process of looping in Python. The documentation for the `random` module can be found at `http://docs.scipy.org/doc/numpy/reference/routines.random.html`. The documentation is also included with Sage, and can be accessed by executing the following commands:

```
import numpy
numpy.random?
```

Summary

This chapter covered a broad range of techniques in numerical mathematics. We learned about the tools that Sage offers for:

- Finding the zeros of a function
- Computing integrals and derivatives numerically
- Finding minimum values of functions of one or more variables
- Computing the discrete Fourier transform, and using window functions
- Solving an ordinary differential equation (ODE) numerically

- Numerically solving a higher-order ODE by transforming it into a system of first-order ODEs
- Using optimization techniques for linear programming, fitting curves to data, and finding an optimal solution in the presence of constraints
- Using probability distributions to obtain pseudo-random numbers

By now, you have all the basic information that you need to start using Sage to solve problems in applied mathematics. However, there is still more to learn! Python is a very powerful programming language that makes complex programming tasks possible. We'll learn more about advanced programming techniques in the next chapter.

9

Learning Advanced Python Programming

In Chapter 4, we learned about the basic elements of Python programming that you need to use Sage effectively. Throughout the following chapters, we saw various examples of objects in Sage, such as the `ode_solver` object we used in the last chapter. In this chapter, you will learn how to define your own classes to create custom objects. Objects are a way to bundle data and algorithms together to help you keep your code organized. You will also learn to handle runtime errors in your programs by using exceptions. Finally, you will learn how unit testing can help you avoid bugs in your code. Many of the concepts in this chapter are used by software engineers on large projects. It might seem to be "overkill" to use these principles on the short scripts you have been writing, but short scripts tend to grow into long programs. A little bit of discipline early in the programming process can save a lot of time later on.

In this chapter, you will learn how to:

- Define your own classes
- Use inheritance to expand the usefulness of your classes
- Organize your class definitions in module files
- Bundle module files into packages
- Handle errors gracefully with exceptions
- Define your own exceptions for custom error handling
- Use unit tests to make sure your package is working correctly

Let's see how object-oriented programming can help us write code more effectively.

How to write good software

Writing good software requires a combination of creativity and discipline. This section is a brief overview of the discipline of software development. There are many approaches to developing software, and the subject can be highly controversial! Look at what others have done and develop a process that works for you or your team. A good place to start is `http://en.wikipedia.org/wiki/Software_development_methodology`. First, we'll outline the formal software development process that is used for large projects. Then, we'll see how elements of this process can be applied to any project.

The first stage is requirements analysis, which is the process of defining and documenting exactly what the software is supposed to accomplish. The requirements are used to write a specification for the project. The specification is then used to define the structure of the program, such as functions, classes, data, methods, and so on. The next stage is writing the actual code, which is followed by testing to ensure that the software meets the specification. A critical aspect of the project is writing documentation, which ideally takes place while the code is being written. Once the software is working correctly and released to the users, it enters the maintenance phase. Bugs are fixed as they are reported, improvements are made, and new features may be added. The maintenance phase can be easy or it can be a nightmare, depending on the quality of the software design, implementation, and documentation.

All of these concepts can (and should) be applied to the short scripts that you write on a daily basis. Requirements analysis can be as simple as pausing before implementing a function or class to think about what it needs to accomplish. One trick is to write the docstring before writing the actual code. Use the docstring to organize your thoughts and document what the inputs and outputs of the code will be. Before you jump into writing code, think about the approach you're going to take. For more complex code, you might want to consult books, journal articles, or open-source projects to see how others have approached the subject (and make sure that you are not re-inventing the wheel). In practice, a lot of projects start off as little scripts or snippets of code, and gradually grow into monsters. It's important to recognize when your code is getting out of control. Take a short break from programming, and ask yourself how to organize the code more effectively. Do you need to define a function to replace redundant code? Would it help to use an object represent this concept? Do the variable names make sense? Do you have enough comments to make it clear what's going on? If you have to fix a bug in this code six months from now, will you understand how it works? If not, take the time to improve the documentation *right now*. In the long run, it will save you a lot of time if you develop the discipline to write clean, organized, well-documented code.

Version control (also known as revision control or source control) is a process of tracking and managing changes in programs and documentation. Version control tools can be very helpful even for small projects, and they are essential for large projects with multiple developers. For example, the Sage project uses an open-source version control tool called Mercurial. The Web interface at `http://hg.sagemath.org/` allows you to browse the Sage source code and track changes. Sage also provides functions that allow you to work with Mercurial from within the notebook interface. The documentation for the Mercurial interface is available at `http://www.sagemath.org/doc/reference/sage/misc/hg.html`. Other popular open-source version control tools include Bazaar, Git, and Subversion.

Object-oriented programming

An object is a construct that contains data and has methods that operate on its data. A class defines how data is stored in an object, and what methods are available to work with the data. A class is like a blueprint that describes how a house is to be built. An object is like a house that is constructed from the blueprint. Many houses can be constructed from the same blueprint. Although the houses are built from the same plans and have the same structure, each house is an independent entity, and the contents of each house can be different. In Python, an object is known as an *instance* of a *class*. If you're new to object-oriented programming, a good starting point is to use objects as models of concrete objects in the real world. Once you've become familiar with the concept, you can use objects to represent all kinds of concepts. For more information about the general principles of object-oriented programming, read `http://en.wikipedia.org/wiki/Object-oriented_programming`.

Time for action – defining a class that represents a tank

To start out, we will define a class that models a tank (meaning a tracked, armored fighting vehicle). A tank typically runs on two continuous tracks, and it has a rotating turret that houses a powerful cannon. The relationship between the various components of a tank is shown in the following diagram:

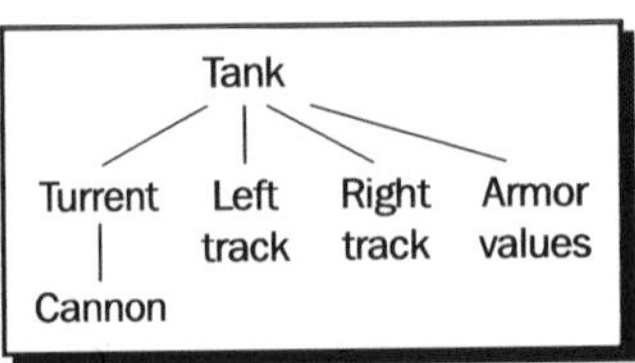

Based on this conceptual representation, we will define classes to represent the cannon, the tracks, and turret. We will then define another class that utilizes these classes to model a tank. To keep the example simple, we'll use point values to represent the relative strength of the tank's armor and the damage inflicted by its main gun. Although this is a simple "toy" example, a class like this could be used as the foundation of a video game or a simulator for military training:

```
class Cannon():
    """Model of a large cannon."""
    def __init__(self, damage):
        """Create a Cannon instance
          Arguments:
              damage      Integer that represents
                  the damage inflicted by the cannon
        """
        # _damage   amount of damage inflicted by cannon (integer)
        # _operational  True if operational, False if disabled
        self._damage = damage
        self._operational = True
    def __str__(self):
        return 'Damage value:' + str(self._damage)

class Track():
    """Model of a continuous track."""
    def __init__(self):
        # _operational  True if operational, False if disabled
        self._operational = True
class Turret():
    """Model of a tank turret."""
```

```
    def __init__(self, gun):
        """Create a Turret instance
            Arguments:
                gun       instance of Gun class
        """
        # _gun   instance of Gun class
        # _operational  True if operational, False if disabled
        self._gun = gun
        self._operational = True

    def __str__(self):
        return(str(self._gun))

class Tank():
    """Model of an armored fighting vehicle."""

    def __init__(self, armor_values, cannon_damage_value):
        """Create a tank instance
            Arguments:
                armor_values    A dictionary of armor values
                    of the form:
                    {'front' : 100, 'side' : 50, 'rear' : 25,
                        'turret' : 75}
                cannon_damage_value     Integer that represents
                    the damage inflicted by the main gun
        """
        # Initialize armor
        self._frontal_armor = armor_values['front']
        self._left_armor = armor_values['side']
        self._right_armor = armor_values['side']
        self._rear_armor = armor_values['rear']
        self._turret_armor = armor_values['turret']

        # Add tank components
        main_gun = Cannon(cannon_damage_value)
        self._turret = Turret(main_gun)
        self._left_track = Track()
        self._right_track = Track()

    def __str__(self):
        import os
        ls = os.linesep
        description = 'Tank parameters:' + ls
        description += '  Armor values:' + ls
```

```
        description += '    Front:' + str(self._frontal_armor) + ls
        description += '    Left:' + str(self._left_armor) + ls
        description += '    Right:' + str(self._right_armor) + ls
        description += '    Rear:' + str(self._rear_armor) + ls
        description += '    Turret:' + str(self._turret_armor) + ls
        description += '  Weapons:' + ls
        description += '    Main cannon:' + ls
        description += '    ' + str(self._turret) + ls
        return description

# Define parameters for the tank
armor_values = {'front' : 100, 'side' : 50, 'rear' : 25,
    'turret' : 75}
main_gun_damage = 50

# Create a tank object
tank = Tank(armor_values, main_gun_damage)
print(tank)
```

Use the `load` command on the Sage command line or in a cell in a worksheet to run the code. If you run it from the command line, the output should look like this:

```
sage: load("4460_9_1.py")
Tank parameters:
  Armor values:
    Front:100
    Left side:50
    Right side:50
    Rear:25
    Turret:75
  Weapons:
    Main cannon:
    Damage value:50
```

What just happened?

We used our knowledge of a real-world object (an armored fighting vehicle) to construct a conceptual model of a tank. We then used Python to implement an object-oriented representation of a tank. We defined a `Tank` class, which uses point values to keep track of the amount of armor on the tank. Each instance of the `Tank` class has an associated instance of the `Turret` class, which in turn has an instance of a `Cannon`. Each `Tank` instance also has two instances of the `Track` class, to represent the left and right tracks.

The keyword `class` is used to start each class definition, followed by the name of the class, and a set of parenthesis and a colon. By convention, Python class names start with an upper-case letter, and use a mix of upper- and lower-case letters, rather than underscores, to separate words (known as camel case, because the upper-case letters can resemble the humps of a camel). This convention helps us distinguish between an object named `tank` and a class named `Tank`. The pair of parenthesis is used for inheritance, which we'll get to in moment. Methods for the class are defined using function definition syntax, and they are indented to show that they are part of the class definition. The first argument to a method is special, and by convention the name `self` is used. `self` refers to the instance itself. The `self` argument allows a method to access data and call other methods from the class or instance, using the syntax `self.method_name()`. However, when the methods are called from outside of the class, the `self` keyword is omitted.

The first method we defined for each class is called `__init__`. In Python, the `__init__` method is automatically called when an instance is first created. This special method has the same purpose as a constructor in other object-oriented languages. If data needs to be initialized every time an instance is created, that code should go into `__init__`. If no initialization needs to be done, then you can omit this method from the class definition. The `Tank` class and the `Turret` class have additional arguments to `__init__` that are used to set initial values for the data in the objects, while the `Cannon` and `Track` classes do not have any arguments. Keyword arguments can also be used with the `__init__` method. An instance of the `Tank` class can be created using function call syntax. The name of the class is used instead of a function name, and the argument list must match the arguments required by the `__init__` method (ignoring `self`, as previously mentioned).

Instance variables are created in the `__init__` method with the syntax `self.var_name = value`. Instance variables can be public or non-public. Public instance variables can be modified by code outside of the class, while non-public variables are only supposed to be modified within the class. By convention, public instance variables have regular names, and non-public instance variables have names that start with a single underscore. We defined our class with non-public instance variables to encourage users to use methods to get and set the values. Methods can also be non-public, in which case their names also start with a single underscore. Note that Python does not prevent outside code from modifying non-public variables or calling non-public methods. That is why they are called non-public, rather than private. Python doesn't have truly private instance variables or methods.

Another special method is called `__str__`, which is an optional method that returns a string representation of an object. Because we have defined this method for the `Tank` and `Cannon` classes, we can use the syntax `print(tank)` to display useful data about the instance. This method is also called when the instance is an argument to the `str` function. Notice how the `__str__` method of the `Tank` class actually calls the `str` function to get a text representation of the `Cannon` instance. It would be possible for the `__str__` method of the `Tank` class to go and get the value of `_damage` directly from the `Cannon` object and convert it to a string, but this would be an unwise shortcut. In the future, we might decide to completely change the internal structure of the `Cannon` class, and the variable `damage_value` may go away. By using methods to access the data from an object, we keep our code more organized and prevent bugs. If we try to use `print` with an instance that does not have a `__str__` method, we will only get a cryptic message about the type of object and its memory address. For example:

```
sage: print(tank._left_track)
<__main__.Track instance at 0x100463440>
```

Note that the memory address that is printed on your system will probably be different.

Immediately after each class definition and function definition, there is a triple-quoted string called a *docstring*. This string is used to document the purpose of the class or function. When you ask for help on a class or instance, Sage and Python use the docstring to provide help. For example:

```
sage: Tank?
Type:        classobj
String Form:    __main__.Tank
Namespace:    Interactive
File:        /Applications/sage/local/lib/python2.6/site-packages/IPython/
FakeModule.py
Docstring:
    Model of an armored fighting vehicle.


Constructor information:
Definition:  Tank(self, armor_values, cannon_damage_value)
Docstring:
    Constructs a tank instance
       Arguments:
          armor_values    A dictionary of armor values of the form:
             {'front' : 100, 'side' : 50, 'rear' : 25, 'turret' : 75}
```

```
        cannon_damage_value     Integer that represents the damage
          inflicted by the main gun
```

You should write docstrings for all public modules, functions, classes, and methods. A general guide to writing good docstrings can be found at `http://www.python.org/dev/peps/pep-0257/`. Our Tank class is useful for organizing and displaying data, but the instances don't do much. Let's make them do something useful.

Making our tanks move

At a simplistic level, a tank only has to do two things: move and shoot. Let's start by giving our tank model the ability to move.

Time for action – making the tanks move

To start out, we will define attributes and methods that allow the tank instances to move. Execute this enhanced version of the previous example:

```
class Cannon():

    """Model of a large cannon."""

    def __init__(self, damage):
        """Create a Cannon instance
            Arguments:
                damage      Integer that represents
                    the damage inflicted by the cannon
        """
        # _damage   amount of damage inflicted by cannon (integer)
        # _operational  True if operational, False if disabled
        self._damage = damage
        self._operational = True

    def __str__(self):
        return 'Damage value:' + str(self._damage)

class Track():

    """Model of a continuous track."""

    def __init__(self):
        # _operational  True if operational, False if disabled
        self._operational = True

class Turret():

    """Model of a tank turret."""

    def __init__(self, gun):
        """Create a Turret instance
```

```
            Arguments:
                gun      instance of Gun class
        """
        # _gun   instance of Gun class
        # _operational  True if operational, False if disabled
        self._gun = gun
        self._operational = True

    def __str__(self):
        return(str(self._gun))

class Tank():

    """Model of an armored fighting vehicle."""

    def __init__(self, armor_values, cannon_damage_value, position):
        """Create a tank instance
            Arguments:
                armor_values    A dictionary of armor values
                    of the form:
                    {'front' : 100, 'side' : 50, 'rear' : 25,
                        'turret' : 75}
                cannon_damage_value     Integer that represents
                    the damage inflicted by the main gun
position    (x,y) tuple of coordinates
        """
        # Initialize armor
        self._frontal_armor = armor_values['front']
        self._left_armor = armor_values['side']
        self._right_armor = armor_values['side']
        self._rear_armor = armor_values['rear']
        self._turret_armor = armor_values['turret']

        # Add tank components
        main_gun = Cannon(cannon_damage_value)
        self._turret = Turret(main_gun)
        self._left_track = Track()
        self._right_track = Track()

        # Intialize position
        self._x = position[0]
        self._y = position[1]

    def __str__(self):
        import os
        ls = os.linesep
        description = 'Tank parameters:' + ls
```

```
        description += '  Armor values:' + ls
        description += '    Front:' + str(self._frontal_armor) + ls
        description += '    Left:' + str(self._left_armor) + ls
        description += '    Right:' + str(self._right_armor) + ls
        description += '    Rear:' + str(self._rear_armor) + ls
        description += '    Turret:' + str(self._turret_armor) + ls
        description += '  Weapons:' + ls
        description += '    Main cannon:' + ls
        description += '    ' + str(self._turret) + ls
        return description

    def move(self, direction, distance):
        """Move the tank.
            Arguments:
                direction   floating-point number representing
                    the compass angle of movement in degrees. North is
0,
                    east is 90, south is 180, and west is 270.
                    0 <= direction < 360
                distance       distance to move (in meters)
        """
        if (direction < 0) or (direction >= 360):
            print("Error: Direction must be greater than or equal \
to zero and less than 360.")
        elif distance < 0:
            print("Error: Negative distance.")
        else:
            self._x += n(distance * cos(direction * pi / 180))
            self._y += n(distance * sin(direction * pi / 180))

    def get_position(self):
        """Returns a tuple with the (x,y) coordinates of the tank's
        current location.
        """
        return (float(self._x), float(self._y))

# Define parameters for the tank
armor_values = {'front' : 100, 'side' : 50, 'rear' : 25,
    'turret' : 75}
main_gun_damage = 50
initial_position = (0.0, 0.0)

# Create a tank object
tank = Tank(armor_values, main_gun_damage, initial_position)

pos = tank.get_position()
print("Initial position: x = {0:.2f}m  y = {1:.2f}m".format(pos[0],
pos[1]))
```

```
# Move 10m north
tank.move(0.0, 10.0)
pos = tank.get_position()
print("Current position: x = {0:.2f}m  y = {1:.2f}m".format(pos[0],
pos[1]))

# Now move 10m east
tank.move(90.0, 10.0)
pos = tank.get_position()
print("Current position: x = {0:.2f}m  y = {1:.2f}m".format(pos[0],
pos[1]))

# Move southwest, back to the origin
tank.move(225.0, sqrt(10.0**2 + 10.0**2))
pos = tank.get_position()
print("Current position: x = {0:.2f}m  y = {1:.2f}m".format(pos[0],
pos[1]))

# Try a move which doesn't make sense
tank.move(-2,-1)
```

If you run this example from the command line, you should get the following results:

```
sage: load("4460_9_2.py")
Initial position: x = 0.00m  y = 0.00m
Current position: x = 10.00m  y = 0.00m
Current position: x = 10.00m  y = 10.00m
Current position: x = -0.00m  y = 0.00m
Error: Direction must be greater than or equal to zero and less than 360.
```

What just happened?

We defined two new methods, and made some changes to `__init__`. If our tanks are going to move, they must have an initial position, so we added an argument called `position` to `__init__`. This argument is a tuple, which is used to initialize two new attributes, `x` and `y` (for simplicity, we'll assume the tank is located on a plane). We also added a method called `get_position`, which simply returns the current location of the tank as a tuple of Python `float` values. We have to force the return values to be floats to ensure that they will be formatted correctly when the values are printed. Sage `RealNumber` objects evaluate to strings when used as arguments to `format`, so they must be converted to Python floating-point numbers in order to use Python's format specifications for real numbers.

The new method called move is a little more interesting. It accepts a direction and a distance, and updates the x and y coordinates of the tank accordingly. However, this method checks to ensure that the direction and distance are valid before the tank is moved. If the arguments are not valid, an error message is printed and the tank does not move. This method illustrates a principle of object-oriented programming: whenever possible, define methods and use them to interact with the data in an object. Utilize the input methods to make sure the inputs are valid before you accept them. move calculates a new position for the tank (in Cartesian coordinates) using the Sage functions sin and cos. The n function (short for numerical_approx) is used to ensure that the x and y values are stored as Sage RealNumber objects.

Have a go hero – checking the values passed to __init__

The __init__ method doesn't check whether or not the armor values, cannon damage value, and initial position are valid. You could accidentally construct a tank with a negative armor value, for example. It's also a good idea to check the type of the arguments, or force them to have the correct type, to avoid unexpected results. The armor value and cannon damage value should be integers and the position should be a tuple of real numbers. Add code to validate the values that are passed to __init__.

Creating a module for our classes

Our classes are getting to the point where they are useful, but the code is also getting rather lengthy. With each new example, we find ourselves duplicating much of the code from the previous example. Python provides modules to help us re-use code without duplication.

Time for action – creating your first module

Create a new Python file called **tank.py** that contains the following code:

```
import sage.all

class Cannon():
    """Model of a large cannon."""
    def __init__(self, damage):
        """Create a Cannon instance
            Arguments:
                damage      Integer that represents
                    the damage inflicted by the cannon
        """
        # _damage   amount of damage inflicted by cannon (integer)
        # _operational  True if operational, False if disabled
        self._damage = damage
```

```
        self._operational = True

    def __str__(self):
        return 'Damage value:' + str(self._damage)

class Track():
    """Model of a continuous track."""

    def __init__(self):
        # _operational  True if operational, False if disabled
        self._operational = True

class Turret():
    """Model of a tank turret."""

    def __init__(self, gun):
        """Create a Turret instance
            Arguments:
                gun      instance of Gun class
        """
        # _gun   instance of Gun class
        # _operational  True if operational, False if disabled
        self._gun = gun
        self._operational = True

    def __str__(self):
        return(str(self._gun))

class Tank():
    """Model of an armored fighting vehicle."""

    def __init__(self, armor_values, cannon_damage_value, position):
        """Create a tank instance
            Arguments:
                armor_values    A dictionary of armor values
                    of the form:
                    {'front' : 100, 'side' : 50, 'rear' : 25,
                        'turret' : 75}
                cannon_damage_value     Integer that represents
                    the damage inflicted by the main gun
                position    (x,y) tuple of coordinates
        """
        # Initialize armor
        self._frontal_armor = armor_values['front']
        self._left_armor = armor_values['side']
        self._right_armor = armor_values['side']
        self._rear_armor = armor_values['rear']
        self._turret_armor = armor_values['turret']
```

```
        # Add tank components
        main_gun = Cannon(cannon_damage_value)
        self._turret = Turret(main_gun)
        self._left_track = Track()
        self._right_track = Track()

        # Intialize position
        self._x = position[0]
        self._y = position[1]

    def __str__(self):
        import os
        ls = os.linesep
        description = 'Tank parameters:' + ls
        description += '  Armor values:' + ls
        description += '    Front:' + str(self._frontal_armor) + ls
        description += '    Left:' + str(self._left_armor) + ls
        description += '    Right:' + str(self._right_armor) + ls
        description += '    Rear:' + str(self._rear_armor) + ls
        description += '    Turret:' + str(self._turret_armor) + ls
        description += '  Weapons:' + ls
        description += '    Main cannon:' + ls
        description += '    ' + str(self._turret) + ls
        return description

    def move(self, direction, distance):
        """Move the tank.
            Arguments:
                direction   floating-point number representing
                    the compass angle of movement in degrees. North is
0,

                    east is 90, south is 180, and west is 270.
                    0 <= direction < 360
                distance        distance to move (in meters)
        """
        if (direction < 0) or (direction >= 360):
            print("Error: Direction must be greater than or equal \
to zero and less than 360.")
        elif distance < 0:
            print("Error: Negative distance.")
        else:
            self._x += n(distance * cos(direction * pi / 180))
            self._y += n(distance * sin(direction * pi / 180))

    def get_position(self):
        """Returns a tuple with the (x,y) coordinates of the tank's
```

```
        current location.
        """
        return (float(self._x), float(self._y))
```

In the same directory, create another Python file that contains the following code:

```
import tank
# Define parameters for the tank
armor_values = {'front' : 100, 'side' : 50, 'rear' : 25,
    'turret' : 75}
main_gun_damage = 50
initial_position = (0.0, 0.0)
# Create a tank object
tank_1 = tank.Tank(armor_values, main_gun_damage, initial_position)
pos = tank_1.get_position()
print("Initial position: x = {0:.2f}m  y = {1:.2f}m".format(pos[0],
pos[1]))
# Move 10m north
tank_1.move(0.0, 10.0)
pos = tank_1.get_position()
print("Current position: x = {0:.2f}m  y = {1:.2f}m".format(pos[0],
pos[1]))
# Now move 10m east
tank_1.move(90.0, 10.0)
pos = tank_1.get_position()
print("Current position: x = {0:.2f}m  y = {1:.2f}m".format(pos[0],
pos[1]))
# Move southwest, back to the origin
tank_1.move(225.0, sqrt(10.0**2 + 10.0**2))
pos = tank_1.get_position()
print("Current position: x = {0:.2f}m  y = {1:.2f}m".format(pos[0],
pos[1]))
# Try a move which doesn't make sense
tank_1.move(-2,-1)
```

Execute the script you just created. You should see the following results, which are identical to the previous example:

```
sage: load 4460_9_3.py
Initial position: x = 0.00m  y = 0.00m
Current position: x = 10.00m  y = 0.00m
Current position: x = 10.00m  y = 10.00m
Current position: x = -0.00m  y = 0.00m
Error: Direction must be greater than or equal to zero and less than 360.
```

What just happened?

We took the code from the previous example and split it into two files. The first one, which we called **tank.py**, is a module that contains our class definitions. The name of this file becomes the name of the module, so it should follow the Python naming conventions for modules: use lower-case letters, with underscores if necessary, and keep the name as short as possible while still being clear about what the module contains.

We have to make one important change to the code in the tank module. We now have to import names from Sage using the syntax `import sage.all`. We can then access Sage variables and functions with the following syntax:

```
sage.all.cos(direction * sage.all.pi / 180)
```

To understand why we have to do this, we have to know a little bit about namespaces and scope in Python. A *namespace* is a conceptual space that maps names to objects. A *scope* is a portion of a Python program in which names from a certain namespace are directly accessible. When working on the Sage command line, all of the built-in names (of classes, functions, instances, variables, and so on) are accessible. Our module has its own, separate namespace, so names that we take for granted on the command line aren't directly accessible in the module. Hence, we use the `import` statement to make all the standard Sage names available throughout our module. In fact, each time a function or class is defined, a new local namespace is created. That's why the names you create within a function definition are only visible within that function (and functions declared within that function). The technical aspects of namespaces and scoping are explained in the Python documentation.

Ideally, a Python package would be designed so that the user only has to import the sub-packages or modules that are required to use a subset of its functionality. However, the only way to use Sage names in a Python module (as of Sage version 4.6.1) is to `import sage.all`. There is no way to import a subset of Sage's functionality. Since Sage is rather large, we placed the import statement at the beginning of the class definition so that Sage is imported only once, when the `tank` module is loaded. If we placed the `import` statement in method `move`, it could potentially be imported more than once (although the Python interpreter tries to avoid this), slowing down the function call.

The second file is a script that imports the module and uses the classes to create and move a tank instance. We use the syntax `import tank` to import the module called **tank.py**. We can then use the syntax `tank.Tank` to access the `Tank` class from the `tank` module. We don't have to import any of the other classes, because we don't access them outside of the `tank` module. Note that we have also changed the name of the `tank` instance to `tank_1` so that it does not conflict with the module name. This makes it possible to use the command `reload(tank)` to reload the module (see tip).

`reload` the module after making changes

Let's say you created the module **tank.py** and used `import tank` to make its names available in a Sage script, or on the Sage command line. During testing, you found and fixed a bug, and saved the module file. However, Sage won't recognize that you changed anything unless you use the command `reload(tank)` to force it to reload the module. When working with multiple modules in a package, you may need to `import` a module on the command line (or in a worksheet cell) before reloading it.

Expanding our simulation to other kinds of vehicles

So far, we have defined a rudimentary framework for a simulation of tank combat. What if we want to include other types of military vehicles in our simulation, such as armored personnel carriers (APCs), armored cars, and supply trucks? We could define a class for each of those vehicles, but there would certainly be some duplication between the classes. For example, every vehicle class would need to define a method to get the vehicle position and move the vehicle. How can we avoid this duplication?

Time for action – creating a vehicle base class

We can avoid duplicating code in related classes by applying the object-oriented principle of inheritance. Inheritance allows a class to be derived from a base class. The derived class inherits the methods and attributes of the base class, and adds its own attributes and methods. This can be rather confusing, so we'll jump into a concrete example. Since tanks, APCs, armored cars, and trucks are all vehicles, we will create a base class for ground vehicles. Then, we will define derived classes to represent various types of vehicles. Enter the following code into a file called **vehicle.py**:

```
import sage.all

class Cannon():
    """Model of a large cannon."""

    def __init__(self, damage):
        """Create a Cannon instance
            Arguments:
                damage      Integer that represents
                    the damage inflicted by the cannon
        """
        # _damage   amount of damage inflicted by cannon (integer)
        # _operational  True if operational, False if disabled
        self._damage = damage
```

```
        self._operational = True

    def __str__(self):
        return 'Damage value:' + str(self._damage)

class Track():

    """Model of a continuous track."""

    def __init__(self):
        # _operational  True if operational, False if disabled
        self._operational = True

class Turret():

    """Model of a tank turret."""

    def __init__(self, gun):
        """Create a Turret instance
            Arguments:
                gun      instance of Gun class
        """
        # _gun   instance of Gun class
        # _operational  True if operational, False if disabled
        self._gun = gun
        self._operational = True

    def __str__(self):
        return(str(self._gun))

class Ground_Vehicle():
    """Base class for all ground vehicles"""
    def __init__(self, position):
        """Create a vehicle instance
                position    (x,y) tuple of coordinates
        """
        # Intialize position
        self._x = position[0]
        self._y = position[1]

    def move(self, direction, distance):
        """Move the tank.
            Arguments:
                direction   floating-point number representing
                    the compass angle of movement in degrees. North is
0,

                    east is 90, south is 180, and west is 270.
                    0 <= direction < 360
                distance        distance to move (in meters)
```

```
        """
        if (direction < 0) or (direction >= 360):
            print("Error: Direction must be greater than or equal \
to zero and less than 360.")
        elif distance < 0:
            print("Error: Negative distance.")
        else:
            self._x += sage.all.n(distance * sage.all.cos(direction *
sage.all.pi / 180))
            self._y += sage.all.n(distance * sage.all.sin(direction *
sage.all.pi / 180))

    def get_position(self):
        """Returns a tuple with the (x,y) coordinates of the tank's
        current location.
        """
        return (float(self._x), float(self._y))

class Tank(Ground_Vehicle):
    """Model of an armored fighting vehicle."""
    def __init__(self, armor_values, cannon_damage_value, position):
        """Constructs a tank instance
            Arguments:
                armor_values    A dictionary of armor values
                    of the form:
                    {'front' : 100, 'side' : 50, 'rear' : 25,
                        'turret' : 75}
                cannon_damage_value     Integer that represents
                    the damage inflicted by the main gun
                position    (x,y) tuple of coordinates
        """
        # Initialize armor
        self._frontal_armor = armor_values['front']
        self._left_armor = armor_values['side']
        self._right_armor = armor_values['side']
        self._rear_armor = armor_values['rear']
        self._turret_armor = armor_values['turret']

        # Add tank components
        main_gun = Cannon(cannon_damage_value)
        self._turret = Turret(main_gun)
        self._left_track = Track()
        self._right_track = Track()

        Ground_Vehicle.__init__(self, position)

    def __str__(self):
```

```
        import os
        ls = os.linesep
        description = 'Tank parameters:' + ls
        description += '  Armor values:' + ls
        description += '    Front:' + str(self._frontal_armor) + ls
        description += '    Left:' + str(self._left_armor) + ls
        description += '    Right:' + str(self._right_armor) + ls
        description += '    Rear:' + str(self._rear_armor) + ls
        description += '    Turret:' + str(self._turret_armor) + ls
        description += '  Weapons:' + ls
        description += '    Main cannon:' + ls
        description += '    ' + str(self._turret) + ls
        return description
```

Now, we need to modify the script that creates Tank instances so that the tank class is imported from the `vehicle` module instead of the `tank` module:

```
import vehicle

# Define parameters for the tank
armor_values = {'front' : 100, 'side' : 50, 'rear' : 25,
    'turret' : 75}
main_gun_damage = 50
initial_position = (0.0, 0.0)

# Create a tank object
tank_1 = vehicle.Tank(armor_values, main_gun_damage, initial_position)

pos = tank_1.get_position()
print("Initial position: x = {0:.2f}m  y = {1:.2f}m".format(pos[0],
pos[1]))

# Move 10m north
tank_1.move(0.0, 10.0)
pos = tank_1.get_position()
print("Current position: x = {0:.2f}m  y = {1:.2f}m".format(pos[0],
pos[1]))

# Now move 10m east
tank_1.move(90.0, 10.0)
pos = tank_1.get_position()
print("Current position: x = {0:.2f}m  y = {1:.2f}m".format(pos[0],
pos[1]))

# Move southwest, back to the origin
tank_1.move(225.0, sqrt(10.0**2 + 10.0**2))
pos = tank_1.get_position()
print("Current position: x = {0:.2f}m  y = {1:.2f}m".format(pos[0],
pos[1]))
```

```
# Try a move which doesn't make sense
tank_1.move(-2,-1)
```

When we run this script, we should get the same results as the previous example:

```
sage: load("4460_9_4.py")
Initial position: x = 0.00m  y = 0.00m
Current position: x = 10.00m  y = 0.00m
Current position: x = 10.00m  y = 10.00m
Current position: x = -0.00m  y = 0.00m
Error: Direction must be greater than or equal to zero and less than 360.
```

What just happened?

We created a base class called `Ground_Vehicle` to contain methods and attributes that are common to all ground vehicles. For now, every ground vehicle has a position that is stored as a pair of coordinates, a method to update the position, and a method that returns the current position. Since a vehicle has to have a defined position for movement to make any sense, the `__init__` method accepts one argument that sets the initial position.

The first line of the `Tank` class definition was modified to show that the class is derived from the class `Ground_Vehicle`:

```
class Tank(Ground_Vehicle):
```

Since the methods `move` and `get_position` are defined in `Ground_Vehicle`, we removed them from the `Tank` class definition. We say that `Tank` inherits these methods from `Ground_Vehicle`. We can also override inherited methods. For example, let's say that we have defined a class that represents a wheeled vehicle:

```
class Wheeled_Vehicle(Ground_Vehicle):
```

We want to implement a special version of the `move` method that reduces the mobility of wheeled vehicles when they travel off-road. If we define a method called `move` in the `Wheeled_Vehicle` class, it will override the `move` method defined in the base class.

We also made an important change in the `__init__` method of the `Tank` class. We used the following syntax to call the `__init__` method of the base class to set the initial position of the vehicle:

```
Ground_Vehicle.__init__(self, position)
```

You must explicitly call the `__init__` method of the base class (if it has one) from the `__init__` method of the derived class in order to properly initialize the object.

Note that we didn't have to make any changes in the code that creates `Tank` instances, aside from changing the name of the module we are importing. Changes to the class structure were transparent to the code that creates and uses `Tank` instances. A well-designed class implements an *interface*, and all interaction with the class takes place through the interface. If you improve the design of the class without changing its function, a process known as *refactoring*, the interface should not change. Although Python does not have a formal language element for defining interfaces, it's helpful to think in terms of interfaces when designing classes.

Creating a package for our simulation

A logical step in developing our simulation is to add derived classes for different types of vehicles. Before we do that, let's take a minute to improve the organization of the code by creating a package. A package is a collection of modules, organized in a tree of directories.

Time for action – creating a combat simulation package

Create a directory called **combatsim**. The name of the directory is the name of the package, so it should follow the Python naming conventions for packages. The name should use lower-case letters and should be as short as possible, in case someone wants to use your package on a system that doesn't support long names. Underscores are officially discouraged in package names, but don't be afraid to use them if it makes the package name easier to understand. Now, create a new file in the directory called **__init__.py**. Leave this file empty. It only needs to be present to tell the Python interpreter that this directory is a package.

In the directory **combatsim**, enter the following code in a file called **components.py**. Essentially, we're just going to cut and paste to place the definitions for the `Cannon`, `Track`, and `Turret` classes into their own files. We will repeat the process with the definitions of the classes `Ground_Vehicle` and `Tank`.

```
class Cannon():

    """Model of a large cannon."""

    def __init__(self, damage):
        """Create a Cannon instance
            Arguments:
                damage      Integer that represents
                    the damage inflicted by the cannon
        """
        # _damage   amount of damage inflicted by cannon (integer)
        # _operational  True if operational, False if disabled
        self._damage = damage
        self._operational = True

    def __str__(self):
```

```
        return 'Damage value:' + str(self._damage)

class Track():
    """Model of a continuous track."""
    def __init__(self):
        # _operational  True if operational, False if disabled
        self._operational = True

class Turret():
    """Model of a tank turret."""
    def __init__(self, gun):
        """Create a Turret instance
            Arguments:
                gun      instance of Gun class
        """
        # _gun   instance of Gun class
        # _operational  True if operational, False if disabled
        self._gun = gun
        self._operational = True

    def __str__(self):
        return(str(self._gun))
```

Now, create another file in the **combatsim** directory called **vehicle.py**, and enter the following code to define the `Ground_Vehicle` base class:

```
import sage.all

class Ground_Vehicle():
    """Base class for all ground vehicles"""
    def __init__(self, position):
        """Create a vehicle instance
                position    (x,y) tuple of coordinates
        """
        # Intialize position
        self._x = position[0]
        self._y = position[1]

    def move(self, direction, distance):
        """Move the tank.
            Arguments:
                direction   floating-point number representing
                    the compass angle of movement in degrees. North is
0,
                    east is 90, south is 180, and west is 270.
                    0 <= direction < 360
```

```
                distance        distance to move (in meters)
        """
        if (direction < 0) or (direction >= 360):
            print("Error: Direction must be greater than or equal \
to zero and less than 360.")
        elif distance < 0:
            print("Error: Negative distance.")
        else:
            self._x += sage.all.n(distance * sage.all.cos(direction *
sage.all.pi / 180))
            self._y += sage.all.n(distance * sage.all.sin(direction *
sage.all.pi / 180))

    def get_position(self):
        """Returns a tuple with the (x,y) coordinates of the tank's
        current location.
        """
        return (float(self._x), float(self._y))
```

Create another file in the **combatsim** directory called **tank.py**, and enter the following code:

```
import sage.all

class Ground_Vehicle():
    """Base class for all ground vehicles"""
    def __init__(self, position):
        """Create a vehicle instance
                position    (x,y) tuple of coordinates
        """
        # Intialize position
        self._x = position[0]
        self._y = position[1]

    def move(self, direction, distance):
        """Move the vehicle.
            Arguments:
                direction   floating-point number representing
                    the compass angle of movement in degrees. North
                    is 0, east is 90, south is 180, and west is 270.
                    0 <= direction < 360
                distance        distance to move (in meters)
        """
        if (direction < 0) or (direction > 360):
            print("Error: Direction must be greater than or equal \
to zero and less than 360.")
        elif distance < 0:
```

```
            print("Error: Negative distance.")
        else:
            self._x += sage.all.n(distance * sage.all.cos(direction *
                sage.all.pi / 180))
            self._y += sage.all.n(distance * sage.all.sin(direction *
                sage.all.pi / 180))

    def get_position(self):
        """Returns a tuple with the (x,y) coordinates of the tank's
        current location.
        """
        return (float(self._x), float(self._y))
```

Finally, we need to make a slight change in the code that creates instances of the Tank class. Enter the following code in a file that resides in the same directory as **combatsim**. When you are done, the file hierarchy should look like this:

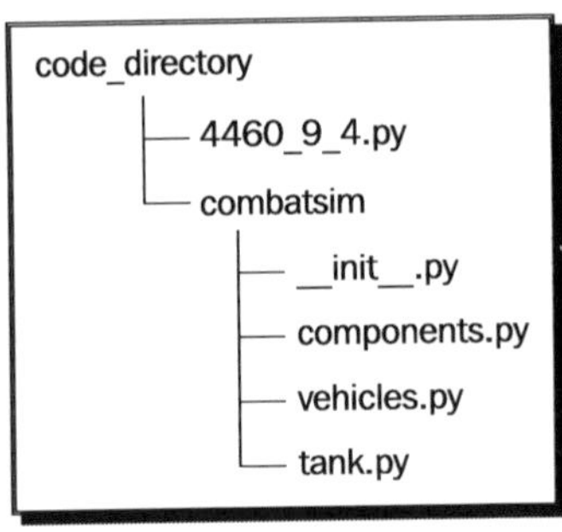


```
from combatsim import tank

# Define parameters for the tank
armor_values = {'front' : 100, 'side' : 50, 'rear' : 25,
    'turret' : 75}
main_gun_damage = 50
initial_position = (0.0, 0.0)

# Create a tank object
tank_1 = tank.Tank(armor_values, main_gun_damage, initial_position)

pos = tank_1.get_position()
print("Initial position: x = {0:.2f}m  y = {1:.2f}m".format(pos[0],
pos[1]))

# Move 10m north
tank_1.move(0.0, 10.0)
pos = tank_1.get_position()
print("Current position: x = {0:.2f}m  y = {1:.2f}m".format(pos[0],
pos[1]))
```

```
# Now move 10m east
tank_1.move(90.0, 10.0)
pos = tank_1.get_position()
print("Current position: x = {0:.2f}m  y = {1:.2f}m".format(pos[0],
pos[1]))

# Move southwest, back to the origin
tank_1.move(225.0, sqrt(10.0**2 + 10.0**2))
pos = tank_1.get_position()
print("Current position: x = {0:.2f}m  y = {1:.2f}m".format(pos[0],
pos[1]))

# Try a move which doesn't make sense
tank_1.move(-2,-1)
```

When you run the code, you should get the same results as before, if you have done everything right:

```
sage: load("4460_9_5.py")
Initial position: x = 0.00m  y = 0.00m
Current position: x = 10.00m  y = 0.00m
Current position: x = 10.00m  y = 10.00m
Current position: x = -0.00m  y = 0.00m
Error: Direction must be greater than or equal to zero and less than 360.
```

What just happened?

We have now split the example into four files. Class definitions reside in a package called **combatsim**, which contains the modules `components`, `vehicle`, and `tank`. The first line of the file **tank.py** is:

```
from components import *
```

This code imports all of the names from the module `components`. Since we are importing names from another module in the same package, and we created both modules, it's okay to use `import *`. In general, you should avoid using `import *` outside of these special circumstances. The reason is that two modules might define functions or classes with the same name. If you `import *` from several packages, you don't know which function or class you are actually using. For example, NumPy and Sage both define the `sin` function, but its behaviour is different. That is why we always `import numpy` and then access individual functions with the syntax `numpy.sin(x)`.

We also had to modify the `import` statements in the file that creates `Tank` instances. The line imports the name `Tank` from the module named `tank` in the package named **combatsim**:

```
from combatsim.tank import Tank
```

The syntax follows this pattern:

```
from package.module import name
```

The following line imports only the class `Ground_Vehicle` from the module called `vehicle`:

```
from vehicle import Ground_Vehicle
```

Importing only the classes you absolutely need makes your code much easier to debug and maintain than using `import *`. Now that we've gotten things organized, it's time to take advantage of our new base classes.

Have a go hero – adding another derived class

Using the Tank class as an example, add a derived class for another type of ground vehicle, such as an armored personnel carrier (APC). Create a new module in the **combatsim** package and use it to define your class. A typical APC is similar to a tank, with two tracks, an armored hull, and a gun turret. However, the APC also carries infantry, and the gun is typically a small-calibre, rapid-fire cannon. You'll need to add component class definitions in the file **components.py** to represent the automatic cannon and the cargo of infantry. Once you have a working APC class, try adding a cargo truck. Since trucks have four or six wheels instead of tracks, you'll have to add a component to represent the wheels.

Potential pitfalls when working with classes and instances

We've learned the general thought processes and the syntax needed to design our own classes, and organize them in modules and packages. In the following example, we're going to move away from our combat simulation and construct some simple test classes to further illustrate how Python classes work. The purpose of these examples is to demonstrate some behavior that may seem strange and cause your programs to behave in unexpected ways if you don't understand the underlying principles.

Time for action – using class and instance attributes

Enter the following code into a text file, or an input cell in a worksheet:

```
class Test():
    class_list = []
    def __init__(self):
        self.instance_list = []

instance_1 = Test()
instance_2 = Test()
instance_1.instance_list.append(1)
instance_2.instance_list.append(2)
print("Instance 1 instance_list:" + str(instance_1.instance_list))
print("Instance 2 instance_list:" + str(instance_2.instance_list))
print("Appending values to class_list:")
instance_1.class_list.append(3)
instance_2.class_list.append(4)
print("Instance 1 class_list:" + str(instance_1.class_list))
print("Instance 2 class_list:" + str(instance_2.class_list))
print("Adding new attributes:")
instance_1.new_list = [5,6]
instance_2.new_list = [7,8]
print("Instance 1 new list:" + str(instance_1.new_list))
print("Instance 2 new list:" + str(instance_2.new_list))
```

The output should look like this:

```
sage: load("4460_9_6.py")
Instance 1 instance_list:[1]
Instance 2 instance_list:[2]
Appending values to class_list:
Instance 1 class_list:[3, 4]
Instance 2 class_list:[3, 4]
Adding new attributes:
Instance 1 new list:[5, 6]
Instance 2 new list:[7, 8]
```

What just happened?

We defined a simple class called Test, which has two data attributes. instance_list is defined in the __init__ method, just like the instance attributes we've used in previous examples. class_list is defined outside of __init__, similar to the way in which methods are defined. This makes class_list a *class attribute*. We then created two instances of the class and performed some experiments with the attributes.

We appended a different number to each of the instance lists, and printed the contents of the list. Because each instance gets its own copy of an instance attribute, each list contains a single value. When we appended numbers to the class_list attribute, the results were very different. The reason is that there is only one copy of a class attribute, which is shared by all instances of that class. Appending a number to the class_list attribute of instance_1 is exactly the same as appending a number to the class_list attribute of instance_2, since both operations work on the same list! Finally, we added a new attribute called new_list to each instance. Attributes that are added after an instance is created are instance attributes, as we can see by their behavior.

Time for action – more about class and instance attributes

Enter the following code into a text file, or an input cell in a worksheet:

```
class Test2():
    value1 = 5

    def method1(self):
        return 'Old Method '
instance_1 = Test2()
instance_2 = Test2()
print("Instance 1, value1 = " + str(instance_1.value1))
print("Instance 2, value1 = " + str(instance_2.value1))
print("Changing value1:")
instance_1.value1 = 6
print("Instance 1, value1 = " + str(instance_1.value1))
print("Instance 2, value1 = " + str(instance_2.value1))
print("Instance 1, method1: " + instance_1.method1())
print("Instance 2, method1: " + instance_2.method1())
def new_method():
    return 'New Method'
print("Adding a new method:")
instance_1.method1 = new_method
print("Instance 1, method1: " + instance_1.method1())
print("Instance 2, method1: " + instance_2.method1())
```

The output should look like this:

```
sage: load("4460_9_7.py")
Instance 1, value1 = 5
Instance 2, value1 = 5
Changing value1:
Instance 1, value1 = 6
Instance 2, value1 = 5
Instance 1, method1: Old Method
Instance 2, method1: Old Method
Adding a new method:
Instance 1, method1: New Method
Instance 2, method1: Old Method
```

What just happened?

This example demonstrates some of the more subtle aspects of class and instance attributes. Class `Test2` has a class data member called `value1` which happens to be an integer. Initially, both instances reported the same value for `value1`. We then used the following statement to assign a new value to `value1`:

```
instance_1.value1 = 6
```

However, when we printed the value from both instances, we got different numbers, even though `value1` was defined as a class attribute. This happens because the statement above replaces the class attribute `value1` with an instance attribute called `value1`. `instance_1` now has its own instance attribute called `value1`, while `instance_2` has a class attribute called `value1`. Recall that in the previous example, the class attribute was a list, and we appended data to the list. This modifies the existing list, rather than replacing it, so it remains a class attribute.

We then demonstrated that class methods follow the same rules as class attributes. All instances of a class share the same methods. We can define a new function and use it to replace an existing method (or add a new method, if we give it a new name). The same rules apply to methods as to attributes. The new method becomes an attribute method, and it is only attached to `instance_1`.

Creating empty classes and functions

There are two circumstances where it is advantageous to define a class without adding any attributes or methods. One is during the initial stage of coding a module or package, when you want to define a class or a function as a "placeholder" or a "stub" and fill it in later. The other is when you need a class to act like a `struct` in C or a `record` in Pascal. Let's look at an example to see how empty classes and functions work.

Time for action – creating empty classes and functions

Enter the following code into a text file, or an input cell in a worksheet:

```
# Create an empty class to use as a data structure
class Struct():
    pass

# Use pass to define empty methods
class VTOL():
    """Class to represent airborne vehicles with VTOL
    (Vertical Take-Off/Landing) capabilities, such as
    helicopters, tilt-rotors, and Harrier jump jets.
    """
    def __init__(self):
        pass

    def move(self, horizontal_angle, vertical_angle, distance):
        pass

data_container = Struct()

data_container.name = "String data"
data_container.count = 14
data_container.remainder = 0.1037

print(data_container.name)
print(data_container.count)
print(data_container.remainder)
```

The output should look like this:

```
sage:  load 4460_9_8.py
String data
14
0.1037
```

What just happened?

If you attempt to define a function or a class with no indented code following it, the Python interpreter will give you an error message. The `pass` keyword allows us to define empty classes and functions. We defined an empty class called `Struct` and created an instance, and then added instance attributes. This is a convenient shortcut when you need to group some different data types together (a dictionary is another option).

We also defined a "skeleton" class that could potentially be added to the `vehicles` module in our **combatsim** package. We used the `pass` keyword to define empty methods. This is a good strategy to use when you are designing a class. Think about all the methods you want to add, and what arguments they will need. If you don't have time to implement them all right away, use the `pass` keyword to define empty methods so that you don't forget about them. It's even better if you add a docstring to each empty method, to describe what it's supposed to do.

Handling errors gracefully

Your programs are eventually going to have errors. Generally, errors fall into two categories: errors in the design of the program logic (bugs), and errors that happen when the code is used incorrectly. The first type of error can be minimized with thoughtful program design, and caught by thorough testing (described in the next section). Errors of the second kind are almost guaranteed to happen. An integer will be passed where a float is expected, a denominator will approach zero, or there won't be enough lines in a data file. In Python, these runtime errors are called *exceptions*, to distinguish them from syntax errors that will prevent a program from running. We can easily generate a few examples on the command line. Here's a `TypeError` exception, which occurs when something has the wrong type:

```
sage: sin("one")
---------------------------------------------------------------------------
TypeError                                 Traceback (most recent call last)


/Users/cfinch/Documents/Articles/Sage Math/Chapters/Chapter 9/
Code/<ipython console> in <module>()


/Applications/sage/local/lib/python2.6/site-packages/sage/symbolic/
function.so in sage.symbolic.function.GinacFunction.__call__ (sage/
symbolic/function.cpp:6572)()


/Applications/sage/local/lib/python2.6/site-packages/sage/symbolic/
function.so in sage.symbolic.function.Function.__call__ (sage/symbolic/
function.cpp:4336)()
```

```
TypeError: cannot coerce arguments: no canonical coercion from <type
'str'> to Symbolic Ring
```

And here's a `ZeroDivisionError` exception, which is self-explanatory:

```
sage: 1/0
---------------------------------------------------------------------------
ZeroDivisionError                         Traceback (most recent call last)

/Users/cfinch/Documents/Articles/Sage Math/Chapters/Chapter 9/
Code/<ipython console> in <module>()

/Applications/sage/local/lib/python2.6/site-packages/sage/structure/
element.so in sage.structure.element.RingElement.__div__ (sage/structure/
element.c:11973)()

/Applications/sage/local/lib/python2.6/site-packages/sage/rings/integer.
so in sage.rings.integer.Integer._div_ (sage/rings/integer.c:11163)()

/Applications/sage/local/lib/python2.6/site-packages/sage/rings/integer_
ring.so in sage.rings.integer_ring.IntegerRing_class._div (sage/rings/
integer_ring.c:5022)()

ZeroDivisionError: Rational division by zero
```

Exceptions don't have to cause the program to come to a sudden halt and spew out incomprehensible error codes to the user. Python provides tools for customizing and handling exceptions that help us manage runtime errors.

Time for action – raising and handling exceptions

Let's go back to the combat simulation example. We wrote code that printed an error message when the `move` method received invalid arguments. We will rewrite the error-handling code to use exceptions. Replace the contents of the file **vehicle.py** in the **combatsim** package with the following code:

```
import sage.all

class Ground_Vehicle():
    """Base class for all ground vehicles"""
    def __init__(self, position):
        """Create a vehicle instance
```

```
                position    (x,y) tuple of coordinates
        """
        # Intialize position
        self._x = position[0]
        self._y = position[1]

    def move(self, direction, distance):
        """Move the vehicle.
            Arguments:
                direction   floating-point number representing
                    the compass angle of movement in degrees. North is
0,
                    east is 90, south is 180, and west is 270.
                    0 <= direction < 360
                distance        distance to move (in meters)
        """
        if (direction < 0) or (direction >= 360):
            raise ValueError("Error: Direction must be greater \
than or equal to zero and less than 360.")
        if distance < 0:
            raise ValueError("Error: Distance must be >= 0.")
        self._x += sage.all.n(distance * sage.all.cos(direction *
            sage.all.pi / 180))
        self._y += sage.all.n(distance * sage.all.sin(direction *
            sage.all.pi / 180))

    def get_position(self):
        """Returns a tuple with the (x,y) coordinates of the tank's
        current location.
        """
        return (float(self._x), float(self._y))
```

Enter the following code into a Python file in the same directory as **combatsim**:

```
from combatsim import tank
# Define parameters for the tank
armor_values = {'front' : 100, 'side' : 50, 'rear' : 25,
    'turret' : 75}
main_gun_damage = 50
initial_position = (0.0, 0.0)
# Create a tank object
tank_1 = tank.Tank(armor_values, main_gun_damage, initial_position)
pos = tank_1.get_position()
```

```
print("Initial position: x = {0:.2f}m  y = {1:.2f}m".format(pos[0],
pos[1]))

# Move 10m north
try:
    tank_1.move(0.0, 10.0)
except ValueError as error:
    print(error.args[0])
else:
    pos = tank_1.get_position()
    print("Current position: x = {0:.2f}m  y = {1:.2f}
m".format(pos[0], pos[1]))

# Try invalid direction
try:
    tank_1.move(361, 10.0)
except ValueError as error:
    print(error.args[0])
else:
    pos = tank_1.get_position()
    print("Current position: x = {0:.2f}m  y = {1:.2f}
m".format(pos[0], pos[1]))

# Try invalid distance
try:
    tank_1.move(90, -1.0)
except ValueError as error:
    print(error.args[0])
else:
    pos = tank_1.get_position()
    print("Current position: x = {0:.2f}m  y = {1:.2f}
m".format(pos[0], pos[1]))
```

The results should look like this:

```
sage: load("4460_9_9.py")
Initial position: x = 0.00m  y = 0.00m
Current position: x = 10.00m  y = 0.00m
Error: Direction must be greater than or equal to zero and less than 360.
Error: Distance must be >= 0.
```

What just happened?

We modified the `move` method in the `Ground_Vehicle` class so that it raises an exception when it encounters an invalid argument. An exception is an object that gets passed up the chain of calling functions until it gets handled or causes the program to terminate. When an exception is raised, execution stops and the exception is immediately passed to the calling code. For example, if the `direction` argument to the move `method` is invalid, an exception will be raised and the value of `distance` will not be checked. The following syntax raises an exception:

```
raise ExceptionType(args)
```

There are many types of pre-defined exceptions, which we'll describe soon. In this case, we chose the `ValueError` exception, since we are checking for invalid values of the arguments. `ValueError` exceptions accept a single optional argument, which is a string that describes the error in more detail.

The general syntax for handling exceptions looks like this:

```
try:
    statement 1
    statement 2
     ...
except ExceptionType1 as error:
    handle exception
except ExceptionType2:
    handle exception
else:
    statements
finally:
     clean up
```

To handle exceptions raised by one or more statements, enclose the statements in a `try` block. After the `try` block, enclose exception-handling code in one or more `except` blocks. If you want access to the exception object, you can use the following syntax which assigns the name `error` to the exception object:

```
except ExceptionType1 as error:
```

We can then access a tuple containing the exception's arguments with `error.args`. Since this exception has a single string argument, we printed the value of the first argument in the tuple. You can handle multiple exception types with the following syntax:

```
except (ExceptionType1, ExceptionType2) as error:
```

The `else` keyword is used to indicate code that should only be executed if there is no exception. In this example, we only want to print the position of the tank if it has changed. We only want to print the location if there is no exception and the tank moves, so we placed the `print` function in the `else` clause. You can also include a `finally` clause, which is a good place to put clean-up statements like closing open files. The code in a `finally` clause will be executed whether or not an exception is raised.

Using exceptions has improved our simulation in several ways. The classes defined in the **combatsim** package no longer rely on the `print` function to pass error messages to the user. This makes the package much more flexible. If the combat simulator is eventually used with a graphical user interface, printing error messages to the terminal won't be very effective. Handling exceptions also allows the code to continue running after an exception occurs. If we didn't handle exceptions, execution would have stopped the first time `move` was called with invalid arguments.

Exception types

The following exceptions are built in to Python. Try to raise the most appropriate error to inform your users what the problem is. More information on any exception type can be found using the Sage help system, or the Python documentation.

AssertionError	KeyError	RuntimeError	UnicodeDecodeError
AttributeError	KeyboardInterrupt	StopIteration	UnicodeTranslateError
EOFError	MemoryError	SyntaxError	ValueError
FloatingPointError	NameError	SystemExit	VMSError
GeneratorExit	NotImplementedError	TypeError	WindowsError
IOError	OSError	UnboundLocalError	ZeroDivisionError
ImportError	OverflowError	UnicodeError	
IndexError	ReferenceError	UnicodeEncodeError	

Have a go hero – raising exceptions in the __init__ method of Tank

In a previous exercise, you were asked to check for valid arguments in the `__init__` method of the `Tank` class. While this was good practice, it wasn't very practical, because the instance was created even if you caught an error. Now, modify the `__init__` method again to raise exceptions when errors are found.

Creating your own exception types

You can also create your own exception types by defining an exception class that is derived from one of the existing exception types. This is handy when you want to distinguish categories of errors that are unique to your program.

Time for action – creating custom exception types

We will finally give our tanks the ability to fire their cannons. Adding a `fire` method means that we will need to raise exceptions related to cannon fire, in addition to exceptions that come from movement. To handle this situation, we will define custom error classes. Create a file called **exceptions.py** in the **combatsim** directory and enter the following code:

```
class CombatsimError(Exception):
    """Base class for exceptions generated by combatsim"""

    def __init__(self, value):
        """Create a CombatsimError exception.
        Arguments:
            value   String describing the error
        """
        Exception.__init__(self, value)

class MoveError(CombatsimError):
    def __init__(self, value):
        CombatsimError.__init__(self,value)

class ShootError(CombatsimError):
    def __init__(self, value):
        CombatsimError.__init__(self,value)
```

Enter the following code in **vehicle.py** in the **combatsim** directory:

```
import sage.all
from exceptions import *

class Ground_Vehicle():
    """Base class for all ground vehicles"""
    def __init__(self, position):
        """Create a vehicle instance
                position    (x,y) tuple of coordinates
        """
        # Intialize position
        self._x = position[0]
        self._y = position[1]

    def move(self, direction, distance):
        """Move the vehicle.
```

```
            Arguments:
                direction   floating-point number representing
                    the compass angle of movement in degrees. North is
0,
                    east is 90, south is 180, and west is 270.
                    0 <= direction < 360
                distance        distance to move (in meters)
        """
        if (direction < 0) or (direction >= 360):
            raise MoveError("Error: Direction must be greater \
than or equal to zero and less than 360.")
        if distance < 0:
            raise MoveError("Error: Distance must be >= 0.")

        self._x += sage.all.n(distance * sage.all.cos(direction *
            sage.all.pi / 180))
        self._y += sage.all.n(distance * sage.all.sin(direction *
            sage.all.pi / 180))

    def get_position(self):
        """Returns a tuple with the (x,y) coordinates of the tank's
        current location.
        """
        return (float(self._x), float(self._y))
```

Enter the following code in **tank.py** in the **combatsim** directory:

```
from components import *
from exceptions import *
from vehicle import Ground_Vehicle

class Tank(Ground_Vehicle):
    """Model of an armored fighting vehicle."""
    def __init__(self, armor_values, cannon_damage_value, position):
        """Constructs a tank instance
            Arguments:
                armor_values    A dictionary of armor values
                    of the form:
                    {'front' : 100, 'side' : 50, 'rear' : 25,
                        'turret' : 75}
                cannon_damage_value     Integer that represents
                    the damage inflicted by the main gun
                position    (x,y) tuple of coordinates
        """
        # Initialize armor
        self._frontal_armor = armor_values['front']
```

```
        self._left_armor = armor_values['side']
        self._right_armor = armor_values['side']
        self._rear_armor = armor_values['rear']
        self._turret_armor = armor_values['turret']

        # Add tank components
        main_gun = Cannon(cannon_damage_value)
        self._turret = Turret(main_gun)
        self._left_track = Track()
        self._right_track = Track()

        Ground_Vehicle.__init__(self, position)

    def __str__(self):
        import os
        ls = os.linesep
        description = 'Tank parameters:' + ls
        description += '  Armor values:' + ls
        description += '    Front:' + str(self._frontal_armor) + ls
        description += '    Left:' + str(self._left_armor) + ls
        description += '    Right:' + str(self._right_armor) + ls
        description += '    Rear:' + str(self._rear_armor) + ls
        description += '    Turret:' + str(self._turret_armor) + ls
        description += '  Weapons:' + ls
        description += '    Main cannon:' + ls
        description += '    ' + str(self._turret) + ls
        return description

    def fire(self, direction, elevation):
        """ Fire the cannon.
            Arguments:
            direction   degrees, 0 <= direction < 360
            elevation   degrees, 0 <= direction < 90
        """
        if (direction < 0) or (direction >= 360):
            raise ShootError("Error: Firing direction must be \
greater than or equal to zero and less than 360.")
        if (elevation < 0) or (elevation >= 90):
            raise ShootError("Error: Firing elevation must be \
greater than or equal to zero and less than 90.")

        print "Bang!"
```

Enter the following code in a new Python file in the same directory as **combatsim**:

```
from combatsim import tank
import combatsim.exceptions as ex
# Define parameters for the tank
armor_values = {'front' : 100, 'side' : 50, 'rear' : 25,
    'turret' : 75}
main_gun_damage = 50
initial_position = (0.0, 0.0)
# Create a tank object
tank_1 = tank.Tank(armor_values, main_gun_damage, initial_position)
pos = tank_1.get_position()
print("Initial position: x = {0:.2f}m  y = {1:.2f}m".format(pos[0],
pos[1]))
# Move 10m north
try:
    tank_1.move(0.0, 10.0)
except ex.MoveError as error:
    print(error)
else:
    pos = tank_1.get_position()
    print("Current position: x = {0:.2f}m  y = {1:.2f}
m".format(pos[0], pos[1]))
# Valid arguments to fire method
try:
    tank_1.fire(325,24)
except ex.ShootError as error:
    print(error.args[0])
# Invalid arguments to fire method
try:
    tank_1.fire(325,-1)
except ex.CombatsimError as error:
    print(error.args[0])
# Invalid arguments to move and fire methods
try:
    tank_1.move(-1,1)
    tank_1.fire(325,97)
except (ValueError, ex.ShootError) as error:
    print("Firing error.")
    print(error.args[0])
except ex.MoveError as error:
    print("Movement error:")
    print(error.args[0])
```

The results should look like this:

```
sage: load("4460_9_10.py")
Initial position: x = 0.00m  y = 0.00m
Current position: x = 10.00m  y = 0.00m
Bang!
Error: Firing elevation must be greater than or equal to zero and less
than 90.
Movement error:
Error: Direction must be greater than or equal to zero and less than 360.
```

What just happened?

We added a new module called `exceptions` to the **combatsim** package. This module defines a base class called `CombatsimError`, which is derived from the Python base class `Exception`. In general, custom exceptions are derived from `Exception`. We then derived two new classes, `MoveError` and `ShootError`, which are derived from `CombatsimError`. It is convention to create a custom base class for all exceptions raised by a module or package, and to use the word "Error" when naming exception classes.

We added one line at the top of **vehicle.py** to import all of the new exception definitions. Remember that, in general, it is best to avoid the syntax `import *`. In this case, we are importing names from another module within the same package, so it is unlikely that names will conflict. We changed the `move` method so that it raises a `MoveError` exception, instead of a `ValueError` exception, if either of the parameters is invalid. We also `import` the new exception classes in **tank.py**, and we added a method called `fire`. This method accepts two arguments, `direction` and `elevation`, which are the compass direction (in degrees) in which the cannon is pointing and the elevation of the gun above horizontal (in degrees), respectively. For simplicity, we assume that the elevation must be greater than or equal to 0 degrees and less than 90 degrees. If either the direction or elevation is incorrect, the method raises a `ShootError` exception.

In the file **4460_9_10.py**, we `import` the module containing our custom exception classes. Each `try` block that contains a call to the `move` method now catches exceptions of the `MoveError` class. We added a `try` block containing a call to the new `fire` method, which catches exceptions of type `ShootError`. We also called the `fire` method inside a `try` block that catches errors of the exception base class, `CombatsimError`. This works because `ShootError` is derived from `CombatsimError`, and the exception handler for a base class will also handle any derived exceptions.

Finally, we called both the `move` method and the `fire` method in the same `try` block. We use two `except` statements to catch two different exception classes and handle them differently. This is a good reason to define your own exception classes—if we had just raised `ValueError` exceptions, we would have had no way to know where an exception came from (other than looking at its argument). Note that the output only shows a `MoveError`, even though the call to `tank.fire` would have produced an error as well (elevation > 90). Because the `move` method raised an exception, the interpreter skipped directly to the `except` block, ignoring the rest of the statements in the `try` block.

Tips for using exceptions correctly

The whole idea of using exceptions is to make it easier to identify and handle specific runtime errors in your programs. You defeat the purpose of using exceptions if you place too many lines of code in a `try` block, because then it's hard to tell which statement raised the exception. It's also a bad idea to have a bare `except:` statement that doesn't specify the exception type that is being caught. This syntax will catch any type of exception, including `SystemExit` and `KeyboardInterrupt` exceptions, making it hard to terminate a misbehaving program. It's also considered bad practice to catch an exception without properly handling it, as this practice can mask errors.

Unit testing

As object-oriented programs get larger and more complicated, debugging can become more difficult. Unit testing is a paradigm for verifying and validating software. A unit is the smallest part of the program that can be tested, such as an individual function or method. Unit testing is the practice of testing each individual unit, by itself, to ensure that it responds correctly. Python has a package in the standard library called `unittest` to help you implement unit tests for your code.

Time for action – creating unit tests for the Tank class

Let's see how `unittest` can help us test the Tank class. Enter the following code into a text file in the same directory as the **combatsim** package:

```
import combatsim
import combatsim.exceptions as ex
import unittest

class TestTank(unittest.TestCase):
    """Tests for the combatsim package."""

    def setUp(self):
        """Called before EACH test is run."""
        # Define parameters for the tank
```

```
        armor_values = {'front' : 100, 'side' : 50, 'rear' : 25,
            'turret' : 75}
        main_gun_damage = 50
        initial_position = (0.0, 0.0)

        # Create a tank object
        self.tank = combatsim.tank.Tank(armor_values, main_gun_damage,
initial_position)

    def test_get_position(self):
        """Test method get_position"""
        position = self.tank.get_position()
        self.assertEqual(position, (0.0, 0.0))

    def test_move(self):
        """Test method move"""
        self.tank.move(0, 1)
        position = self.tank.get_position()
        self.assertEqual(position, (1, 0))

    def test_move_arg1(self):
        """Test method move, arg 1 invalid"""
        self.assertRaises(ex.MoveError, self.tank.move, 360, 1)

    def test_move_arg2(self):
        """Test method move, arg 2 invalid"""
        self.assertRaises(ex.MoveError, self.tank.move, 159, -1)

    def test_fire(self):
        """Test method fire.  This test is designed to FAIL \
so you can see what a failed test looks like."""
        result = self.tank.fire(90,30)
        self.assertEqual(result, True)

suite = unittest.TestLoader().loadTestsFromTestCase(TestTank)
unittest.TextTestRunner(verbosity=2).run(suite)
```

Run the script. You should get output like this:

```
sage: load("4460_9_11.py")
Test method fire.  This test is designed to FAIL so you can see what a
failed test looks like. ... Bang!
FAIL
Test method get_position ... ok
Test method move ... ok
Test method move, arg 1 invalid ... ok
```

```
Test method move, arg 2 invalid ... ok

======================================================================
FAIL: Test method fire.  This test is designed to FAIL so you can see
what a failed test looks like.
----------------------------------------------------------------------
Traceback (most recent call last):
  File "./4460_9_11.py", line 42, in test_fire
    self.assertEqual(result, True)
AssertionError: None != True

----------------------------------------------------------------------
Ran 5 tests in 0.006s

FAILED (failures=1)
```

What just happened?

We started out by importing the `Tank` class from `combatsim.tank` and importing the `combatsim.exceptions` module, just like we did before. We also imported the `unittest` module. We created a class called `TestTank`, which is derived from `unittest.TestCase`, for the purpose of testing the `Tank` class. Each of the methods of `TestTank` tests a specific feature of the Tank class. However, we need to create an instance of the Tank class before we can start testing. The method called `setUp` is called before each test is run. If we had to do some cleanup (such as closing a file or a database connection) after each test, we would have placed this code in a method called `tearDown`.

Each test method has a docstring that explains what it does. The docstring is especially important for test methods because it is used to document the result of the test. The method `test_get_position` starts by calling the `get_position` method of a `Tank` instance created by `setUp`. The next statement uses `assertEqual` to check that the position returned by `get_position` matches the position specified in `setUp`. This is all you have to do—the rest is handled automatically by `unittest`. The next method, `test_move`, works in a similar way.

The methods `test_move_arg1` and `test_move_arg2` are somewhat different. These methods intentionally cause the `move` method to raise an exception by passing invalid arguments. The syntax for this is slightly different. The `assertRaises` method takes three arguments: the name of the exception that should be raised, the method to be tested, and any arguments for the method to be tested. In this case, the arguments are two numbers that represent direction and distance. I also included a method called `test_fire`, which fails because the fire method doesn't really do anything. This method was included so that you can see what happens when a test fails. Notice that the test method docstring is printed to help you understand which test failed.

The final two lines of the example are shortcuts to help us create a test suite and run the tests. The following statement creates a test suite called `suite`:

```
suite = unittest.TestLoader().loadTestsFromTestCase(TestTank)
```

The following line calls the `run` method of a class called `TextTestRunner` that comes with `unittest`:

```
unittest.TextTestRunner(verbosity=2).run(suite)
```

This class provides a simple text interface that runs the tests and prints the results.

This short example demonstrates only the most basic features of `unittest`. Look at the `unittest` documentation to get an idea of what it can do to help you test larger and more complex packages. There are more `assert` methods to handle various types of output from the methods you are testing. Here is a list of the assert methods available in Python 2.6; even more are available in Python 2.7 and higher:

assertTrue(expr)	Test fails if `expr` is False
assertEqual(first, second)	Test fails if `first` is not equal to `second`
assertNotEqual(first, second)	Test fails if `first` is equal to `second`
assertAlmostEqual(first, second, [,places])	Test fails if the difference between `first` and `second` is greater than `places` decimal places (default 7)
assertNotAlmostEqual(first, second[,places])	Test fails if the difference between `first` and `second` is smaller than `places` decimal places (default 7)
assertRaises(exception, callable [,args])	Test fails unless `exception` is raised by `callable` (with optional `args` passed to `callable`)
assertFalse(expr)	Test fails if `expr` is True

Strategies for unit testing

Defining unit tests requires careful thought and a fair amount of judgement. It's impossible, or at least highly impractical, to test every possible execution path in most programs. Before writing tests, the developer should think about the intended use of the code and refer back to the requirements that may have been defined before the code was written. The following are some suggestions for unit tests:

- Boundary (or edge) cases test how the code performs when one of its parameters reaches an extreme value
- A corner case tests what happens when all of the parameters take on extreme values
- Branch testing attempts to test all branches of the source code at least once
- Exception tests check to make sure that exceptions are raised and handled properly
- Run the code with a set of fixed inputs to ensure that it reproduces known results (such as published results)
- Randomly generate valid inputs and run the code to see if certain combinations of parameters lead to an error

For some types of tests, such as corner cases, the author of the code is the best person to write the test. On large projects, unit tests are often written by someone other than the author of the code. The tests are written to cover the requirements that were defined for the software. This approach has the advantage that the tests may uncover assumptions that were made by the person who wrote the code.

If you have written some code that you would like to have included in the Sage library, you will have to become familiar with the testing standards of the Sage project. The Sage project uses a type of testing called doctesting to ensure quality. The docstring for each function or module is written in a special format that includes a section with examples. Doctesting automatically searches for examples in the docstring (hence the name), runs them, and verifies that the results are correct. More information about doctesting Sage modules and the conventions for writing docstrings is available at:

`http://www.sagemath.org/doc/developer/doctesting.html`

`http://www.sagemath.org/doc/developer/conventions.html`

Have a go hero – creating some unit tests

Define two methods to verify that the `fire` method of the `Tank` class raises the right exception when invalid arguments are passed to the method. Use `test_move_arg1` as an example.

Summary

This chapter introduced you to the principles of object-oriented programming. You have learned how to create classes in Python, and how to use them to organize your code. We also touched on some general software engineering principles, including the concept of unit testing. Specifically, we:

- Defined classes to represent an armoured fighting vehicle
- Used inheritance to represent other types of military vehicles
- Organized the class definitions into modules
- Created a package to contain our modules
- Learned how to handle exceptions
- Defined our own exceptions specific to the Vehicle and Tank classes
- Created unit tests to make sure our classes are working correctly

Now, we'll move on to some advanced techniques to help you get the most out of Sage.

10

Where to go from here

The previous chapters have introduced you to many aspects of Sage. This chapter contains a collection of topics that you may find useful after you have become familiar with the basics of Sage. Specifically, we will learn how to:

- Export equations as PNG and PDF files
- Export vector graphics and typeset mathematical expressions for inclusion in LaTeX documents
- Use LaTeX to document Sage worksheets
- Speed up collision detection using NumPy vector operations and Cython
- Create a Python script that uses Sage functionality
- Create interactive graphical examples in the notebook interface

Let's get started.

Typesetting equations with LaTeX

Sage makes it easy to document and publish mathematical results with a document mark-up language called LaTeX. The TeX typesetting system is used to process LaTeX files to create documents, in much the same way that web browsers parse HTML documents to create web pages. A plain text file containing LaTeX markup is passed to the TeX processor. The processor parses the source file, includes graphics from other files, and produces a vector graphics file in a format such as DVI (Device Independent), Postscript, or PDF. Other types of documents can also be created. Many publishers of mathematical and scientific books and journals encourage authors to submit their work as LaTeX files, and some journals require authors to use it. Both TeX and LaTeX are available under open-source licenses. LaTeX requires an entire book of its own; this section will only give you the bare minimum of information you need to use LaTeX with Sage. Sage does not include LaTeX, so we will start by installing LaTeX.

Installing LaTeX

In order for the following examples to run, you need to have LaTeX installed on your system. If you are building Sage from source, it is recommended that you install LaTeX before building Sage. For UNIX operating systems like Solaris and OpenSolaris, and UNIX-like systems such as Linux, install the TeX Live distribution. If it is not available through your distribution's package manager, it can be downloaded directly from `http://www.tug.org/texlive/`. For OS X, install MacTeX, which is based on TeX Live. MacTex can be found at `http://www.tug.org/mactex/`.

You can install TeX on Windows, but Sage will not be able to access it because Sage runs in a Linux virtual machine. You will have to install a Linux version of TeX within the virtual machine. If you simply want to run TeX on Windows, try MiKTeX (`http://www.miktex.org/`). proTeXt (`http://www.tug.org/protext/`) is another distribution for Windows that is based on MiKTeX and includes some additional tools.

First, let's verify that the basic tools are installed. The following commands can be entered on the command line, or in an input cell in a worksheet. The results will vary, depending on which operating system you are using. On OS X, you will see:

```
sage: print latex.engine()
latex
sage: print sage.misc.viewer.viewer()
sage-open
sage: print sage.misc.viewer.pdf_viewer()
sage-native-execute sage-open
sage: print sage.misc.viewer.dvi_viewer()
sage-native-execute sage-open
```

The first line shows that an external LaTeX processor is available, and will be used as the engine for processing LaTeX. The next three lines show that sage-open will be used to view both PDF and DVI files. This means that the default applications for OS X will be used to open PDF and DVI files. On Ubuntu Linux (or Windows, since Sage runs in a Linux virtual machine), you will see:

```
sage: print latex.engine()
latex
sage: print sage.misc.viewer.viewer()
xdg-open
sage: print sage.misc.viewer.pdf_viewer()
sage-native-execute xdg-open
sage: print sage.misc.viewer.dvi_viewer()
sage-native-execute xdg-open
```

OpenSolaris:

```
sage: print latex.engine()
latex
sage: print sage.misc.viewer.viewer()
xdg-open
sage: print sage.misc.viewer.pdf_viewer()
sage-native-execute xdg-open
sage: print sage.misc.viewer.dvi_viewer()
sage-native-execute xdg-open
sage: print sage.misc.viewer.pdf_viewer()
sage-native-execute xdg-open
```

If you have set the SAGE_BROWSER environment variable to force Sage to use a particular web browser, you might have trouble viewing PDF or DVI files in an external viewer. If this occurs, unset SAGE_BROWSER, and change the default web browser for your operating system so that Sage will use the correct browser.

Time for action – PDF output from the notebook interface

Enter the following code into an input cell in a worksheet, and evaluate the cell.

```
var('n,x,t')
J_n(n,x) = 1/pi*integral(cos(n*t-x*sin(t)), t)
J_n
show(J_n)
view(J_n)
view(J_n, mode='display'))
```

You should see the following results in your worksheet:

$$(n,x) \mapsto \frac{\int_0^{\pi} \cos(-nt + x\sin(t))\, dt}{\pi}$$

$$(n,x) \mapsto \frac{\int_0^{\pi} \cos(-nt+x\sin(t))\, dt}{\pi}$$

$$(n,x) \mapsto \frac{\int_0^{\pi} \cos(-nt + x\sin(t))\, dt}{\pi}$$

Let's say you want to generate a PDF file. Enter the following code after evaluating the code from the first example:

```
restore('i'))
J_n_2(n, x) = 1 / (2 * pi) * integral(exp(-i * (n * t - x * sin(t))),
t, -pi, pi)
view([J_n, J_n_2], title='Representations of the Bessel function',,
sep='\hrule', viewer='pdf', mode='display')
```

You will not see any output in the worksheet. Instead, the external viewer should open a new window with a PDF file that contains the following content:

Representations of the Bessel function

$$(n,x) \mapsto \frac{\int_0^{\pi} \cos(-nt + x\sin(t))\, dt}{\pi}$$

$$(n,x) \mapsto \frac{\int_{-\pi}^{\pi} e^{(-i\,nt + i\,x\sin(t))}\, dt}{2\,\pi}$$

If you only want to output a single equation as a PDF file, rather than an entire page, try this:

```
view(J_n, viewer='pdf', tightpage=True, mode='display')
```

The results should look like this:

$$(n, x) \mapsto \frac{\int_0^{\pi} \cos(-nt + x\sin(t))\, dt}{\pi}$$

Now, try this:

```
sage.misc.latex.png(J_n, 'J_n.png')
```

You should see this:

$$(n, x) \mapsto \frac{\int \cos\left(-nt + x\sin\left(t\right)\right)\, dt}{\pi}$$

What just happened?

In the first example, we defined a function `J_n` that represents a Bessel function of the first kind. Bessel functions are a type of "special function" that are used to represent solutions to certain types of partial differential equations. You don't need to know any more than that to understand this example, but you can find more information at `http://en.wikipedia.org/wiki/Bessel_function`.

We used the familiar `show` function to display the Bessel function, and we demonstrated how to use the `view` function. `view` returns a LaTeX representation of its argument. When called from the notebook interface, the LaTeX mark-up is automatically parsed by jsMath, which produces an HTML expression that your browser can display. jsMath is a collection of JavaScript programs that display mathematical content on web pages. It is installed on the server side, so the user doesn't need to install any software to view mathematical expressions. However, mathematical expressions will look much better if the user downloads a set of TeX fonts.

You may have noticed the little jsMath button on the lower right-hand corner of every Sage worksheet. When you click the button, you get a control panel that allows you to set various options. Click the button labelled **Hi-Res Fonts for Printing** to download the TeX fonts (if the button is greyed out, you already have the fonts). You can find out more about jsMath and download the TeX fonts directly at:

`http://www.math.union.edu/~dpvc/jsMath/`

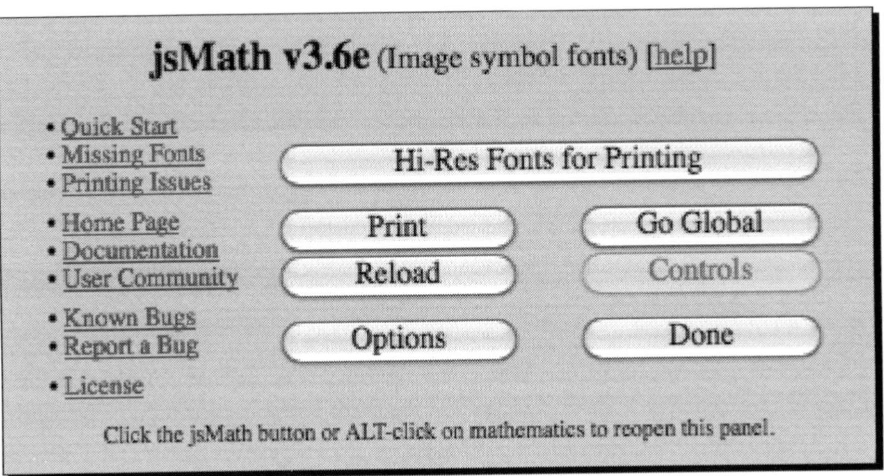

The output from `show` is somewhat larger than the output produced by `view`. The reason is that LaTeX has two modes for displaying mathematics: inline and display. Inline mode is used when you want to put mathematical symbols on the same line as text, and display mode is used when you want to display an expression on a line by itself. By default, `view` uses inline mode, but we can change that with the `mode` keyword. When we used the `mode` keyword to set the mode to `'display'`, the output from `view` was equivalent to the output from `show`.

The next part of the example showed how to generate a PDF file containing mathematical expressions. We defined another callable symbolic expression called `J_n_2`, which is an alternative representation of a Bessel function. Note that we started the example with the line `restore('i')`. By default, Sage defines the symbol `i` as the square root of negative one, which is how we intend to use it in this example. However, `i` is frequently used as a counting variable in `for` loops. We used the `restore` function to restore the symbol to its default value, to ensure that the code runs correctly even if `i` has already been used as a counting variable in a previous calculation.

When `view` receives the keyword argument `viewer='pdf'`, the LaTeX output is used to create an external PDF file instead of being passed to jsMath. This part of the example also showed how to typeset multiple expressions in the same PDF document. We created a list containing both equations, and used this list as the first argument to `view`. When `view` receives a list of objects for output to a PDF file, it typesets each one on its own line. The `sep` keyword argument specifies what kind of separation should be used between the expressions. In this case, the LaTeX command `\hrule` creates a horizontal line. Sometimes, we don't want to generate a whole page of output for a single equation. The third part of the example shows how the keyword argument `tightpage=True` shrinks the page to fit tightly around a single typeset expression.

In the fourth part of the example, we used the `png` function to create a bitmap image of a mathematical expression. Bitmaps are not the best way to represent mathematical expressions, but sometimes they might be the only option. The `png` function uses the system TeX installation to create a DVI file, and then uses an external program called **dvipng** to convert it to a PNG bitmap. This will only work if an external installation of LaTeX is present.

The view function in the interactive shell

You can also use the `view` function on the Sage command line. However, you will need to have a LaTeX distribution installed on your system in order to see the output.

LaTeX mark-up in the notebook interface

The previous example produced some nice output, but it was not very flexible. What if we are writing an entire paper or book with LaTeX, and we want to integrate equations from Sage into our work? Let's see what else we can do with LaTeX.

Time for action – working with LaTeX markup in the notebook interface

Enter the following into an input cell in the worksheet:

```
var('n, x, t')
J_n(n, x) = 1 / pi * integral(cos(n * t - x * sin(t)), t, 0, pi)
latex(J_n)
```

You will get a string of LaTeX mark-up that represents the object `J_n`:

```
\left( n, x \right) \ {\mapsto} \ \frac{\int_{0}^{\pi} \cos\left(-n t + x
\sin\left(t\right)\right)\,{d t}}{\pi}
```

You can paste this text directly into an existing LaTeX document. This function will also work on the Sage command line.

You can also use the notebook interface to evaluate LaTeX expressions. Enter this into an input cell (you can copy and paste the markup for the mathematical expression from the previous example):

```
%latex
You can paste LaTeX markup directly into a cell:
\[
\left( n, x \right) \ {\mapsto} \ \frac{\int \cos\left(-n t + x \sin\
left(t\right)\right)\,{d t}}{\pi}
\]
You can also put expressions like \(y=x^3\) inline.
```

The result should be:

You can paste LaTeX markup directly into a cell:

$$\left(n, x \right) \ {\mapsto} \ \frac{\int \cos\left(-n t + x \sin\left(t\right)\right)\,{d t}}{\pi}$$

You can also put expressions like $y=x^3$ inline.

Another neat trick is that we can actually embed Sage commands into LaTeX mark up. Enter the following code into another input cell:

```
%latex
You can also embed Sage commands in LaTeX markup like this:
\[
\sage{latex(J_n(n,x))}
\]
```

The result should be:

You can also embed Sage commands in LaTeX markup like this:

$$\frac{\int_{0}^{\pi} \cos\left(-n t + x \sin\left(t\right)\right)\,{d t}}{\pi}$$

We can also use LaTeX to typeset mathematical expressions in text cells in the notebook. Use shift-click to insert a new text cell, and enter the following text:

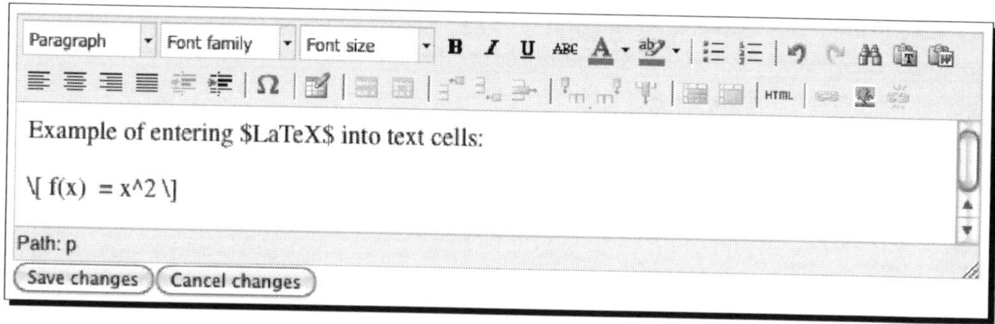

When you save the text, the cell should look like this:

Example of entering *LaTeX* into text cells:

$$f(x) = x^2$$

What just happened?

Every Sage object is required to provide a LaTeX representation of itself. In the previous examples, we saw how to use the `view` function to generate LaTeX and automatically process it to create graphics. In this example, we used the `latex` function to return a string of LaTeX commands that represent a mathematical expression. We then created a new cell in the worksheet and entered `%latex` in the first line. This directs Sage to evaluate the rest of the cell as a LaTeX expression. We pasted in the output from the `latex` function, adding `\[` before the markup and `\]` after. The backslash with square brackets tells the LaTeX processor that the enclosed commands should be processed in "math mode." Square brackets cause the expression to be rendered in display mode, while parenthesis are used to indicate inline mode. This example uses both modes to illustrate the differences. You will sometimes see two dollar signs `$$` used to indicate math display mode, and a single dollar sign `$` used to indicate inline mode. Using dollar signs is discouraged, since it can cause problems with certain LaTeX packages. While you wouldn't want to typeset a whole document in a Sage notebook cell, the ability to process LaTeX mark-up is very useful for previewing snippets of LaTeX to make sure it will display correctly.

The next block of code shows how to embed a Sage command into LaTeX mark-up. The LaTeX command `\sage{sage_command}` tells the TeX processor to run `sage_command` using Sage, insert the results into the LaTeX mark-up, and continue processing. In this case, we simply used the `latex` function to return the LaTeX representation of a function. This is handy, because your LaTeX output will automatically incorporate any changes you make in your mathematical expressions. We can take this a step farther, and use the `\sage` command in LaTeX mark-up outside of Sage. This requires some extra configuration of your TeX distribution; more details can be found at:

`http://www.sagemath.org/doc/tutorial/sagetex.html`

Time for action – putting it all together

Let's produce a simple document with LaTeX that incorporates typeset equations and graphics. This is a suitable starting point for a report, journal article, or homework assignment. First, let's make a plot of the Bessel function of the first kind for three values of n.

```
from matplotlib import pyplot as plt
import numpy

def J_n_numerical(n, x):
    integrand(n1, x1, t) = cos(n1 * t - x1 * sin(t))
    J_n = numpy.zeros(len(x))
    for j in range(len(x)):
        J_n[j] = 1 / pi.n() * integrand(n1=n, x1=x[j]).nintegrate(t, 
0, pi)[0]
    return J_n

n_values = [0, 1, 2]
x = numpy.arange(0.0, 10.0, 0.1)

plt.figure()
for n in n_values:
    plt.plot(x, J_n_numerical(n, x), label='n=' + str(n))
plt.xlabel('x')
plt.ylabel('J(x)')
plt.legend(loc='upper right')
plt.savefig('J_n.pdf')
plt.close()
```

The plot will be saved as a PDF file in the SAGE_TEMP directory, so you won't see the plot in your browser. Instead, you will see a link to the file. Click this link to open the file in a PDF viewer, and save a copy in a convenient location. Now, create a plain text file and save it with a `.tex` extension in the same directory as the PDF plot. Enter the following LaTeX mark-up in the text file:

```
\documentclass{report}
\usepackage{graphicx}

\begin{document}

\title{A Simple \LaTeX{} Document}
\author{Your Name}

\maketitle

\begin{abstract}
The abstract text goes here.
\end{abstract}

\section{Introduction}
Write your introduction here.

\section{Mathematics}
Some text...

\subsection{Subsection Heading Here}
Equations...

\begin{equation}
    \label{simple_equation}
    \left( n, x \right) \ {\mapsto} \ \frac{\int_{0}^{\pi} \cos\
left(-n t + x \sin\left(t\right)\right)\,{d t}}{\pi}
\end{equation}

\subsection{Subsection Heading Here}
Graphics...

\begin{figure}
    \centering
    \includegraphics[width=3.0in]{J_n.pdf}
    \caption{Bessel function of the first kind}
\end{figure}

\section{Conclusion}
Write your conclusion here.

\end{document}
```

The exact method you will use to process the LaTeX document depends on which operating system and TeX distribution you are using. On Linux or OS X, you can use the command line. In a terminal window, change to the directory where you saved the LaTeX source file and PDF file. On the command line, enter:

```
pdflatex Bessel_functions.tex
```

Your TeX distribution may include other applications that eliminate the need to use the command line. You will get a bunch of text output in the terminal that can be safely ignored as long as no errors are generated. A new PDF file should be created in the same directory. The PDF file should look like this:

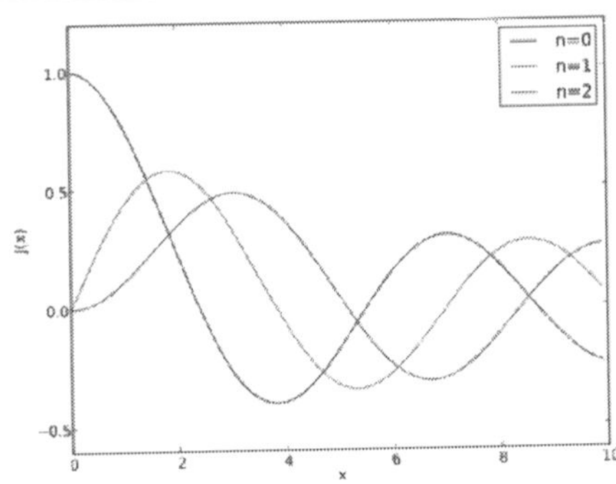

Figure 1: Bessel function of the first kind

1 Bessel functions

Some text...

1.1 Bessel functions of the first kind

Graphics...

1.2 Subsection Heading Here

Equations...

$$(n, x) \mapsto \frac{\int_0^\pi \cos\left(-nt + x\sin\left(t\right)\right) dt}{\pi} \tag{1}$$

2 Conclusion

Write your conclusion here.

What just happened?

This example used information from several previous chapters. We'll start by reviewing how we plotted the Bessel function. Because the integral used to define the Bessel function does not have an analytical solution, we had to use numerical integration. We used matplotlib for plotting because it is better than the built-in `plot` function for numerical data, and gives us the option to save the plot in various file formats. We defined a function called `J_n_numerical` that accepts an array of x values and returns an array of values of the Bessel function. Within this function, a NumPy array is created using the `zeros` function, and a `for` loop is used to iterate over the x values. The `nintegrate` method is used for numerical integration. The resulting array of function values was plotted using the `plot` command from Matplotlib, and we added axes labels and a legend. Finally, we saved the plot as a PDF file. If you are comfortable with LaTeX, an alternative procedure is to save the data in a file so that it can be read and plotted with a LaTeX package called PGFPlots (`http://pgfplots.sourceforge.net/`).

We then created a fairly minimal LaTeX source file. The source file begins with the `\documentclass{article}` command, which sets the document class to `article`. There are many other classes, but the basic options are `article`, `report`, and `book`. This command is required in all LaTeX source files. Your document is also required to include a pair of commands: `\begin{document}` at the beginning and `\end{document}` at the end. The other commands are optional. We also chose to use the command `\usepackage{graphicx}`, that is similar in concept to the `import` statement in Python, to use the package called `graphicx`. We will use this package to import the graphics we saved with Sage.

We copied the LaTeX mark-up that represents our equation from the Sage worksheet, and pasted it between the commands `\begin{equation}` and `\end{equation}`. We then used the commands `\begin{figure}` and `\end{figure}` to define a figure, and used the `\includegraphics[width=3.0in]{J_n.pdf}` command to include the PDF file we saved. If the PDF file isn't in the same directory as the LaTeX source file, then you must include the path to the file. The `\caption{}` command adds a caption to the figure.

This section is only a brief introduction to LaTeX, which requires a book or two of its own. This example demonstrates how LaTeX can produce a beautiful document with a minimum of effort. It will be worth your time to learn more about this powerful tool. A list of LaTeX resources can be found at `http://www.latex-project.org/guides/`

Have a go hero – Bessel functions of the second kind

Using the previous example as a foundation, add a section that documents Bessel functions of the second kind. Define a symbolic function, get its LaTeX representation, and paste it into a new section of the LaTeX document. Then, define a numerical function that can be used for plotting and plot the graph using Matplotlib. Include the plot in your LaTeX document. You may find this Wikipedia article useful as a reference, and to make sure your plot is correct:

`http://en.wikipedia.org/wiki/Bessel_function`

Speeding up execution

In this section, we're going to learn how to make Sage and Python code run faster. This section has been left until the last chapter because optimizing the speed of your code is only important in a few specific circumstances. This philosophy is summarized in a famous quote from Donald Knuth, author of the TeX typesetting system: "We should forget about small efficiencies, say about 97% of the time: premature optimization is the root of all evil." If you consider the amount of time that you spend on a programming project, from start to finish, only a small portion is usually spent waiting for the program to run. Most of the time is spent writing the program, testing it, fixing bugs, and going back into the code a year later and trying to figure out why you wrote it a certain way. To truly save time, the most important thing you can do is to write neat, legible code, and document it well. However, in mathematical and scientific computing, there are circumstances where it is helpful to reduce a program's runtime. For example, climate simulations and some number theory calculations can consume days of time on massively parallel clusters. Testing and debugging also go much faster when a program runs in seconds instead of minutes. Keep these general principles in mind as we go through the following series of examples.

Time for action – detecting collisions between spheres

We will use collision detection as an example to demonstrate some common optimization techniques. Detecting collisions is an important part of Monte Carlo simulations, that are used in physics and chemistry to simulate the motion of molecules and particles. Collision detection is also used in flight simulators and video games. It is easy to detect collisions between spheres, so most collision detection algorithms define a "bounding sphere" around each complex object, and check for intersections between the bounding spheres. If the bounding spheres intersect, then more computationally expensive calculations are used to determine whether or not the objects themselves actually overlap.

This example is designed to be run from the notebook interface. First, let's create a box full of randomly placed spheres. The number of spheres is set so that the example runs in a reasonable length of time on a 2009 MacBook Pro. You may need to adjust the number of spheres to get reasonable runtimes on your particular system. Enter the following code into an input cell in a worksheet:

```
dimension = 20
num_particles = 500
radius = 1.0

rng = RealDistribution('uniform', [0,dimension], seed=1)

x = [rng.get_random_element() for i in range(num_particles)]
y = [rng.get_random_element() for i in range(num_particles)]
z = [rng.get_random_element() for i in range(num_particles)]
```

We can visualize the particles in three dimensions using the following code. Rendering 500 spheres in 3D takes a while, so you may not want to run this part of the example on an older system.

```
grobs = []
for i in range(num_particles):
    grobs.append( sphere((x[i], y[i], z[i]), size=radius,
color='red'))
show(sum(grobs))
```

Finally, check for collisions by running the following code from a worksheet cell:

```
%time
import numpy
collisions_1 = numpy.zeros(num_particles, dtype=numpy.bool)
for i in range(num_particles):

    for j in range(0,i):
        r = sqrt((x[i] - x[j])**2 + (y[i] - y[j])**2 + (z[i] -
z[j])**2)
        if r < 2*radius:
            collisions_1[i] = True

    for j in range(i+1,num_particles):
        r = sqrt((x[i] - x[j])**2 + (y[i] - y[j])**2 + (z[i] -
z[j])**2)
        if r < 2*radius:
            collisions_1[i] = True
```

The spheres look like this:

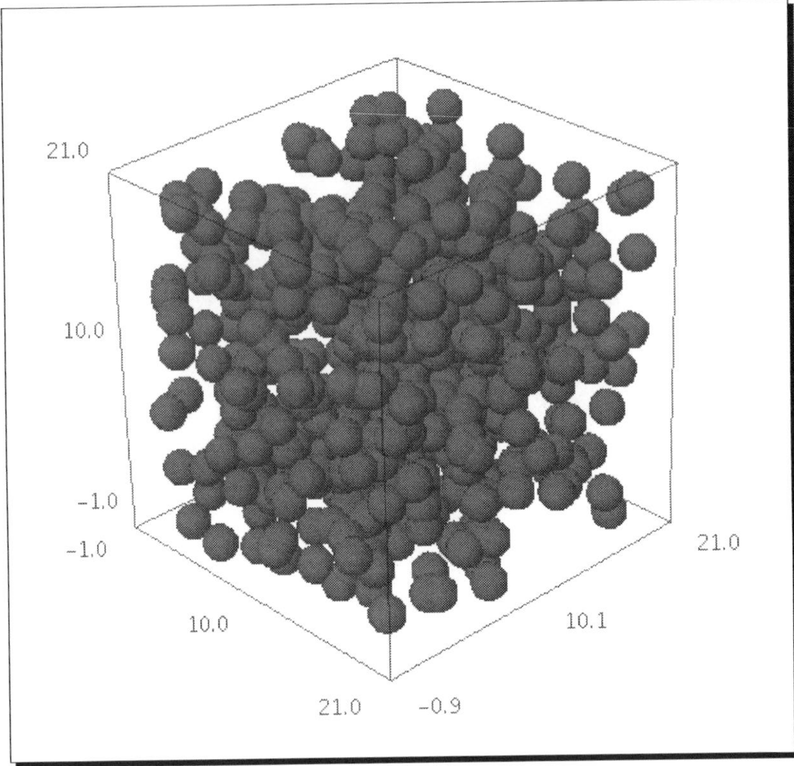

The collision detection itself doesn't give any output; it stores the results in an array of Boolean values. The execution time is printed:

```
CPU time: 3.93 s,  Wall time: 3.98 s
```

As we optimize the code in the following examples, we will check to make sure the results match the results from this example.

What just happened?

We started out by using list comprehensions and the `RealDistribution` class (introduced in Chapter 8) to obtain three lists of x, y, and z coordinates that represent the centres of the spheres. 500 spheres were randomly distributed throughout a cubic region of space. We then used the `sphere` function to obtain a 3D graphical representation of each sphere, and displayed them together. The `sphere` function accepts the following arguments:

Keyword	Default value	Description
`center`	(0,0,0)	Position of the centre of the sphere (x, y, z)
`radius`	1	Radius of the sphere
`color`	blue	Color of the sphere
`opacity`	1	Floating point number between 0 (transparent) and 1 (opaque)

The input cell that contains the actual collision detection algorithm starts with `%time` on the first line. This tells Sage to time the execution of the code in the cell. We placed the code to create and plot the spheres in separate cells because we only want to measure the runtime of the collision detection. We then created a NumPy array of Boolean values, initialized to False, using the `zeros` function (we would have used `ones` if we wanted the default values to be True). Later on, you'll see why we used a NumPy array for this purpose instead of a list.

The actual collision detection algorithm is simple. The outer `for` loop iterates over each sphere in the list. The formula:

$$d = \sqrt{(x_1 - x_2)^2 + (y_1 - y_2)^2 + (z_1 - z_2)^2}$$

is used to compute the distance between the centre of sphere `i` and each of the other spheres. If the centre-centre distance is less than twice the radius, then the spheres intersect and the value of `collisions_1[i]` is set to `True`. This approach is conceptually simple and computationally inefficient. If there are N particles in the list, the collision detection must be performed N2 times. The performance of the algorithm scales poorly as the number of particles increases. Fortunately, there is a lot we can do to improve this!

The Sage notebook interface reports two runtimes for the code: CPU time and wall time. The CPU time is the amount of time that code actually ran on the processor, while the wall time is simply the total time required for the code to run (as it would be measured by a clock on the wall). For this example, the two are almost identical. If the CPU had to wait on another operation to finish, such as accessing a file on disk, the wall time could be considerably longer than the CPU time.

Time for action – detecting collisions: command-line version

This example repeats the previous example using the command-line interface. Create a script in a plain-text editor and enter the following code:

```
dimension = 20
num_particles = 500
radius = 1.0

rng = RealDistribution('uniform', [0,dimension], seed=1)
```

```
x = [rng.get_random_element() for i in range(num_particles)]
y = [rng.get_random_element() for i in range(num_particles)]
z = [rng.get_random_element() for i in range(num_particles)]

import numpy
collisions_1 = numpy.zeros(num_particles, dtype=numpy.bool)

start_time = walltime()
for i in range(num_particles):

    for j in range(0,i):
        r = sqrt((x[i] - x[j])**2 + (y[i] - y[j])**2 + (z[i] -
z[j])**2)
        if r < 2*radius:
            collisions_1[i] = True


    for j in range(i+1,num_particles):
        r = sqrt((x[i] - x[j])**2 + (y[i] - y[j])**2 + (z[i] -
z[j])**2)
        if r < 2*radius:
            collisions_1[i] = True


print(walltime(start_time))
```

Save it with a `.sage` extension, and use the `load` command to run it in the interactive shell. The runtime will be displayed when the script is finished:

```
sage: load collision_detection_1_Sage.sage
4.08416008949
```

What just happened?

This example is very similar to the previous example. The major difference is the way in which the run time is measured. The function `wall_time(t)` returns the length of time that has elapsed since time `t`. We called `wall_time` at the beginning of the block of code to determine the start time. We then called `wall_time` again at the end of the block, passing the start time as an argument, to get the amount of time required to run the block of code. This process can be used to adapt the following notebook examples so they can be run on the command line. The function `cputime` can be used to obtain the CPU time in the same way. The `cputime` function has one additional optional keyword argument called `subprocesses`, which is `False` by default. If set to `True`, `cputime` will also measure the CPU time used by any subprocesses that are spawned by Sage (Sage creates subprocesses to run tools such as Gap or Singular).

Tips for measuring runtimes

Measuring run times can be tricky. Here are a few tips to make your measurements as accurate as possible:

1. Make sure nothing else is using the CPU while you run the code. This may seem obvious, but you need to be especially careful if your code is running for a long period of time. Make sure a scheduled process, like a virus scan, doesn't start in the middle of the run. On OS X or Linux, use the `top` command (in a terminal) to see information about running processes. In Solaris or OpenSolaris, use `prstat`. For Windows, use the Task Manager.
2. Disk access is much slower than calculations on the CPU. Avoid reading or writing files, and don't use so much memory that your program has to swap to disk (unless, of course, you're trying to benchmark disk access).
3. Disable writing to the screen when benchmarking—this is also slow.
4. Run the code several times and average the results. You might have to discard the timing value for the first run, which may be much slower because it has to compile code, or load libraries or data into memory.
5. Optimization can be very specific to a particular language, operating system, and type of CPU. Your results may vary!

Optimizing our algorithm

The algorithm you use to solve a problem has a major impact on the time required to solve the problem, so improving the algorithm is one of the things you should consider when you need to reduce the run time. However, optimizing an algorithm may require a lot of your time, and the resulting code may be much harder to debug (which is why premature optimization is considered to be the root of all evil). Before you start optimizing, try to take advantage of the many optimized routines that are built into Sage. Also, look at journal articles, books, and open-source projects to see if an optimized algorithm already exists.

Time for action – faster collision detection

In this example, we are going to apply a couple of simple tricks and see how they impact the runtime. Assuming you've already defined the spheres in the previous example, you can enter and run the following code in a worksheet cell:

```
%time
import numpy
collisions_2 = numpy.zeros(num_particles, dtype=numpy.bool)
r_min = 4*radius**2
for i in range(num_particles):
```

```
    for j in range(0,i):
        r_squared = (x[i] - x[j])**2 + (y[i] - y[j])**2 + (z[i] -
z[j])**2
        if r_squared < r_min:
            collisions_2[i] = True

    for j in range(i+1,num_particles):
        r_squared = (x[i] - x[j])**2 + (y[i] - y[j])**2 + (z[i] -
z[j])**2
        if r_squared < r_min:
            collisions_2[i] = True
```

The code will print the runtime:

```
CPU time: 2.04 s,  Wall time: 2.07 s
```

It's about twice as fast! Not bad for two minor changes. Now, try this:

```
%time
import numpy
collisions_3 = numpy.zeros(num_particles, dtype=numpy.bool)

r_min = 4*radius**2

for i in range(num_particles):
    for j in range(0,i):
        r_squared = (x[i] - x[j])*(x[i] - x[j]) + \
            (y[i] - y[j])*(y[i] - y[j]) + (z[i] - z[j])*(z[i] -z[j])
        if r_squared < r_min:
            collisions_3[i] = True

    for j in range(i+1,num_particles):
        r_squared = (x[i] - x[j])*(x[i] - x[j]) + \
            (y[i] - y[j])*(y[i] - y[j]) + (z[i] - z[j])*(z[i] - z[j])

        if r_squared < r_min:
            collisions_3[i] = True
```

```
CPU time: 0.80 s,  Wall time: 0.81 s
```

Let's check to make sure we are still getting the right answers:

```
print((collisions_1 == collisions_2).all())
print((collisions_2 == collisions_3).all())
```

The result should be `True` for both lines.

What just happened?

We made two changes in this example that significantly reduced the runtime. First, we realized that we don't actually have to calculate the square root of the distance between the centres of the spheres. We can compare the squared distance to $(2r)^2$:

$$d^2 = (x_1 - x_2)^2 + (y_1 - y_2)^2 + (z_1 - z_2)^2$$

The square root is a computationally intensive operation. Eliminating the square root cut the execution time in half, which is a pretty good return for such a simple change. We also moved the calculation of the squared radius out of the loop so that it only has to be computed once. In the second part of the example, we used multiplication instead of the exponential operator to perform the squaring operation. This change again decreased the runtime by more than 50%.

The final step of this example was to compare the results from these two runs to the results from the first example. Using NumPy arrays to store the results makes the comparison a lot easier. We can test for equality between two arrays with the `==` operator. The result is a NumPy array of Boolean values that are `True` where the two arrays match and `False` where they do not. If the two arrays are identical, the result should be `True` everywhere. Since the result is an array, we used the `all` method, which returns `True` if all the values of the array are `True`.

Optimizing with NumPy

So far, we have been using NumPy because of its useful features, but it can also help us speed up our code. Using NumPy, you can perform operations on arrays without using Python `for` loops. NumPy operations are much faster than Python loops, because the critical parts of NumPy are written in C and optimized for speed.

Time for action – using NumPy

Enter the following code in a new cell in the worksheet to define the spheres using NumPy:

```
import numpy

dimension = 20
num_particles = 500
radius = 1.0

rng = numpy.random.mtrand.RandomState(seed=[1])
x_np = rng.uniform(0, dimension, num_particles)
```

```
y_np = rng.uniform(0, dimension, num_particles)
z_np = rng.uniform(0, dimension, num_particles)
```

Now, enter the following code in another cell to detect collisions:

```
%time
collisions_4 = numpy.zeros(num_particles, dtype=numpy.bool)
r_min = numpy.float64(4*radius**2)
for i in range(num_particles):
    for j in range(0,i):
        r_squared = (x_np[i] - x_np[j])*(x_np[i] - x_np[j]) \
            + (y_np[i] - y_np[j])*(y_np[i] - y_np[j]) \
            + (z_np[i] - z_np[j])*(z_np[i] - z_np[j])
        if r_squared < r_min:
            collisions_4[i] = True
    for j in range(i+1,num_particles):
        r_squared = (x_np[i] - x_np[j])*(x_np[i] - x_np[j]) \
            + (y_np[i] - y_np[j])*(y_np[i] - y_np[j]) \
            + (z_np[i] - z_np[j])*(z_np[i] - z_np[j])
        if r_squared < r_min:
            collisions_4[i] = True
```

The notebook prints the runtime:

```
CPU time: 2.38 s,  Wall time: 2.48 s
```

In another cell, try using NumPy this way:

```
%time
collisions_5 = numpy.zeros(num_particles, dtype=numpy.bool)
r_min = numpy.float64(4*radius**2)
for i in range(num_particles):
    if i>0:
        d2 = numpy.power((x_np[i]-x_np[0:i]),2) \
            + numpy.power((y_np[i]-y_np[0:i]),2) \
            + numpy.power((z_np[i] - z_np[0:i]),2)
        if d2.min() < r_min:
            collisions_5[i] = True

    if i+1 < num_particles:
        d2 = numpy.power((x_np[i]-x_np[i+1:]),2) \
            + numpy.power((y_np[i]-y_np[i+1:]),2) \
            + numpy.power((z_np[i]-z_np[i+1:]),2)
```

```
        if d2.min() < r_min:
            collisions_5[i] = True
```

The notebook prints the runtime:

```
CPU time: 0.31 s,  Wall time: 0.34 s
```

Finally, let's make sure that both computations return the same results:

```
print((collisions_4 == collisions_5).all())
```

As before, the result should be `True` for both cases.

What just happened?

We started out by creating spheres using NumPy's random number capabilities. We created an instance of `RandomState` and initialized it with a seed so that it would provide repeatable, pseudo-random numbers. `RandomState` has methods that return numbers drawn from various types of random distributions. In this case, we used the `uniform` method to obtain numbers drawn from a uniform distribution between zero and the maximum size of the box. The first two arguments to `uniform` define the lower and upper limits, and the third argument defines the number of random numbers to generate. The function returns a NumPy array containing the random numbers. Dozens of other distributions are available; a complete list is available in the NumPy Reference.

In the first part of the example, replacing Sage functions and operators with NumPy functions actually *increased* the runtime! This example demonstrated that simply replacing Sage functions with NumPy functions doesn't speed up the code. However, this attempt did not utilize the full power of NumPy. The second part of the example showed how to use NumPy to optimize execution speed. The inner `for` loops were replaced with NumPy vector operations. The expression `x_np[i]-x_np[0:i]` computes the difference between the single value of `x_np[i]` and all the values in the array `x_np[0:i]`, and returns an array. The NumPy function `power` squares all of these values, and + operator performs element-by-element addition on the results from each `power` operation. In the end, the array `d2` held the square of the distance from particle `i` to each of the other particles. We then used the `min` method of the `array` class to find the minimum squared distance between sphere centers. If this value is less than (2r)2, then the spheres overlap.

Many numerical algorithms consist of nested loops. The statements in the innermost loop are executed more times than statements in the outer loops, so you will get the most "bang for your buck" by focusing your optimization efforts on the innermost loop.

More about NumPy

NumPy vector operations are fast because the NumPy library consists of highly optimized, compiled code. Instead of spending your time figuring how to optimize a mathematical operation, you can take advantage of the hard work that has already been done. One of the reasons that compiled code is fast is because it utilizes parallel processing. Modern CPUs (even single-core units) have the ability to execute multiple instructions in parallel. When you define a loop in an interpreted language like Python, the interpreter executes the loop operations sequentially. When you compile code that contains a loop, the compiler checks to see if the loop operations have to be executed sequentially. If not, the loop is converted to a different form and its instructions are executed in parallel on the CPU. By using vector operations on NumPy arrays, you can take advantage of parallel execution to speed up mathematical operations.

Just about every common mathematical operation is implemented as a function or method in NumPy. Mathematical operations such as addition, subtraction, multiplication, division, and exponents are performed element by element. The result is an array with the same length as the original. In previous chapters, we have already touched on a few, such as the fast Fourier transform and window functions. A categorized list of all the NumPy functions is available at:

`http://www.scipy.org/Numpy_Functions_by_Category`

Optimizing with Cython

Cython is a language for writing C extensions for the Python language. The Cython language is very similar to Python, but supports some additional features that allow it to be compiled to highly optimized C code. It is very easy to use Cython from Sage.

Time for action – optimizing collision detection with Cython

1. Define a function with Cython:

```
%cython
import numpy

def cython_collisions(x, y, z, radius):
    num_particles = len(x)
    collisions = numpy.zeros(num_particles, dtype=numpy.bool)

    r_min = numpy.float64(4*radius**2)

    for i in range(num_particles):
        if i>0:
            d2 = numpy.power((x[i]-x[0:i]),2) \
                + numpy.power((y[i]-y[0:i]),2) \
                + numpy.power((z[i] - z[0:i]),2)
```

```
            if d2.min() < r_min:
                collisions[i] = True

        if i+1 < num_particles:
            d2 = numpy.power((x[i]-x[i+1:]),2) \
                + numpy.power((y[i]-y[i+1:]),2) \
                + numpy.power((z[i]-z[i+1:]),2)
            if d2.min() < r_min:
                collisions[i] = True

    return collisions
```

When you run this cell, it may take a minute or two to compile for the first time. The results will look similar to this:

```
Users cf...0 code sage27 spyx.c    Users cf...ode sage27 spyx.html
```

2. In another cell, enter the following code to create the particles and call the Cython function:

```
%time
import numpy

dimension = 20
num_particles = 500
radius = 1.0

rng = numpy.random.mtrand.RandomState(seed=[1])
x_np = rng.uniform(0, dimension, num_particles)
y_np = rng.uniform(0, dimension, num_particles)
z_np = rng.uniform(0, dimension, num_particles)

collisions_6 = cython_collisions(x_np, y_np, z_np, radius)
```

3. The results should look like this:

```
CPU time: 0.08 s,  Wall time: 0.08 s
```

4. Verify that the results are correct:

```
print((collisions_4 == collisions_6).all())
```

The result should be `True`.

What just happened?

We created a Cython cell by placing `%cython` on the first line. We then defined a function that checks for collisions between hard spheres, using essentially the same code from the previous example. When we ran the cell, Cython compiled the code into a C extension. The only visible result of the computation is two links that appeared in the worksheet. Clicking the left-hand link will show you the C code that Cython generated. The right-hand link will take you to an optimization report that shows your Cython source code with color highlighting. Code that has a white or lightly colored background is highly "typed," meaning that it translates to almost pure C without any calls to the Python API. Code that is more brightly colored requires more calls to Python, and therefore runs slower. The optimization report for this code shows that there is plenty of room for improvement in the optimization. However, when we ran the code to test the Cython function, the execution was more than three times faster than the previous example. We also verified that the results are the same. This brief demonstration shows how useful Cython can be for optimizing code, and how easy it is to use Cython from Sage. You can learn more about the Cython project at `http://cython.org/`

Have a go hero – further optimization with Cython

Increase the number of particles in the example until it takes several seconds for the Cython code to run on your computer. Then, continue optimizing the Cython code, following the instructions and examples on the Cython website. Use the optimization report as a guide to tell you which parts of the code are closest to pure C.

Calling Sage from Python

You may want to create Python scripts that take advantage of the functionality of Sage, without having to run Sage itself. You can think of Sage as a giant module that can be imported into a Python program, which can then be run from the command line. We briefly used this capability in Chapter 9, when we imported some simple mathematical functions from Sage to use in a Python module.

Time for action – calling Sage from a Python script

Sage has advanced numerical integrators that adapt to the rate of change in the function being integrated. Let's say that you want to use one of these integrators to integrate an analytical function. You only want to use the integrator, so you don't want to manually start Sage and load a script just to access one function. We can create a stand-alone Python script that calls Sage when necessary. Create a new plain text file, enter the following code, and save it with a `.py` extension.

```
#!/usr/bin/env sage -python
from sage.all import *

vars={}

# Define limits of integration
vars['a'] = 0
vars['b'] = 8

sage_eval('None', cmds='f(x)=e^x*cos(x)', locals=vars)
print vars['f']

sage_eval('None', cmds='value, tol = numerical_integral(f,a,b)',
locals=vars)
print(vars['value'])
```

There are two ways to run this script. One option is to open a terminal and enter the following command. If the Sage installation is on your path, you can simply type:

```
$ sage -python /path/to/script/4460_10_8.py
```

in which you specify the full or relative path to the script. If Sage is not on your path, you will have to either provide the full path to the Sage executable, or change to the top-level directory of your Sage installation. For example:

```
$ $ /Applications/sage_source/sage-4.6.1/sage -python 4460_10_8.py
```

The result should be:

```
x |--> e^x*cos(x)
1257.25293971
```

You can also set up the script so that it can be executed directly. On Solaris, OS X, or Linux, use the `chmod` command on the command line:

```
bash$ chmod u+x 4460_10_8.py
```

The directory where Sage is installed also has to be in your system PATH variable. For example, on a UNIX or UNIX-like system:

```
bash$ echo $PATH
/usr/bin:/bin:/usr/sbin:/sbin:/usr/local/bin:/usr/texbin:/usr/X11/bin
bash$ PATH=$PATH:/Applications/sage
bash$ export PATH
bash$ echo $PATH
/usr/bin:/bin:/usr/sbin:/sbin:/usr/local/bin:/usr/texbin:/usr/X11/bin:/
Applications/sage
```

Run the script from the command line by typing:

```
bash$ ./4460_10_8.py
```

The result should be:

```
x |--> e^x*cos(x)
1257.25293971
```

What just happened?

Writing a Python script that uses Sage requires a different approach than writing a Sage script. Our script has to be valid Python, so we can't directly use Sage-specific syntax, like a mathematical function definition: `f(x)=e^x*cos(x)`. First, we have to use the statement `from sage.all import *` to access names from Sage. Then, we have to use the `sage_eval` function to "wrap" Sage expressions. This function accepts four arguments:

Argument	Keyword	Default	Description
source			A string to be evaluated
local variables	locals	None	A dictionary of variables for Sage to use
commands	cmds	''	A string of commands to be executed before the source is evaluated
pre-parse source	preparse	True	Disable the Sage pre-parser

We created an empty dictionary called `vars`, and created items `a` and `b` to contain integers that define the interval of integration. We then used the function call:

```
sage_eval('None', cmds='f(x)=e^x*cos(x)', locals=vars)
```

to define the function we want to integrate. Note that the source was set to 'None', and the function definition was passed as a command string. After this function call, the dictionary of variables contains a new item called `f`, which holds the Sage function. We then performed the integration with:

```
sage_eval('None', cmds='value, tol = numerical_integral(f,a,b)',
locals=vars)
```

Once again, the integration function call is passed as a command string. Basically, any expression that involves variable assignment needs to be passed with the `cmd` keyword. The source string is only used to evaluate expressions that don't involve assigning values to variables. When this command string is executed, Sage gets the values of `a` and `b` from the dictionary of variables, and computes the integral. Afterwards, you can see that the variables `value` and `tol` have been added to the dictionary.

In this example we used the `all` module to import everything from Sage at once. This may cause you a little concern since Sage is huge, and it is considered good practice to import only the functions and classes that you actually need. At this point, Sage is not structured in such a way that you can import a subset of packages and modules and expect that it will work correctly. You have to import everything.

If you want to try this example interactively on the Python command line, run Sage with the **–python** option to get an interactive Python shell. You can then run each of these expressions on the command line and see the results.

Have a go hero – solving an ODE symbolically from Python

In Chapter 8, we learned how to solve an ordinary differential equation with the `desolve` function. Repeat that example using a Python script to access Sage functions to solve the equation. You won't be able to view plots from the Python script, so don't try to plot the solution.

Introducing Python decorators

We need to take a little detour here to introduce one of the newer features of the Python language: the Python decorator. This is not an implementation of the "decorator" design pattern, although the concepts are similar. We'll need decorators to implement the interactive graphics that will be introduced in the next section.

Time for action – introducing the Python decorator

Enter the following code into a cell in a workbook and run it. You can also run this on the Sage command line, but the HTML formatting will not look nice!

```
def html_table(func):

    def display_output(*args):
        result = func(*args)
        html_string = '<table border=1><tr>'
        for item in result:
            html_string += '<td>' + str(item) + '</td>'
        html_string += '</tr></table>'
        html(html_string)
        return result

    return display_output
```

```
@html_table
def square_list(my_list):
    for i in range(len(my_list)):
        my_list[i] = my_list[i]**2
    return my_list

x = square_list([1.0, 2.0, 3.0])
print x
```

The result should be:

```
1.00000000000000 | 4.00000000000000 | 9.00000000000000

[1.00000000000000, 4.00000000000000, 9.00000000000000]
```

What just happened?

We defined a simple function called `square_list`, that accepts a list as an argument, squares every item in the list, and returns the squared list. Since you've just been introduced to NumPy, you should recognize that this is not really a useful function in Sage, but it will serve to illustrate how decorators work. We defined a *decorator function* called `html_table` that accepts a function as an argument called `func`. The decorator function defines and returns a new function called `display_output` that accepts the same arguments as `func` and returns the same results as `func`. However, before it returns, `display_output` creates and displays an HTML table that shows the values in the list. We use the `@` symbol to indicate that `html_table` *decorates* `square_list`. The syntax:

```
@decorator_function
def my_function():
    pass
```

is simply a shortcut for:

```
def my_function():
    pass

decorator_function(my_function)
```

When we call `square_list`, the call is intercepted and `html_table` is called with `square_list` as its argument. `html_table` returns an "improved" version of `square_list` which is then called with the appropriate arguments. The result is the formatted list that you see in the output.

This has been only a brief introduction to function decorators. Class decorators were introduced in Python 2.6. If you're going to be writing your own decorators, you will need to learn more about how to do it correctly. Python decorators are very flexible and powerful, and they give you the power to write convoluted code. The following resources should help you:

http://docs.python.org/release/2.4/whatsnew/node6.html

http://docs.python.org/release/2.6/whatsnew/2.6.html#pep-3129-class-decorators

http://wiki.python.org/moin/PythonDecoratorLibrary

Pop quiz – understanding function decorators

What is the output from the following code? Try to figure it out, and then run it to check your answer.

```
def decorator(func):

    def print_value(*args):
        print "Value is:"
        result = func(*args)
        return result

    return print_value

@decorator
def my_function(my_arg):
    print my_arg
    return my_arg

x = my_function('text')
```

Have a go hero – improving the decorator

The `html_table` decorator can only handle a one-dimensional list, but it could easily be extended to multi-dimensional lists, Sage matrices, or NumPy matrices. Extend the decorator function so that it displays two-dimensional data as an HTML table. Use the starting tag `<tr>` and ending tag `</tr>` to create a new row in the table. For help with HTML tables, check out:

http://www.w3schools.com/html/html_tables.asp

Have a go hero – the memoize decorator

The optimization technique known as "memoization" speeds up function calls by caching the results of previous function calls and returning a saved value when the function is called again when the same arguments are used. A Python decorator is a good way to add this ability to existing Python functions. Look at the examples in the links below, and implement a "memoize" decorator that you can use to speed up function calls.

`http://en.wikipedia.org/wiki/Memoization`

`http://wiki.python.org/moin/PythonDecoratorLibrary#Memoize`

Making interactive graphics

The Sage notebook interface can be used to make interactive examples that are controlled by simple graphical controls. This feature is comparable to the `Manipulate` function in *Mathematica*. Interactive graphics are especially useful for creating teaching tools to help students learn new mathematical concepts. We will make extensive use of the Python decorators that were introduced in the previous section.

Time for action – making interactive controls

This example consists of a gallery of all the basic controls that can be used in the Sage notebook interface. The code is followed by the result from running that code in an input cell.

```
@interact
def _(t=text_control('Static text goes here')):
    pass
```

Static text goes here

```
@interact
def _(value = slider(vmin=0, vmax=10, step_size=1, default=5,
    label='Slide me:', display_value = True)):
    print value
```

Here is a shorthand way to create the same type of control:

```
@interact    # Shortcuts
def _(value1=(1..10), value2=(0,100,10), value3=(1,10)):
    print value1
    print value2
    print value3
```

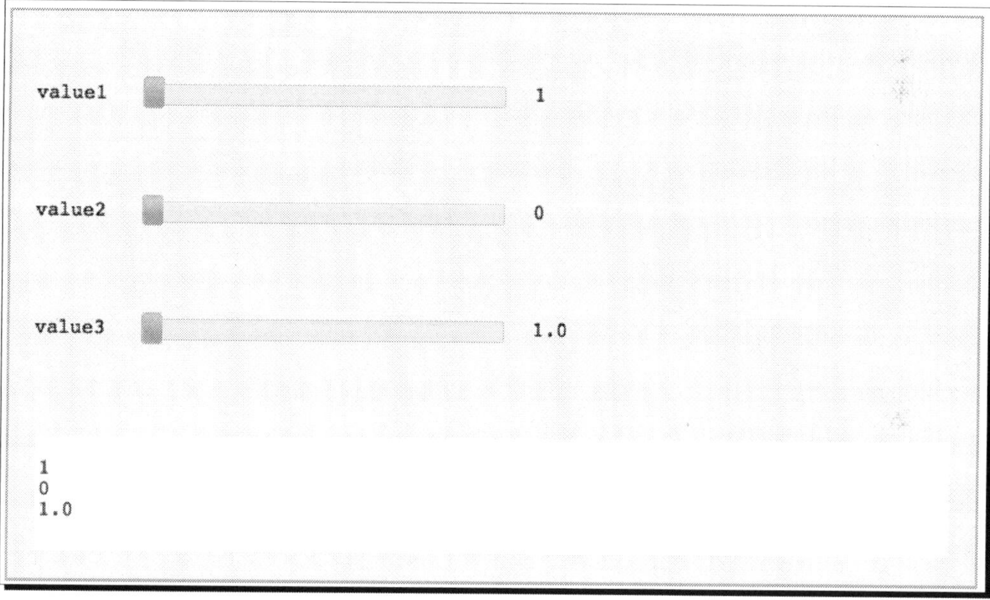


```
@interact
def _(value = range_slider(0, vmax=10, step_size=1, default=(3,7),
    label='Slide me:', display_value = True)):
    print value
```

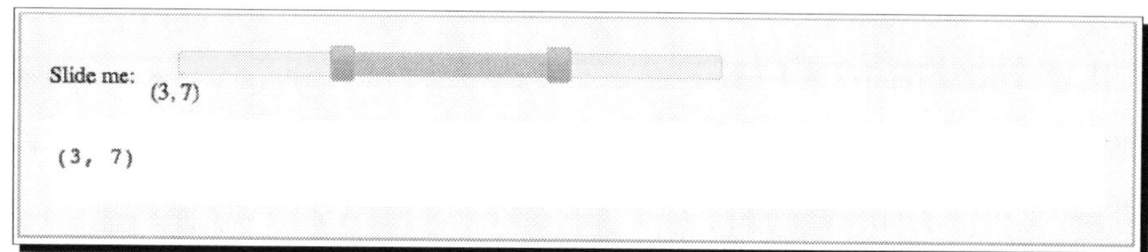

```
@interact
def _(checked = checkbox(True, "Check the box:")):
    print checked
```

```
Check the box: ☑

True
```

Here is a shorthand way to create the same type of control:

```
@interact
def _(check_value = True):     # Shortcut
    print check_value
```

```
check_value ☑

True
```

```
@interact
def _(value1 = selector(['a','b','c'], label='Choose one:',
        default='b'),
    value2 = selector(['a','b','c','d'], label='Choose one:',
        default='b', nrows=2, ncols=2)):
    print value1
    print value2
```

```
Choose one: b
Choose one: a b
            c d

b
b
```

Here is a shorthand way to create the same type of control:

```
@interact     # Shortcuts
def _(value1 = ['a','b','c'], value2=[1,2,3,4,5,6]):
```

```
    print value1
    print value2
```

value1 a b c

value2 1

a
1

```
@interact
def _(s = input_box(default='type here', label='Type something: ',
    type=str, width=40)):
    print s
```

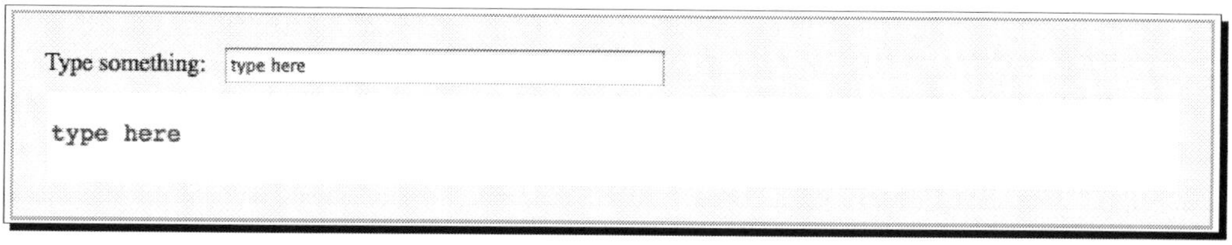

Type something: type here

type here

Here is a shorthand way to create the same type of control:

```
@interact    # Shortcut
def _(s1, s2 = 'type here'):
    print s1
    print s2
```

s1 None
s2 type here

None
type here

```
@interact
def _(m = input_grid(nrows=2, ncols=2, default=0,
```

```
        label='Input matrix:')):
        print m
```

Input matrix:

0	0
0	0

```
[[0, 0], [0, 0]]
```

Here is a shorthand way to create the same type of control:

```
default_matrix = Matrix(QQ, 2, 4)

@interact    # Shortcut
def _(input_matrix = default_matrix):
    print input_matrix
```

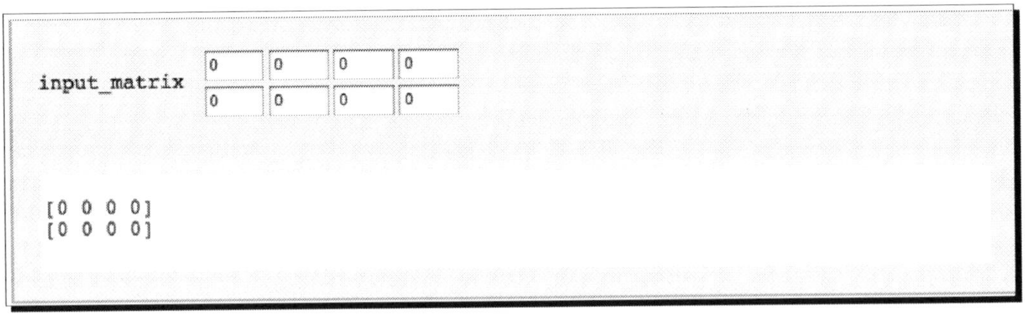

input_matrix

0	0	0	0
0	0	0	0

```
[0 0 0 0]
[0 0 0 0]
```

```
@interact
def _(color = color_selector(default=(1,0,0),
    label='Choose a color:', widget='farbtastic', hide_box=False)):
    print color
```

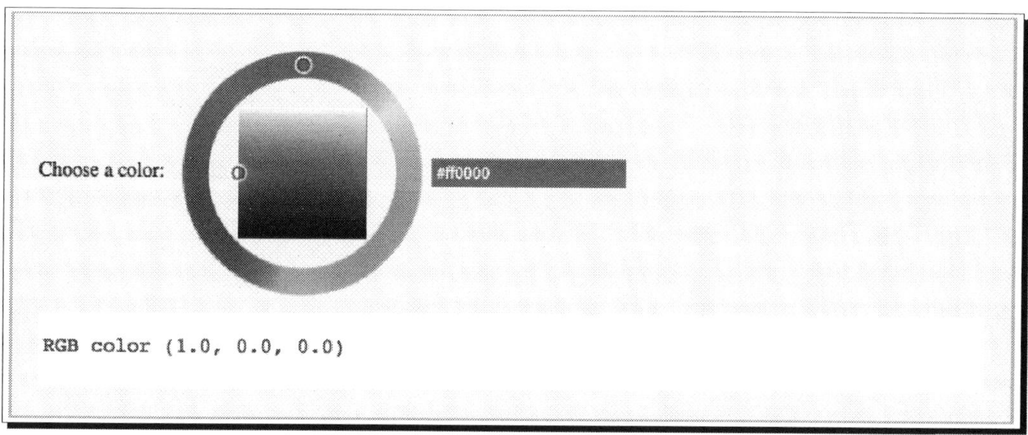

Here is a shorthand way to create the same type of control:

```
@interact    # Shortcut
def _(color = Color('red')):
    print color
```

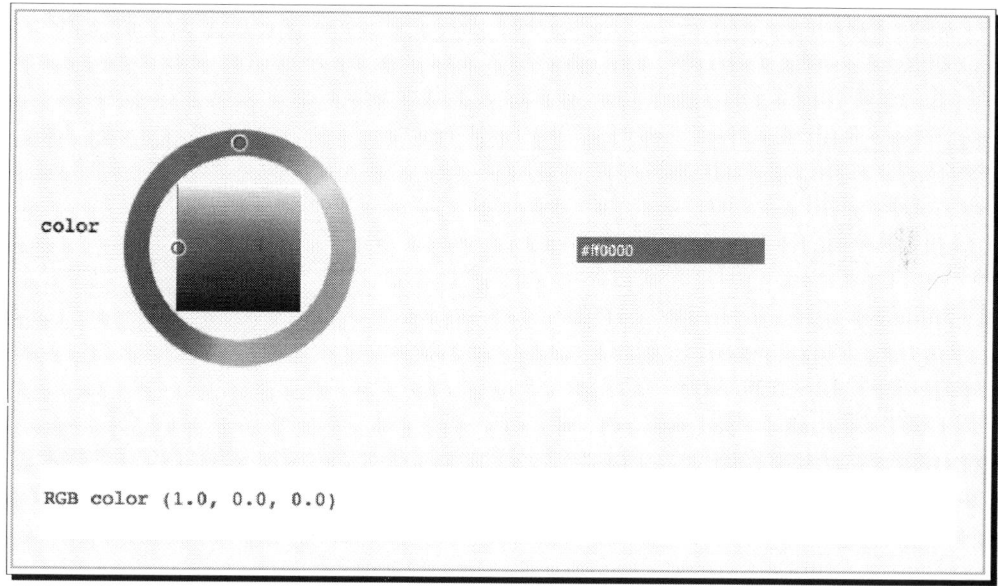

What just happened?

This example makes use of Python function decorators, that were introduced in the previous example. Sage defines a decorator called `interact`. When you decorate a function with `@interact`, `interact` is called, and the function you defined is passed as an argument. `interact` uses your function to construct an interactive graphical user interface. The syntax for doing this is somewhat unusual. The keyword arguments of your function define the elements of the interface, and the statements in the body of the function determine what happens when the user interacts with the controls. The code that creates a check box is a good place to start:

```
@interact
def _(checked = checkbox(True, "Check the box:")):
    print checked
```

The name of the function we define doesn't really matter, as long as it doesn't conflict with any other names, so the convention is to use a single underscore. There's nothing magical about the underscore; you could give the function any name. The function has a single keyword argument. The keyword is the variable name that will contain the result from the control, and `checkbox` is the function that creates the control. `checkbox` takes two optional arguments: the default value, and a label for the control. When the user clicks on the checkbox, the statements in the function body are executed. In this case, the value returned by the control is just printed below the control.

There are also shortcuts for creating many of the controls. The shortcuts typically give you less control over the appearance of the controls. I don't recommend using the shortcuts, because someone who is unfamiliar with the shortcut will have no idea how the code works until they study the documentation for the `interact` module. Code should generally be self-explanatory. The shortcuts are listed here so that you can understand what is going on if you come across them in other examples.

Using interactive controls

Time for action – an interactive example

Let's take an example from Chapter 8 and make it interactive. Run the following code in a worksheet:

```
var('x,y')

@interact
def _(c1 = slider(vmin=0, vmax=3, default=2, label='c1:'),
        c2 = slider(vmin=-3, vmax=3, default=1, label='c2:'),
        c3 = slider(vmin=-3, vmax=3, default=1, label='c3:'),
```

```
        c4 = slider(vmin=0, vmax=3, default=2, label='c4:')):
    c=vector(RDF,[-4,-5])
    G=matrix(RDF,[[c1,c2],[c3,c4],[-1,0],[0,-1]])
    h=vector(RDF,[3,3,0,0])
    sol=linear_program(c,G,h)
    print "Minimum:" + str(sol['x'])
    print "Slack variables: " + str(sol['s'])
    c1_plot = implicit_plot(c1*x + c2*y ==3, (x,0,6), (y,0,6))
    c2_plot = implicit_plot(c3*x + c4*y == 3, (x,0,6), (y,0,6))
    c3_plot = implicit_plot(x == 0, (x,0,6), (y,0,6))
    c4_plot = implicit_plot(y == 0, (x,0,6), (y,0,6))
    min_plot = point(sol['x'], color='red', size=50)
    rp = region_plot([c1*x + c2*y <= 3, c3*x + c4*y <= 3, x >= 0,
        y >= 0], (x,0,6), (y,0,6))

    g = graphics_array([c1_plot+c2_plot+c3_plot+c4_plot+min_plot,
        rp],1,2)
    g.show(aspect_ratio=1)
```

The results should look like this:

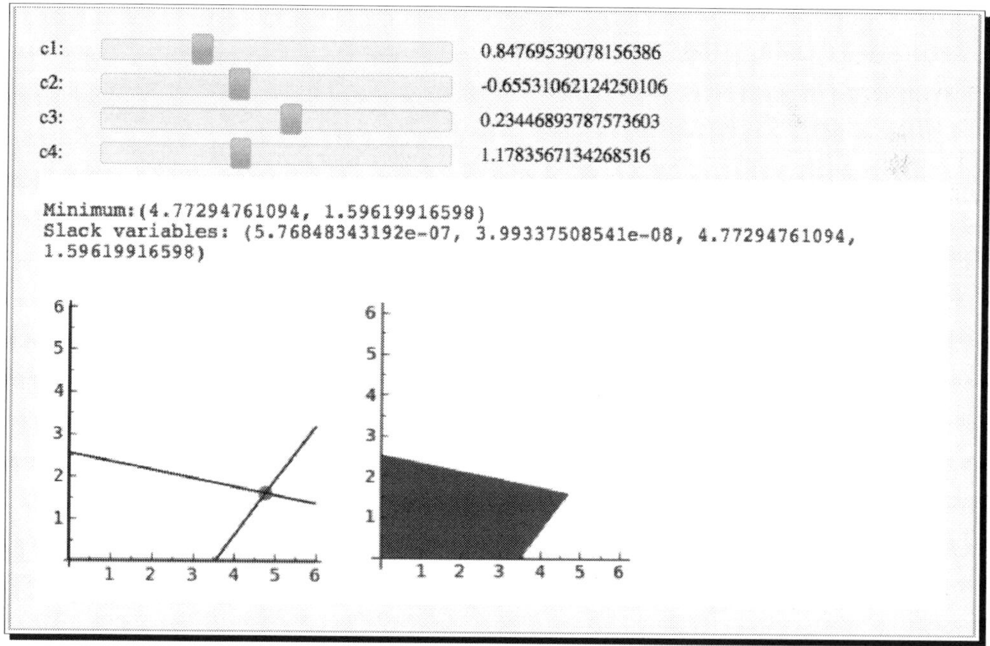

Play with the sliders to adjust two of the lines that constrain the minimization problem. Notice that the coordinates of the minimum are printed every time you move a slider, and the plots change to reflect the new constraints and the location of the minimum.

What just happened?

We started with an example from Chapter 8, and made it interactive. We defined a function with a single underscore as its name, and used the decorator syntax to decorate the function with `interact`. We created four slider controls, using the syntax described in the previous example. We then pasted the code from Chapter 8 into the function body and made a few changes. The linear constraints are represented as a matrix `G` and a vector `h`. We changed four of the entries in the matrix to be variables rather than hard-coded values. The slider controls set the values for these variables. When you move a slider, the constraints change, the minimum is recalculated, and the plots are redrawn. Note that this example is a good choice for user interaction because the linear program can be solved quickly; if the code took minutes or hours to run, there would be no point in making it interactive!

The complete documentation of the `interact` module can be found at:

`http://sagemath.org/doc/reference/sagenb/notebook/interact.html`

`Many interactive examples, along with source code, can be found at:`

`http://wiki.sagemath.org/interact`

Have a go hero – Taylor series

In Chapter 7, we used an example to demonstrate a Taylor series converges to a function in a region as the number of terms in the series increases. Convert this example so that it is interactive. Allow the user to change the number of terms in the series, and update the graph to show how the series converges to the function.

Summary

This chapter provided you with advanced tools that will help you get the most out of Sage. We learned about:

- Exporting mathematical expressions in PDF files and PNG bitmaps
- Generating LaTeX mark-up that describes a mathematical expression
- Incorporating LaTeX mark-up into a text cell in a workbook
- Processing LaTeX mark-up in a workbook
- Using NumPy to improve the execution speed of your code

- Using Sage from a stand-alone Python script
- Creating interactive graphical examples in the notebook interface

I hope you have found Sage to be a useful tool that takes much of the pain out of mathematics. This book has only scratched the surface of its capabilities, especially if you are interested in advanced mathematics. Refer to the online documentation for Sage and Python to learn more. The Sage worksheets published at `http://www.sagenb.org/pub/` can also be an excellent resource.

Index

Symbols

A

B

C

D

G

H

I

J

K

L

M

N

O

P

Q

R

S

T

U

V

W

X

Y

Z

Thank you for buying

Sage Beginner's Guide

About Packt Publishing

Packt, pronounced 'packed', published its first book "*Mastering phpMyAdmin for Effective MySQL Management*" in April 2004 and subsequently continued to specialize in publishing highly focused books on specific technologies and solutions.

Our books and publications share the experiences of your fellow IT professionals in adapting and customizing today's systems, applications, and frameworks. Our solution based books give you the knowledge and power to customize the software and technologies you're using to get the job done. Packt books are more specific and less general than the IT books you have seen in the past. Our unique business model allows us to bring you more focused information, giving you more of what you need to know, and less of what you don't.

Packt is a modern, yet unique publishing company, which focuses on producing quality, cutting-edge books for communities of developers, administrators, and newbies alike. For more information, please visit our website: `www.packtpub.com`.

About Packt Open Source

In 2010, Packt launched two new brands, Packt Open Source and Packt Enterprise, in order to continue its focus on specialization. This book is part of the Packt Open Source brand, home to books published on software built around Open Source licences, and offering information to anybody from advanced developers to budding web designers. The Open Source brand also runs Packt's Open Source Royalty Scheme, by which Packt gives a royalty to each Open Source project about whose software a book is sold.

Writing for Packt

We welcome all inquiries from people who are interested in authoring. Book proposals should be sent to author@packtpub.com. If your book idea is still at an early stage and you would like to discuss it first before writing a formal book proposal, contact us; one of our commissioning editors will get in touch with you.

We're not just looking for published authors; if you have strong technical skills but no writing experience, our experienced editors can help you develop a writing career, or simply get some additional reward for your expertise.

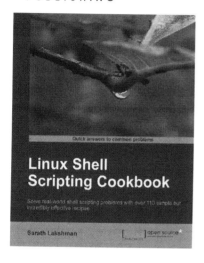

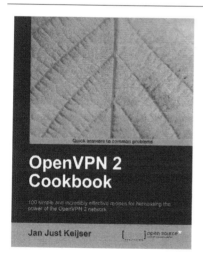

Made in the USA
Lexington, KY
19 July 2014